D0236341

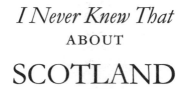

I Never Knew That ABOUT SCOTLAND

Christopher Winn

I Never Knew That ABOUT SCOTLAND

ILLUSTRATIONS
BY
Mai Osawa

EBURY
PRESS

This edition published for The Book People Ltd
Hall Wood Avenue, Haydock, St Helens, WA1 1UL

5 7 9 10 8 6

Published in 2007 by Ebury Press, an imprint of Ebury Publishing

Ebury Publishing is a division of the Random House Group

The Random House Group Limited Reg. No. 954009

Addresses for companies within the Random House Group can be found at www.randomhouse.co.uk

A CIP catalogue record for this book is available from the British Library

The Random House Group Limited makes every effort to ensure that the papers used in our books are made from trees that have been legally sourced from well-managed and credibly certified forests. Our paper procurement policy can be found on www.randomhouse.co.uk

Typeset by Palimpsest Book Production Limited,
Grangemouth, Stirlingshire

Printed and bound in the UK by
CPI Mackays, Chatham ME5 8TD

ISBN 9780091910242

For Mum and Dad

Contents

Perkill Castle, Ayrshire

Preface

'. . . I feel a sort of reverence in going over these scenes in this most beautiful country . . .' So wrote Queen Victoria in 1873 while travelling through Scotland on a visit to her beloved Balmoral. For many people, and for every Scot, Scotland is without doubt the most beautiful country in the world.

There is greater variety and contrast in Scotland than almost anywhere, from the glorious gold and purple heather moorlands of the Borders to the quiet blue and green rivers and woods of the southwest. From the brooding grandeur of Britain's highest mountains, magnificent and stark, to Britain's furthest west and furthest north, the bleak splendour and golden beaches of Scotland's islands, mystical and remote.

Then there are the cities: Edinburgh, 'Athens of the North', home of the world's largest arts festival; Glasgow, workshop of the world and city of culture; Aberdeen, the Granite City, sparkling and oil rich.

The images, the sights and sounds of Scotland are more instantly recognisable and distinctive than those of anywhere else on earth, from tartan and kilts to whisky and bagpipes, Edinburgh Castle and Eilean Donan. Scotland's history is more savage and romantic, her legends and her heroes more colourful and more tragic. William Wallace, Robert the Bruce, Mary Queen of Scots, Bonnie Prince Charlie.

Scottish engineering and ingenuity have built the world. Thomas Blake Glover, the 'Scottish Samurai', drove the industrial development of modern Japan. Major-General Lachlan Macquarie, the 'Father of Australia', turned that land from a penal colony into a nation. Nine Governors of the original 13 American states were Scots. Canada is the true 'Nova Scotia'. Engineers such as Thomas Telford, the Stevensons, William Arrol and John Loudon McAdam created roads and bridges and harbours. Scottish inventors gave the world the telephone, the bicycle, television, the pneumatic tyre, radar, steam engines, penicillin, savings banks, logarithms and radar.

Scotland bestrides the world of literature; Walter Scott, Robert Burns, James Barrie, Arthur Conan Doyle, Robert Louis Stevenson, JK Rowling, John Buchan, Alastair Maclean.

Scotland may not be big, but her heart, like her landscapes, is mighty. So many different worlds in one small but captivating country. To explore and to discover all of these bewitching and unexpected Scotlands is truly an adventure and a delight.

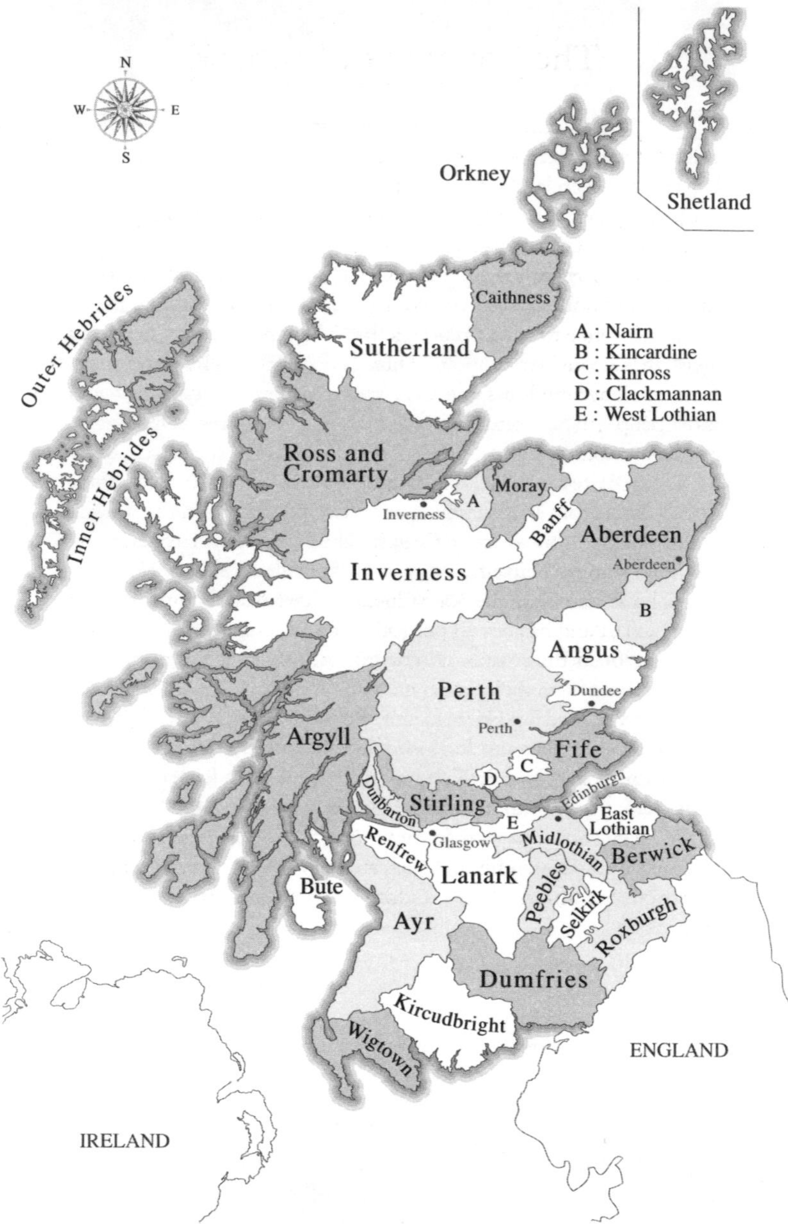
N
W
E
S
Orkney
Shetland
Outer Hebrides
Inner Hebrides
Caithness
Sutherland
A : Nairn
B : Kincardine
C : Kinross
D : Clackmannan
E : West Lothian
Ross and Cromarty
Moray
A
Inverness
Banff
Aberdeen
Aberdeen
Inverness
B
Angus
Perth
Dundee
Perth
Argyll
Fife
C
D
Edinburgh
Dunbarton
Stirling
E
East Lothian
Glasgow
Midlothian
Renfrew
Berwick
Lanark
Bute
Peebles
Selkirk
Roxburgh
Ayr
Dumfries
Kircudbright
Wigtown
ENGLAND
IRELAND

The Counties of Scotland

I Never Knew That About Scotland is divided into the 33 counties that existed between 1889 and 1974, before the Local Government (Scotland) Act of 1973, which introduced new administrative regions, districts and islands. These vast new units, designed by bureaucrats for their own convenience, mean nothing in terms of history, tradition, loyalties or geographical orientation and hence are of no relevance to a book such as this, which takes its flavour from all of these considerations. The pre-1975 counties grew organically from ancient kingdoms and parishes, are instantly recognisable to most people in Scotland, and are of a manageable and human size.

At various times over the years, some counties took the name of their county town. Angus, for example, was for a while known as Forfarshire, from its county town of Forfar. However, the ancient name of Angus, by which the area had been known for generations, soon re-established itself.

I have also bent the rules slightly when dealing with Scottish islands. Scotland has 787 islands, all of them distinctive and all very different from the mainland. For this reason I have removed the Western Isles from their parent counties and grouped them together in a chapter called The Hebrides. This chapter features stories from Lewis, which belongs to Ross and Cromarty, Skye, Harris, Eriskay, South Uist, Barra and St Kilda, all from Inverness-shire, and Mull, Iona, Jura, Islay and Staffa from Argyll.

The island groups that make up Orkney and Shetland are counties in their own right. Arran, Bute, Great Cumbrae and Little Cumbrae, Inchmarnock and Pladda together make up the county of Buteshire.

Aberdeenshire

County Town: Aberdeen

Aber Don – 'At the mouth of the Don'
(Celtic or Old British)

Drum Castle, with one of the three oldest tower house keeps in Scotland, is the oldest intact building in the care of the National Trust for Scotland

Aberdeen

'The one haunting and exasperatingly lovable city in Scotland'
Lewis Grassic Gibbon

Aberdeen, The Granite City, is the old county town, Scotland's third largest city and second largest fishing port, a holiday resort and the capital of Europe's oil industry. When the sun shines after it rains, the whole city glistens like silver as the granite buildings, flecked with mica, sparkle in the light. The pale grey of the granite is agreeably softened with myriad green spaces and glorious displays of flowers – Duthie Park Winter Gardens are the largest in Europe and Aberdeen has won the Britain in Bloom contest a record ten times.

Aberdeen has been a royal burgh since the reign of David I in the 12th century and the burgh records, dating from 1398, are the oldest in Scotland. There has also been an important harbour here since that time, and Aberdeen's Harbour Board, established in 1136, is the oldest recorded business in Britain. Aberdeen is also the home of the

WORLD'S OLDEST DOCUMENTED TRANSPORT COMPANY, The Shore Porters Society of Aberdeen, which was founded in 1498 and is still trading today. Aberdeen now has SCOTLAND'S LARGEST FISH MARKET.

In 1337, Aberdeen was burned to the ground by Edward III. When it was rebuilt it was divided into Old Aberdeen, around the cathedral precincts, and 'New' Aberdeen with the harbour and commerce.

Union Street, the main thoroughfare, runs for one mile (1.6 km) east to west over a series of viaducts above numerous deep watercourses. It was laid out in 1805 to link the north and south of the city and the name commemorates the union of Britain and Ireland in 1801. Although thronged with shops, Union Street has a pleasing uniformity to it thanks to the consistent use of granite and the restrained Georgian design of most of the buildings, and compares favourably with Edinburgh's Prince's Street.

Midway along Union Street is Union Bridge, which takes the road across the Denburn. It was built in 1805 and, with a span of 130 ft (40 m), is THE LARGEST SINGLE-SPAN GRANITE ARCH IN THE WORLD.

Housed in the Old Tolbooth on the north side of Union Street at its eastern end is the infamous Aberdeen Maiden, prototype for the French guillotine. This was used in 1562 to execute Sir John Gordon, a younger son of the 4th Earl of Huntly, in front of a weeping Mary, Queen of Scots.

Further east is the Mercat Cross, regarded as THE FINEST OF ITS KIND IN SCOTLAND. It was put up in 1686 in the market-place on the site of the now vanished city castle. This was destroyed in 1308 by supporters of Robert the Bruce as they ejected the English garrison of Edward I. Their rallying cry of 'Bon Accord' is now Aberdeen's motto.

A noted Aberdeen landmark is the slender granite spire of ST NICHOLAS KIRK, which soars 195 ft (59 m) into the sky above Union Street. This replaced a wooden one burned down in 1874 and the tower beneath houses A CARILLON OF 48 BELLS, THE LARGEST IN BRITAIN. There has been a church here since at least as far back as the 12th century and St Nicholas was once THE BIGGEST PARISH KIRK IN SCOTLAND but was divided in two, East and West, at the Reformation. The West church was rebuilt in 1763 by James Gibbs, the East in the 19th century. Inside the East Church, in the south transept, is SCOTLAND'S ONLY MEDIEVAL BRASS, bearing an inscription to Sir Alexander de Irwyn, who died in 1457.

The granite from which most of Aberdeen is built comes from the RUBISLAW QUARRY, off Queen's Road to the west of the city. With a depth of 465 ft (142 m) this was THE DEEPEST QUARRY IN BRITAIN and one of the biggest man-made holes in all of Europe. Granite from here went to make the Forth Bridge, Waterloo Bridge and the terraces of the Houses of Parliament in London, the docks at Southampton and Portsmouth and, further afield, Sebastopol docks and a temple in Japan. Rubislaw closed in 1970 and is now fenced off and partially flooded to a depth of 180 ft (55 m).

ABERDEEN FIRSTS

BRITAIN'S FIRST CHAIR OF MEDICINE was established at the University of Aberdeen in 1497.

In 1784, in Aberdeen's St Andrew's Cathedral, SAMUEL SEABURY was consecrated as AMERICA'S FIRST EPISCOPALIAN BISHOP and THE FIRST ANGLICAN BISHOP OF A DIOCESE OUTSIDE THE BRITISH ISLES. St Andrew's is the Mother Church of the Episcopalian Communion in America.

In 1825, JOHN MOIR of Aberdeen produced THE FIRST CANNED SALMON.

In 1868, *Thermopylae*, THE FASTEST SAILING BOAT EVER BUILT, was launched at Aberdeen.

While on tour in Aberdeen in 1897, MINNIE PALMER became BRITAIN'S FIRST WOMAN CAR OWNER AND DRIVER, when she took possession of a French Rougement.

The maze in Hazlehead Park was planted in 1935 and is THE OLDEST IN SCOTLAND.

In the 1970s, Aberdeen Football Club's Pittodrie became BRITAIN'S FIRST ALL-SEATER STADIUM. It was also THE FIRST STADIUM TO INTRODUCE DUG-OUTS.

Thanks to the oil industry, and the need to travel between the city and the oil rigs out in the North Sea, Aberdeen has THE WORLD'S BIGGEST AND BUSIEST CIVILIAN HELIPORT.

BORN IN ABERDEEN

GEORGE JAMESONE (1588–1644), BRITAIN'S FIRST PORTRAIT PAINTER. His father Alexander built Aberdeen's oldest residential building, PROVOST ROSS'S HOUSE, in 1594.

Robert Davidson (1804–94), chemist and electrical pioneer, educated at Marischal College. In 1839 Davidson built BRITAIN'S FIRST PRACTICAL ELECTRIC MOTORS, used to power a lathe and a small printing machine. He also designed an electric railway locomotive that ran for nearly two miles (3.2 km) at a speed of 4 mph (6.4 kph) on a stretch of the Edinburgh to Glasgow line in 1842, nearly 40 years before the first effective electric railway demonstration by Seimens in 1879.

SIR DAVID GILL (1843–1914), Astronomer Royal for Scotland, educated at Marischal College. In 1868 he took THE FIRST-EVER PHOTOGRAPH OF THE MOON.

'SCOTTY', the engineer from the first *Star Trek* series who spawned the much-quoted catch-phrase 'Beam me up, Scotty', claimed to be a native of Aberdeen in one episode.

Old Aberdeen

A Granite Cathedral, a Medieval Bridge and a Crown Spire

After the bustle and activity of 'New' Aberdeen, the narrow cobbled streets and winding alleyways of OLD ABERDEEN, a mile to the north, seem eerily quiet, almost comatose. A pleasant walk past elegant 18th-century houses with high stone walls and scented trees leads to ST MACHAR'S, THE ONLY GRANITE MEDIEVAL CATHEDRAL IN THE WORLD, teetering on the edge of a small hill above a park.

The somewhat truncated building we see today is the nave and west end of a 15th-century structure. The great west window, consisting of seven lancets of equal height, is spectacular and unique. Flanking the window are two towers with spires added in 1532. If you are lucky enough to find the cathedral open and awake, the interior is delightfully Romanesque in appearance, with lots of rounded pillars and arches. The colourfully painted heraldic ceiling is unexpected and in striking contrast to the slightly gloomy grandeur.

St Machar was a disciple of St Columba, and was told by God in a dream to leave Iona, go east, and found a church by a river shaped like a bishop's crook, precisely the shape of the River Don at this point. A short walk north through woods, beside the curve of the river, takes you to THE LOVELIEST MEDIEVAL ARCH IN SCOTLAND, the BRIG O' BALGOWNIE, completed in the early 14th century on the orders of Robert the Bruce.

Back in the heart of Old Aberdeen, the area around King's College, established in 1494 as Scotland's third university, is slightly more lively. Now united with Marischal College as the University of Aberdeen, King's College was founded by the Chancellor of Scotland, Bishop William Elphinstone, who produced SCOTLAND'S FIRST BOOK OF LITURGY, the Aberdeen Breviary, in 1510. The only original building remaining is the Chapel, distinguished by a delicate crown spire, erected in the 17th century in honour of James VI. The interior is a splendid display of SCOTLAND'S FINEST SURVIVING MEDIEVAL WOODWORK, with a great oak screen, choir stalls, misericords, a pulpit out of St Machar's and a magnificent vaulted wooden roof.

Royal Deeside

'Every year my heart becomes more fixed on this dear paradise'
QUEEN VICTORIA

The River Dee flows for 85 miles (137 km) from the Cairngorms to the North Sea at Aberdeen and is SCOTLAND'S FIFTH LONGEST RIVER. It is also SCOTLAND'S FASTEST-FLOWING RIVER and its source, the Wells of Dee is, at 4,000 ft (1,216 m), THE HIGHEST SOURCE OF ANY RIVER IN BRITAIN.

Queen Victoria first came to the area in 1848 and fell in love with the countryside. Prince Albert purchased the Balmoral estate for her and they made it into their summer home. The Royal Family have been coming ever since, hence the name 'Royal' Deeside.

Kincardine O'Neil

Kincardine O'Neil is THE OLDEST VILLAGE ON DEESIDE. It was here, in 1057, that Malcolm III 'Canmore' was handed the head of Macbeth, his father Duncan's killer, on a plate, after defeating him in battle near Lumphanan, just up the road. On a farmland slope just north of Lumphanan, there is a cairn ringed with trees which is said to mark the spot where Macbeth fell. It is a cold and sorrowful spot, hard to reach, and steeped in melancholy.

Ballater

Ballater is a lovely, small, stone town set amongst hills of pine trees and birch, mostly a 19th-century creation and benefiting as a resort from the nearby springs at Pananich and the presence of royalty at Balmoral. The station at Ballater used to be one of the most recognised in Britain, the backdrop to many a royal arrival or departure. Queen Victoria insisted that the railway should stop here and not be extended further west to Braemar, past Balmoral. The railway line is now closed, but the specially built Victorian wooden station, painted red and cream, must be the prettiest station in Britain, and has been beautifully preserved.

Birkhall
Two miles to the south of Ballater, hidden amongst trees on the west bank of the River Muick, is Birkhall, home of the Duke and Duchess of Rothesay, as Prince Charles and his wife are styled when in Scotland. Built in 1715, it was described by Queen Elizabeth the Queen Mother as 'a small big house or a big small house'. Prince Albert bought Birkhall from the Gordon of Abergeldie family in 1849 as somewhere for the Prince of Wales, later Edward VII, to stay while his parents were up the road at Balmoral. While Prince Edward was still young, the house was let to the Queen's physician Sir James Clark, who invited Florence Nightingale to come and stay. It was while at Birkhall that Florence, encouraged by Queen Victoria, planned her strategy to go and nurse the troops in the Crimea. Birkhall has been the scene of many royal honeymoons, including that of Prince Charles and Camilla in 2005.

Lochnagar
Views from Ballater are dominated by the three peaks of 'dark Lochnagar', which rises to a height of 3,786 ft (1,154 m) and is now part of the Balmoral estate.

England, thy beauties are tame and domestic
To one who has roamed over mountains afar
Oh! for the crags that are wild and majestic,
The steep frowning glories of dark Lochnagar.

Lord Byron whose mother was a Gordon spent school holidays at a farm called Ballaterich, to the east of Ballater, while he was a child growing up in Aberdeen. The words of his famous poem attest to his love of the place. Written in 1807, 'Dark Lochnagar' was set to music by Beethoven, and Queen Victoria was heard to say that she was inspired to come to Deeside after reading Byron's poem.

Balmoral
The Balmoral estate was leased by Queen Victoria in 1848 after the previous owner of the lease, Sir Robert Gordon, brother of the Prime Minister the 4th Earl of Aberdeen, died choking on a fish bone. The Queen bought the estate outright in 1853 and rebuilt the castle to a design heavily influenced by Prince Albert and carried out by William Smith. Today the present Queen spends most of August at Balmoral and, by tradition, invites the Prime Minister of the day to join her

for some of that time – being invited to Balmoral can be something of an ordeal for those not suited to hearty outdoor pursuits. The grounds and the castle ballroom can be visited when the Royal Family is not in residence.

Crathie

A short walk away from Balmoral, across the River Dee, is CRATHIE CHURCH, where the Royal Family attend Sunday service. So familiar from a million newsreels, it is much more substantial than it appears on the television.

There has been a centre of worship in Crathie since the 6th century, and the remains of a 14th-century church can be seen across the road in the watermeadows. In the old graveyard next to it are buried many local people who served at Balmoral, including Queen Victoria's ghillie (highland servant) and confidant John Brown (1826–83).

The present church was designed by Marshall Mackenzie, the architect of the Marischal College in Aberdeen. Queen Victoria laid the foundation stone in 1893. The interior is noble indeed for a country Scottish church, with soaring pillars of pale grey granite, beautifully carved woodwork, a fine apse and numerous features donated by various members of the Royal Family over the years. Pride of place goes to the magnificent communion table of white Iona marble given by George V in memory of Edward VII. A cross is cleverly picked out in the light green veining on the central panel.

Braemar

Braemar sits at a height of 1,100 feet (335 m) and is officially THE COLDEST PLACE IN BRITAIN, on two occasions the site of THE LOWEST TEMPERATURE EVER RECORDED IN BRITAIN – minus 27.2°C (minus 17°F) in 1895 and 1982, and with an average temperature of 6.4°C (43°F).

Malcolm Canmore camped at Braemar in 1057 before his defeat of Macbeth at Lumphanan, and is thought to have held the first Braemar Games as a means of determining which were his most accomplished soldiers. In 1715, the Braemar Gathering was used as a front by the 6th Earl of Mar to assemble his troops and raise the standard for the first Jacobite uprising. A stone commemorating the event stands opposite the Invercauld Arms Hotel at the entrance to the village which stands on the spot where the standard was raised. After the 1745 Jacobite uprising such gatherings were banned for a while, along with other Highland customs such as the speaking of Gaelic and the wearing of kilts. The Games were

John Brown, Ghillie and Friend

John Brown was born on a farm at Crathie in 1826 and was already employed at Balmoral by the time it was purchased by Queen Victoria. After Prince Albert died the Queen spent much of her time in mourning at Balmoral and came to rely heavily on the strength and sound common sense of Brown, one of the few people who could get through to her in her grief. This upset the somewhat stuffier element amongst her courtiers and politicians who heartily disliked their monarch being influenced by a 'low-born' servant. After the Queen's death, Edward VII, who had been on the end of many a tongue-lashing from the upright ghillie, gained his revenge by expunging all memory of John Brown from Balmoral, destroying any photographs and trinkets he could find. The statue of Brown that Queen Victoria had erected in his memory outside the garden cottage where she would retire to write, was smuggled out of harm's way to a remote part of the estate behind the dairy, where the King was unlikely to come across it. A pleasant hour or two can be had exploring the grounds of Balmoral trying to find it.

revived in their present form in 1832 by the Braemar Highland Society, SCOTLAND'S OLDEST FRIENDLY SOCIETY, and they gained royal approval in 1848 when Queen Victoria attended, a tradition maintained by Queen Elizabeth II to this day.

In the summer of 1881, ROBERT LOUIS STEVENSON came to stay in a cottage to the south of Braemar and began writing *Treasure Island.*

Braemar boasts BRITAIN'S HIGHEST 18-HOLE GOLF COURSE and is THE HIGHEST PARISH IN BRITAIN, containing within its borders three mountains over 4,000 ft (1,216 m) and 24 Munros – a Munro being a Scottish mountain over 3,000 ft, or 914.4 m (*see* Angus).

Craigievar

Disney's Inspiration

Outstanding among Aberdeenshire's many ravishing castles is Craigievar, regarded by many as the loveliest and most perfect castle in the world. Set in lush gardens on a hillside south of Alford, it was built all of a piece from 1600 to 1626 by William Forbes, a Baltic merchant trader known as 'Danzig Willie'. The castle is as comfortable inside as it is satisfying outside, with twisting, narrow stairways leading to light, warm, wood-panelled rooms, all of a sensible size and all with wonderful views. Outside, the rough, pale pink walls are haphazardly pierced with deep-set windows, some

tiny, some huge, and the eye is drawn ever upwards to where the stark, massive keep erupts into a joyous explosion of turrets and pinnacles, balustrades, gables and corbels. There is simply nowhere else like it, and if you think it looks like something out of a fairytale you are not alone – Walt Disney is said to have drawn the inspiration for his magical castles from Craigievar.

Fraserburgh

Scottish Samurai

Fraserburgh, EUROPE'S BIGGEST SHELLFISH PORT, sits on the Buchan coast at the northeast tip of Aberdeenshire, where the Moray Firth meets the North Sea. It was founded in the 16th century by Sir Alexander Fraser. He constructed a harbour in 1546 and a castle on Kinnaird Head in 1572. In 1787 the castle was converted into SCOTLAND'S FIRST LIGHTHOUSE. Still a vital navigational aid today, the lighthouse is now operated automatically, but the keeper's residence has been preserved as a home for the Museum of Scottish Lighthouses.

Fraserburgh's most famous son is THOMAS BLAKE GLOVER (1838–1911), the 'Scottish Samurai'. At the age of 21, while working for the Jardine Matheson trading company, he found himself in Japan, which was just emerging from 300 years of isolation from the West and eager to expand into an industrial power. Seizing his opportunity, Glover began selling arms and ships from Scotland to the Japanese, at the same time arranging for young Japanese to be smuggled out to Britain to be educated. He brought the first steam locomotive to Japan, developed coal mines and helped to found the Mitsubishi shipyards, the first of the great manufacturing concerns upon which industrial Japan is based. His picture still appears on the label of Kirin Beer, which grew out of a brewery he started. Thomas Blake Glover was a Founding Father of modern Japan and THE FIRST NON-JAPANESE PERSON TO BE AWARDED THE ORDER OF THE RISING SUN. He settled in Nagasaki and, in 1863, built himself a house overlooking the harbour. Glover House is still there and is the setting for Puccini's *Madame Butterfly* – Glover married a Japanese girl called Tsura who wore kimonos decorated with butterflies, and the composer used the story of Glover's life as his inspiration.

BORN IN ABERDEENSHIRE

ALEXANDER GARDEN (1730–91), the botanist after whom the flower Gardenia was named, was born at Birse. He lived most of his life in South Carolina, studying the flora and fauna of Cherokee country, and was responsible for introducing THE FIRST ELECTRIC EEL TO BRITAIN.

PETER WILLIAMSON, or 'Indian Peter' (1730–99), was born at Hirnley farm, near Aboyne on Royal Deeside. While visiting his aunt in Aberdeen he was kidnapped and shipped off to America, a fate that was not uncommon for unwary children in the 18th century. He settled down and made a life for himself in America but, in 1754, he was again kidnapped, this time by Cherokee Indians. Impressed by his physique they did not kill him, as was customary, but kept him as a slave. After many adventures, including capture by the French, he finally escaped back to Scotland and settled in Edinburgh. He soon became something of a local legend, often to be seen walking the streets in full Cherokee garb. In 1770 he introduced the first 'penny post' to Edinburgh, and the knowledge gained from providing this service enabled him to produce the first Edinburgh Street Directory. Indian Peter's story served as inspiration for the 1970 film *A Man Called Horse*, starring Richard Harris.

BERTIE CHARLES FORBES (1880–1954), the financial journalist and publisher who founded *Forbes Magazine* in 1917, was born in New Deer and emigrated to New York in 1904. Originally buried in New Jersey, his body was brought back to Scotland in 1988 by his son Malcolm and reinterred in the churchyard at New Deer. Bertie Forbes's grandson Steve Forbes ran for President of the United States in 1996 and 2000 on a flat tax platform.

Well, I never knew this ABOUT ABERDEENSHIRE

BUCHAN NESS, a rocky peninsula with a lighthouse, off the village of Boddam, 2 miles (3.2 km) south of Peterhead, is SCOTLAND'S MOST EASTERLY POINT.

The great treasure of MONYMUSK PRIORY is a small, 8th-century wooden box, covered in silver, bronze and precious stones, and containing a bone relic of St Columba. Known as the Monymusk Reliquary, it was a powerful talisman for Scotland's royal armies and was paraded in front of Robert the Bruce's troops before the Battle of Bannockburn in 1314. It can now be seen at the Museum of Scotland in Edinburgh.

The picturesque conservation fishing village of PENNAN, on Aberdeenshire's north coast, found fame in 1983 as the setting for Bill Forsyth's cult film *Local Hero*, starring Burt Lancaster. The iconic red telephone box used in the film was only a prop, but the village does possess its own red telephone box, located not far from where the prop stood, and fans of the film seem quite happy to take photographs of this.

The BP pipeline for transferring North Sea Oil from Cruden Bay to Grangemouth, was opened in 1975 as BRITAIN'S FIRST OIL PIPELINE. Today some 2.5 million gallons of oil are pumped ashore every day through the pipeline, that runs unseen for 130 miles (209 km) under the golden sands of the bay.

Aberdeen's MARISCHAL COLLEGE is THE SECOND LARGEST GRANITE BUILDING IN THE WORLD, after the Escorial in Madrid.

BRAM STOKER began writing *Dracula* while staying at Cruden Bay in 1895 and is said to have got the inspiration for Dracula's Castle when he visited the bleak ruins of SLAINS CASTLE just up the coast.

The first genetically modified crops in Scotland were secretly planted on a farm in DAVIOT, a small village some 20 miles (32 km) northwest of Aberdeen, some time in 1999 or 2000.

ELVIS PRESLEY, 'The King', has Aberdeen roots. His ancestor, blacksmith Andrew Presley, from Lonmay near Fraserburgh, emigrated to North Carolina in 1745. A number of Presleys lived in the Buchan area of northeast Aberdeenshire during the 18th and 19th centuries, around Lonmay, Old Deer and Tarves.

ANGUS

COUNTY TOWN: FORFAR

Land of Angus, 8th King of the Picts

Glamis Castle – the most haunted castle in the world?

Dundee

Jute, Jam and Journalism

The two Tay bridges provide an exhilarating approach to Scotland's fourth largest city, but DUNDEE can best be appreciated from the summit of Dundee Law, a volcanic rock plug, topped with an ancient hill fort, that rises out of the heart of the city. Dundee is not pretty, most of its old buildings having been destroyed by squabbling between the English and the Scots, but its situation is magnificent, set between the Sidlaw hills and the broad River Tay. Dundee is THE ONLY CITY IN SCOTLAND THAT FACES SOUTH and, as such, claims, slightly cheekily, to be THE COUNTRY'S SUNNIEST CITY.

It is frequently said that Dundee's prosperity is based on Jute, Jam and Journalism. The biggest of these industries was jute, an inexpensive natural fibre that grows mainly in India. Dundee had a large whaling fleet and thus a plentiful supply of the whale oil necessary for processing the jute, which could be easily imported from the

Indian subcontinent through Dundee docks. BROUGHTY FERRY, a suburb to the east of Dundee, became known as 'THE RICHEST SQUARE MILE IN EUROPE' thanks to the vast seaside residences built there by the wealthy jute 'barons'. In the 20th century the industry declined when it became cheaper to produce the cloth in India itself, and the last jute mill closed in 1968. The VERDANT WORKS, a museum housed in a former jute mill, now tells the story of Dundee's jute trade.

Jam refers to KEILLER'S DUNDEE ORANGE MARMALADE, invented in 1797 by thrifty grocer's wife Janet Keiller, when she insisted on boiling up a crate of bitter Seville oranges that her husband was about to throw away. She had long been using the ample fruits of the fertile Carse of Gowrie, west of Dundee, to make jams, and it was through her use of the same technique on the oranges that Dundee orange marmalade was born. Keillers also developed the famous Dundee fruit cake topped with blanched almonds, so that their expanded work-force had something to do while the oranges were out of season.

Journalism came to Dundee in 1905 with the founding of D.C. Thomson & Co., best known for their children's comics, the *Dandy* and the *Beano*, home of beloved characters such as Desperate Dan, Dennis the Menace and Korky the Cat.

In 1922, jute and journalism combined to put Dundee's most famous MP in something of a jam. For 14 years from 1908 until 1922, the 'greatest Briton of all time', Winston Churchill, was Dundee's Member of Parliament, and throughout that time he fought a running battle with David Coupar Thomson's newspapers the *Courier* and the *Advertiser*. Dundee and Churchill did not get on, and in a famous incident during the 1922 general election Churchill's oratory was drowned out and ultimately defeated by Annie Maloney's bell. Annie Maloney was a worker from one of the jute mills and a celebrated heckler – during Churchill's speeches she would ring her bell incessantly until the exasperated candidate was reduced to silence. He lost the seat and never set foot in Dundee again.

Shipbuilding has always been important in Dundee, which even today has over 35 acres of docks. In 1901, RSS *Discovery*, THE LAST WOODEN THREE-MASTED SHIP TO BE BUILT IN BRITAIN, was launched from Dundee, as a scientific research ship for Robert Falcon Scott and Ernest Shackleton on their first Antarctic Expedition. *Discovery* is now the centrepiece of the new Discovery Point and is open as a museum. The American Space Shuttle *Discovery* is the latest in a distinguished line of vessels to

bear the name, including those of Captain Cook and Captain George Vancouver.

Moored in City Quay is the 46-gun frigate *Unicorn*, THE OLDEST BRITISH SHIP STILL AFLOAT. She was launched from Chatham in 1824 and is now refurbished as a museum.

Tay Bridge

A Disaster Waiting to Happen

On 31 May 1878, the TAY BRIDGE, at 3,450 yards or 1.96 miles (3.15 km) THE LONGEST BRIDGE EVER BUILT IN BRITAIN UP TO THAT TIME, was declared open. The bridge, constructed of steel girders, had 85 arches, higher in the middle to allow tall-masted ships to pass underneath, and followed a wide curve at the south end. It all looked frighteningly fragile and there were some who predicted disaster. Passengers complained of uncomfortable vibrations from the high girders, especially when the trains exceeded their 25 mph (40 kph) speed limit, and many felt safer going back on the ferry. Nonetheless, in the summer of 1879 Queen Victoria travelled across the Tay Bridge and the man who designed it, Thomas Bouche, was knighted. A few months later, at 07.20 on the morning of 28 December 1879, in the midst of a violent storm, the 05.20 from Burntisland to Dundee rumbled on to the bridge. In the gloom, the driver failed to see that over 3,000 ft (914 m) of the high bridge had been swept away, and as a result the engine, all five carriages and the guard's van plunged over the edge 90 ft (27 m) into the freezing water below. All 75 people on board died. Only 46 bodies were recovered, along with the steam engine. Sir Thomas Bouche lost the contract to build the new Forth Railway Bridge and retired to Moffat a broken man. He died shortly afterwards.

Perhaps the most poignant memorial to the Tay Bridge disaster was written by Dundee's favourite poet William McGonagall.

Beautiful Railway Bridge of the Silv'ry Tay!
Alas! I am very sorry to say
That ninety lives have been taken away
On the last Sabbath day of 1879,
Which will be remember'd for a very long time.

It is easy to see why McGonagall is known as the world's worst poet, but

somehow these simple, clumsy words seem to express the sorrow and shock felt by the people of Dundee on that frightful night.

Alongside the new railway bridge, the stumps of the old Tay bridge can still be seen, a constant, grim reminder. The second Tay Railway Bridge, opened in 1887, is THE LONGEST RAILWAY BRIDGE IN BRITAIN, with an overall length of 11,653 ft or 2.2 miles (3,552 m), 90 per cent of which is over water.

Arbroath

It is not for glory, nor riches, nor honours that we are fighting, but for freedom – for that alone, which no honest man gives up but with life itself.
from THE DECLARATION OF ARBROATH

ARBROATH has a special place in the hearts of all Scotsmen as the place where Scotland's 'Declaration of Independence', the Declaration of Arbroath, was signed in 1320. The Pope refused to recognise Scottish independence because the Scottish King, Robert the Bruce, had been excommunicated for killing John Comyn at Dumfries in 1306. The Declaration was written by the Abbot, who was also the Chancellor of Scotland, and signed by 8 earls and 31 barons. It was a statement putting the case, in unequivocal terms, for the recognition of Scotland as an independent nation, and for swearing loyalty to Robert the Bruce only as long as he continued to defend Scotland against the English.

The abbey where the declaration was signed dominates Arbroath and was founded in 1178 as the only personal foundation of King William the Lion, who was buried within the precincts in 1214. William was an admirer of Thomas à Becket and dedicated the abbey to him as a tribute, after the Archbishop's murder in 1170. The high Gothic design of Arbroath Abbey is modelled on that of Canterbury Cathedral. The extensive ruins include a great rose window in the south transept known as the 'O of Arbroath', which used to be lit up at night as a beacon for the fishermen out at sea. In 1951, the Stone of Destiny, also known as the Stone of Scone, was discovered beneath the altar, having been symbolically placed there by nationalist students who had stolen it from Westminster Abbey.

The history of Arbroath, short for Aberbrothock, is told in a museum housed in the old signal tower of the Bell Rock lighthouse. THE BELL ROCK LIGHTHOUSE, 118 ft (36 m) high, and situated 12 miles (19 km) off the Angus coast, is THE

WORLD'S OLDEST SURVIVING OFFSHORE LIGHTHOUSE. It was erected between 1807 and 1810 by Robert Stevenson, grandfather of the writer Robert Louis Stevenson. To build such a structure, in the middle of the sea on a rock that was submerged by up to 16 ft (5 m) of water for much of the time, was a remarkable engineering achievement, and the Bell Rock lighthouse is regarded today as one of the wonders of the industrial world.

Arbroath is also known for the ARBROATH SMOKIE, a haddock smoked over a beech-wood fire of a type unique to Arbroath. According to legend the smokie originated in the small fishing village of Auchmithie, a little to the north, when a fisherman's cottage burnt down and the fish which had been stored in the loft were found to taste delicious. Under the same EU law that applies to Champagne, only smokies that come from Arbroath may be called Arbroath Smokies.

In 1842, ALEXANDER SHANKS of Arbroath patented the first lawnmower that effectively cleared up the clippings as it went along. This was a considerable advance on Edwin Budding's invention of 1830. A pony would pull the mower while the operator walked along behind – some say this is the origin of the phrase 'on Shanks's pony', meaning on foot.

KERR'S MINIATURE RAILWAY, which runs along Arbroath on the West Links, was established in 1935 and is THE OLDEST MINIATURE RAILWAY IN SCOTLAND.

Brechin

A Very Small City

BRECHIN is, in fact, a city. It has a cathedral and a football club called Brechin City and therefore it must be. You could be forgiven for not realising, though, for this pretty, red sandstone place, on the side of a hill, has a population of less than 6,000 and exudes the friendly feel of a village.

The cathedral sits at the top of the town, surrounded by houses and not immediately apparent, which is maybe why it is so often overlooked. There has been a church here since at least as early as the 9th century, making Brechin ONE OF THE OLDEST SITES OF CHRISTIAN WORSHIP STILL IN USE IN SCOTLAND. The present cathedral dates from the 12th century but has been heavily restored and from the outside looks like a handsome, but not particularly special, large church. Inside, though, it is gorgeous, with every window a dazzling example of Victorian and Edwardian stained glass, including work by Edward Burne-Jones and William Morris.

Incorporated, slightly reluctantly, into the southwest corner of the cathedral is Brechin's jewel, a simple and utterly beautiful ROUND TOWER, one of only two in Scotland, the other being at Abernethy in Perthshire. Brechin's round tower is the older of the two being built around AD 1000 and is 106 ft (32 m) high. Such towers are more commonplace in Ireland, and Brechin's may have been the gift of Kenneth II's Irish queen who endowed Brechin in the late 10th century. Round towers were used as watch-towers and places of refuge, which is why the doorway is six feet off the ground and reached by a ladder that could be hauled inside. The doorway at Brechin is unique in design and richly decorated.

Kirriemuir

Home of the Wendy House

KIRRIEMUIR was a very important weaving centre for 250 years, up until the First World War, and was the site of Britain's last jute mill, at Marywell Works on the Gairie Burn at the edge of town. Kirriemuir's most famous son was the offspring of a weaver. The ninth of ten children, JAMES MATTHEW BARRIE, the creator of *Peter Pan* and *The Admirable Crichton*, was born at No. 9 Brechin Road in 1860. His birthplace is now a museum. At the back of the house is the original 'Wendy house', the old wash-house that gave Barrie the idea for the little house the lost boys built for Wendy in Never-Never Land. When he was six, Barrie's brother David died and Barrie kept alive his memory as the 'boy who never grew up'. Barrie referred to Kirriemuir as 'Thrums' in his work and in later life donated a camera obscura to the town. ONE OF ONLY THREE IN SCOTLAND, this is located on a hill above Kirriemuir and is close to the New Church Cemetery where Barrie, created a Baronet in 1913 and appointed OM in 1922, was buried in 1937.

Kirriemuir was also the birthplace of BON SCOTT (1946–80), legendary lead singer and front man of the Australian hard rock band AC/DC. Scott died of alcoholic poisoning after a night out in London's Camden Town at the age of 33. His grave in Fremantle Cemetery attracts so many fans that it has been decreed a classified heritage site by the National Trust of Australia.

The actor DAVID NIVEN (1910–83) always claimed to have been born in Kirriemuir – because he thought it sounded more romantic than being born in London.

SIR HUGH MUNRO (1856–1919) was brought up near Kirriemuir on his family estate of Lindertis. A founder member of the Scottish Mountaineering Club, in 1891 he produced a list of mountains in Scotland over 3,000 ft (914.4m) in height, and these became known as 'Munros'. There were thought at one time to be only 30 such mountains, but Munro listed nearly 300 and it is now a popular pastime to try and climb them all. The first person known to have achieved this feat is the Revd A.E. Robertson in 1901. Sir Hugh himself never managed to complete the list.

Glamis Castle

'Very singular and striking in appearance, like nothing I ever saw'
THOMAS GRAY

GLAMIS CASTLE is indeed like nothing you ever saw. That first view of the castle, pink turreted and pinnacled, through the trees at the end of a long, wide, sloping driveway with the blue Angus hills behind is one that can never be forgotten. Glamis, family home of the Bowes Lyons, Earls of Strathmore and Kinghorne, is everything a Scottish castle is meant to be. The core of the present building dates from the 14th century, but most of what we see is 17th century.

Some say it is the most haunted castle in the world. In 1540, Janet Douglas, wife of the 6th Lord Glamis, was burned as a witch on trumped-up charges at the behest of James V, who was determined to wipe out all the Douglases. She was later found innocent, but her soul is said to haunt the chapel where she appears in one particular seat towards the back. Others talk of the dark secret of Glamis, known only to the Earl and his heir. Or of monsters and secret rooms and card games with the Devil. Whether all of these stories are true, or none of them, Glamis looks and feels like the sort of place where they could be true, and that is what makes it one of the most magical and alluring castles in Scotland.

Macbeth was Thane of Glamis, and Duncan's Hall is supposed to have been built where he murdered Duncan, though several other castles claim that accolade, notably Cawdor and Inverness. Duncan's grandfather Malcolm II certainly died at Glamis in 1034, but whether murdered or from a hunting accident is uncertain. His blood is said to seep up through the floor of Duncan's Hall.

The Lyon family has been here since 1372, when Sir John Lyon was given the land by Robert II, first Stewart king and grandson of Robert the Bruce. In 1376 Sir John married the King's daughter Joanna, the first in a long line of royal connections to Glamis. Queen Elizabeth the Queen Mother spent some of her childhood at Glamis, which was her grandfather's and then her father's home. In 1930, she gave birth to Princess Margaret at Glamis, in a comfortable bedroom of the Royal Apartments in the east wing. This was the last time that a Government minister was required to be present at a royal birth to prevent the baby being substituted (*see* Midlothian).

Of great interest to American visitors is the portrait in the billiard room of Frances Smith, wife of the 13th Earl of Strathmore and Queen Elizabeth II's great-grandmother. By an almost direct, if slightly complicated line, through Frances Smith, the present Queen of England is one of the closest living relatives of America's first President George Washington.

Glamis was the last household in Scotland to employ a jester.

Well, I never knew this ABOUT ANGUS

ZOAR, on the outskirts of Forfar, is THE ONLY VILLAGE NAME IN SCOTLAND BEGINNING WITH A 'Z'. The name comes from the Bible, Zoar being the City of the Plain to where Lot escaped from Sodom and Gomorrah.

MONTROSE has THE WIDEST HIGH STREET IN SCOTLAND.

MONTROSE AIR STATION was established by the Royal Flying Corps in 1912 and was BRITAIN'S FIRST OPERATIONAL MILITARY AIRFIELD. Used again in the Second World War, the airfield is now an aviation museum.

The wondrous Renaissance garden at EDZELL CASTLE, once home to the Lindsay family, Earls of Crawford, was laid out in 1604 by Sir David Lindsay, and is THE OLDEST AND BEST-PRESERVED WALLED GARDEN IN SCOTLAND. Called the Pleasance, the garden displays the fleur-de-lis, shamrock, rose and the thistle of France, Ireland, England and Scotland respectively. The garden and the castle ruins are cared for by Historic Scotland.

THE MILLS OBSERVATORY in Dundee's Balgay Park is THE ONLY FULL-TIME PUBLIC OBSERVATORY IN BRITAIN.

CARNOUSTIE has hosted the Open Championship three times, in 1931, 1999 and 2007. Founded in 1842, it is one of the ten oldest golf clubs in the world, and golf has been played at Carnoustie since the 15th century.

The dovecot or doocot at FINAVON, north of Forfar, is THE LARGEST DOVECOT IN SCOTLAND.

JAMES CHALMERS (1782–1853), inventor of the adhesive postage stamp, was born in Arbroath. Although Rowland Hill got all the rewards and publicity for introducing the penny post in 1840, it was James Chalmers's adhesive postage stamp, invented in 1834 and submitted to Parliament in 1837, that made the scheme viable. The first envelope ever posted bearing an adhesive postage stamp was sent by Chalmers to Lt-Col Moberly, Secretary of the GPO, on 2 October 1839. Chalmers is buried in Dundee, and ever since his death his family have fought for his contribution to the postal service to be properly recognised.

DAVID DUNBAR BUICK (1854–1929), engineer and inventor, was born at 26 Green Street, Arbroath. Buick's parents emigrated to America when he was two. He started his career in the plumbing business and is credited with inventing a method for bonding enamel to iron which led to enamel baths and sinks. His interest, however, was always in cars, and in 1903 he formed the Buick Manufacturing Company to build cars and engines. Buick was absorbed by General Motors in 1908.

ARGYLL

COUNTY TOWN: INVERARAY

Earra Ghaidheal – 'Coastline of the Gaels' (Gaelic)

Inveraray Castle, the first major neo-Gothic castle to be built in Britain

Inveraray

A Model Town

INVERARAY, with a population of around 500, is one of Britain's smallest county towns, yet capital of the third largest of Britain's counties. It is a model new town, THE FIRST OF ITS KIND IN SCOTLAND, and was laid out in the mid 18th century by the 3rd Duke of Argyll to replace the original fishing village demolished to make way for the present Inveraray Castle.

It is an enchanting place, beautifully located beside Loch Fyne, with wide Georgian streets and some noble buildings, such as the restored town gaol which is now a major tourist attraction. The neoclassical church, put up in 1798, was divided into two sections to accommodate services in both Gaelic and English. A stiff climb up the detached bell tower of 1914 is rewarded with superb views, but beware the bells – the peel of ten bells is THE SECOND HEAVIEST IN THE WORLD after Liverpool Cathedral.

NEIL MUNRO (1863–1930), author of the 'Para Handy' books, was born in one of Inveraray's 'lands', or apartment buildings, on the edge of the town.

Inveraray Castle is home to the chief of one of Scotland's most powerful clans, the Campbells, Dukes of Argyll. The 2nd Duke was one of the British army's first two field marshals. The 5th Duke was married to one of the 'beautiful Miss Gunnings', sisters from Co. Roscommon in Ireland who were considered to be the most beautiful women in Europe.

Inveraray was THE FIRST MAJOR NEO-GOTHIC CASTLE TO BE BUILT IN BRITAIN, and the State Dining Room is regarded as THE FINEST PAINTED ROOM IN BRITAIN. It was completed in 1784 and is the only surviving work anywhere of the French painters Girard and Guinard.

Ardkinglas

Tall Trees and Oysters

At the head of Loch Fyne is ARDKINGLAS WOODLAND GARDEN, which boasts seven of the widest or tallest trees in Britain, including an *Abies grandis* fir tree, 210 ft (64 m) high, which is thought to be THE TALLEST TREE IN BRITAIN.

The woodland garden lies within the estate of Ardkinglas House, a delightful Scottish-style Edwardian shooting lodge built in 1906–7 by Robert Lorimer for Sir Andrew Noble, who was married to a Campbell.

Born in Greenock in 1831, Noble conducted ground-breaking experiments in explosives and gunnery and is responsible for much of what we know today about ballistics and gun design. He eventually became chairman of Armstrong's, the armaments company.

Perhaps inspired by his former boss Lord Armstrong's success in turning his own weekend retreat in the Northumberland moors, Cragside, into a modern country house, Noble gave Lorimer free rein to design the entire house but asked him 'to get a move on' as he, Sir Andrew, was already in his seventies. Cragside had been the first house in England to be lit by hydro-electricity, and Ardkinglas was very nearly the first house in

Scotland to be lit by electricity, just beaten to it by Mount Stuart (*see* Buteshire).

A recent incumbent of Ardkinglas, John Noble, was responsible, along with local fisherman Andrew Lane, for founding the world-famous Loch Fyne Oyster Company in 1978. In 2004, the first Loch Fyne Oyster Bar, across the loch from Ardkinglas, gained notoriety as the scene of a clandestine summit between Deputy Prime Minister John Prescott and Chancellor of the Exchequer Gordon Brown, to discuss who should be Prime Minister Blair's successor. The meeting has since been dubbed the 'Loch Fyne Accord'.

Strachur

Maclean, Fitzroy Maclean

James Bond is buried in the churchyard at Strachur, on the shores of Loch Fyne. Or rather the man upon whom James Bond may have been modelled: soldier, diplomat, vodka martini connoisseur and MP, SIR FITZROY MACLEAN (1911–96). Educated at Eton and Cambridge, Sir Fitzroy went into the Diplomatic Service, where he met and became friends with James Bond author Ian Fleming. In 1941, as well as being elected MP for Lancaster, he joined the Cameron Higlanders and was recruited by David Stirling as one of the first officers of the newly formed SAS. In 1943, he was chosen by Winston Churchill to be parachuted into Nazi-occupied Yugoslavia to help the partisan leader Tito.

MP for Bute and North Ayrshire from 1959 until 1974, Sir Fitzroy brought his family to live in Strachur House. Included in the property was Creggan's Inn down by Loch Fyne, which ended up being run largely by his wife Veronica, author of a series of popular cookbooks. Creggan's Inn was taken over in 2000 by the Robertson family.

Kintyre

Mull of Kintyre, oh mist rolling
in from the sea,
my desire is always to be here,
Oh Mull of Kintyre
SIR PAUL MCCARTNEY
AND DENNY LAINE

Reached by a bumpy, tortuous track from Southend, that winds across wild moorland and ends in a steep descent, THE MULL OF KINTYRE, on the southwestern tip of the Kintyre peninsula, has been given worldwide fame by Sir Paul McCartney and Wings. They took the song 'Mull of Kintyre' to number one in the charts for 17 weeks in 1977–78, and it became THE FOURTH BEST-SELLING SONG OF ALL TIME.

County Antrim in Ireland is only 12 miles (19 km) across the sea from the Mull of Kintyre and clearly visible on a good day.

However, the 'mist rolling in from the sea' is a common occurrence on this stretch of coast and can make navigation hazardous. In 1994, in thick fog, a Chinook helicopter carrying senior military and security personnel from Northern Ireland flew into the hill above the Mull of Kintyre lighthouse, killing all 29 people on board. A cairn marks the spot.

The largest town on the Kintyre Peninsula is CAMPBELTOWN, one of the remotest towns in Scotland. Although only 60 miles (97 km) from Glasgow as the crow flies, it is 150 miles (240 km) away by road. It is the most southerly town in the Scottish Highlands and lies 25 miles (40 km) further south than Berwick-on-Tweed. Campbeltown's art deco 'Wee Picture House', opened in 1913, is THE OLDEST CINEMA IN SCOTLAND.

The first hole at Machrihanish Golf Course has been regularly been voted 'THE BEST FIRST HOLE IN THE WORLD', an opinion endorsed by none other than Jack Nicklaus.

Until 1997 Campbeltown Airport was RAF MACHRIHANISH, a NATO facility used as a secret operating base for American Stealth bombers during the Gulf War. The runway, at 10,000 ft or 1.9 miles (3,050m) long, is THE SECOND LONGEST IN BRITAIN after No. 1 runway at Heathrow which is 12,800 ft or 2.42 miles (3,900 m) long.

On the southern coast of the peninsula, just west of Southend, is KEIL, where St Columba first set foot in Scotland before heading north for Iona. Near the ruins of a small chapel, on the site of one founded by the saint, is a flat-topped rock on which can be seen two footprints where Columba stood to gaze back at Ireland – he had vowed never to return there after his disgrace at the Battle of the Books.

Dunadd

An Ancient Capital

The name Argyll comes from the Gaelic 'Earra Ghaidheal', meaning 'coastland of the Gaels'. Argyllshire corresponds pretty closely to the ancient Gaelic kingdom of Dalriada, founded around AD 500 by Celtic immigrants from Antrim in Ireland, known to the Romans as 'Scotii', possibly meaning pirates or raiders.

The Scotii established their capital at DUNADD in the west, an isolated, craggy hill fort that rises out of eerie, flat Crinan Moss, once marshland, now brown and barren. A rocky path winds uncertainly upwards, through a series of clearly defended terraces and gateways to the top, where there are signs and markings to indicate that here was a place of some special purpose. There are Ogham writings, rock carvings, a basin scooped out of the rock and what appears to be a seat or a throne. The Kings of Dalriada were crowned here, seated on the Stone of Destiny, brought with them from Ireland. St Columba is believed to have performed THE VERY FIRST CHRISTIAN CORONATION IN BRITAIN here, that of Aidan in 574.

This is a wonderfully evocative place to be at dusk. Apart from a small farm at the foot of the rock, the stupendous view from the summit of Dunadd, birthplace of Scotland, is probably much the same now as it was in the days of Dalriada, The landscape is still, empty, mystical. To the north and east, beyond silent Crinan Moss, the hills of Argyll fade into the twilight. To the west the sea glitters pink and silver beneath the fiery peaks of Jura, as the sun sinks and the ghosts of ancient Scottish kings rise on the gloom from the mossy floor.

The Stone of Destiny was taken from here to Dunstaffnage, north of Oban, another Dalriadan stronghold, now crowned by a mighty castle. From there, in AD 843, the King of the Scots, Kenneth MacAlpin, marched east to Scone in Perthshire to claim, by marriage, the Pictish throne, thus creating the beginnings of the kingdom that was to enshrine his people's name for ever – Scotland.

Glencoe

Accursed Place

Perhaps the most infamous and melancholy place in the Highlands of Scotland is GLENCOE. At 5 a.m. on the morning of 13 February 1692, a regiment of Campbells, under orders from the Secretary of State for Scotland, the 1st Earl of Stair, fell upon their hosts the Macdonalds and 'put all to the sword under seventy'. At least they put 38 to the sword and left countless others to die of exposure in the winter snows.

Although, in terms of numbers, this was by no means the worst of the butcheries that marked the Highland blood feuds of those violent times, the Glencoe massacre takes on a peculiar notoriety because of the collusion of the Crown and the cold-blooded way the honoured guests committed such heinous 'murder under trust'.

King William III of England, keen to quieten the rebellious Highland clans, had offered an amnesty to all those who signed an oath of loyalty by 1 January 1692. Chief MacIan of the Glencoe Macdonalds fully intended to sign the oath but went to Inverlochy to do so, rather than Inveraray, and thereby missed the deadline. The Crown wanted to make an example of somebody, and this unpopular branch of the Macdonalds, little more really than cattle rustlers, had set themselves up nicely. The Campbells saw this as an opportunity to right some wrongs perpetrated on their own farmlands and people. They accepted the Macdonalds' hospitality in the glen for 12 nights and then turned on their hosts. The armorial bearings of the Dalrymples, Earls of Stair, was the Nine of Diamonds, and this has been known ever since as 'the Curse of Scotland'.

Glencoe might have been specially designed by nature as the perfect setting for dark and treacherous deeds. Even on summer days it is a grim, forbidding place, a great cleft driven through the black, sullen mountains, bereft of sunlight or warmth, brooding on misdemeanours. The long, straight approach from the south-west, across the empty wilderness of Rannoch Moor towards the gaping maw of Glencoe, fills the dullest spirit with awe and dread and perfectly sets the mood. In the middle of Rannoch Moor there is a memorial cairn to Peter Fleming, brother of James Bond author Ian Fleming. Peter, himself a well-known writer of travel books, used to love walking here.

Ardnamurchan

Farthest West

The ARDNAMURCHAN PENINSULA stretches like an umbrella over the island of Mull. It is isolated and remote but utterly beguiling, with unexpected sandy beaches, secret hamlets, unbelievable views and a sunset glow. Travelling west, the first civilisation you come to on Ardnamurchan is GLENBORRODALE CASTLE, a castellated Victorian pile set high above the road in glorious gardens. It was once the holiday home of Jesse Boot, founder of the chain of chemists. Today it is a luxury private hotel.

KILCHOAN, the largest community on the Ardnamurchan peninsula, is THE MOST WESTERLY VILLAGE ON THE BRITISH MAINLAND.

Six miles (9.6 km) past Kilchoan, the Point of Ardnamurchan is THE WESTERNMOST POINT ON MAINLAND BRITAIN. It feels like the edge of the world after the long drive on a switchback, single-track road fraught with highland cows and grazing sheep – and at the end of it all a traffic light! The ravishing panoramas from Alan Stevenson's lighthouse make it all worthwhile, with the pencil-slim line of Coll to the west, the humpbacked shapes of Muck and Eigg and Rum jostling to the north, and the Cuillins of Skye visible beyond on a clear day. A visitor centre explains the history and workings of Scotland's lighthouses.

STRONTIAN is a very active community grouped around a large, pleasant village green, established in 1724 to provide accommodation and services for 600 lead miners working the local ore. In 1790, French prisoners of war were employed in the mines, an important source of lead for bullets during the Napoleonic Wars. In the course of their work they discovered a completely new element, which became known as Strontium. Strontium 90 is a powerfully radioactive isotope, while Strontium salts are used for making fireworks burn red.

Well, I never knew this
ABOUT
ARGYLL

AUCHINDRAIN MUSEUM, south of Inveraray, records the life of a pre-20th-century farming community and is THE FIRST OPEN-AIR MUSEUM IN SCOTLAND.

HOLY LOCH, just north of Dunoon, used to be a base for US Polaris nuclear submarines, partly because of the deep water, but also because this part of Argyllshire is cloudy for most of the year, making it difficult for Russian spy satellites to photograph what was going on.

Two of the yachts that competed for Britain in the AMERICA'S CUP were built at Holy Loch.

Buried in the churchyard at Kilmun, just across Holy Loch from Dunoon, is ELIZABETH BLACKWELL (1821–1910), who in 1849 became THE FIRST WOMAN EVER TO GRADUATE IN MEDICINE.

LOCH AWE is THE LONGEST FRESH-WATER LOCH IN SCOTLAND, 24 miles (38 km) in length.

Hidden almost a mile (1.6 km) deep within BEN CRUACHAN, which stands 3,695 ft (1,126 m) high amidst some of the most beautiful scenery in Scotland, is one of Europe's most amazing engineering feats, THE WORLD'S FIRST REVERSIBLE PUMPED STORAGE HYDRO SCHEME, housed in a vast, man-made cavern. Water from Cruachan Reservoir high on the hillside rushes down pipes and turns the turbines before being vented into Loch Awe. Then, at night, using unwanted electricity from the National Grid, the turbines are reversed and water is pumped out of Loch Awe back up the hill to the reservoir, ready to be used again when demand is high. A guided tour takes you by bus into the mountain to see the cavernous turbine house.

Just north of Shiel Bridge, a very narrow, steep, twisting road, hemmed in by tumbledown stone walls and gnarled tree roots, leads down to a beach backed by high, rhododendron-laden cliffs and a couple of quite big houses with unexpectedly smooth velvet lawns. In the far distance, sitting stark on its rocky island at the mouth of Loch Moidart, is CASTLE TIORAM, which can only be reached at low tide, across a natural causeway. It was built in the 13th century and later converted into a modestly comfortable home for Amy, the wife of a Macdonald Lord of the Isles, abandoned here by her husband when he went off to marry Robert II's daughter. The castle is derelict and closed, but you can scramble around the outside on the rocks. With the sea breeze in your face, the view west across ragged islands to the setting sun at the mouth of the bay is achingly beautiful, with the water swirling past on both sides, boats bobbing on the loch, lonely tree-covered headlands, wild flowers and sandy beaches.

Ayrshire

County Town: Ayr

Ar – Gaelic name for a fast running river

Burns Monument, Alloway, the first monument built to honour Scotland's National Poet

Ayr

'Auld Ayr, wham ne'er a town surpasses
For honest men and bonny lasses'
Robert Burns

Bright and breezy Ayr is a historic county town, once the most important harbour on Scotland's west coast. Today, with its long sandy beach, it is Scotland's chief west coast resort, popular with day-trippers from Glasgow. The busy High Street follows a 13th-century plan and winds pleasantly past many fine buildings, including the neo-Gothic Wallace Tower of 1832, its archway striding across the pavement, and Ayr's most prominent landmark, the Town Hall steeple, 225

feet (69 m) high, designed by Thomas Hamilton, and begun in 1827.

It was in Ayr, around 1297, that WILLIAM WALLACE began his campaign when he torched the English garrison of 500 men in an operation known as the 'Burning of the Barns of Ayr'. Wallace watched the flames from a hilltop at Barnweill 6 miles (9.6 km) to the north, and a Victorian memorial tower has been erected there in honour of the occasion.

On 26 April 1315, after the Battle of Bannockburn, Robert the Bruce held his FIRST SCOTTISH PARLIAMENT at St John's Kirk in Ayr, to thrash out the question of the royal succession – it was decided in favour of his brother Edward.

Scotland's national poet, ROBERT BURNS, had strong associations with Ayr (*see* Alloway). He was baptised in the Auld Kirk, and a little further up the High Street you can still enjoy a drink at the Tam o' Shanter Inn, where the hero 'Tam' enjoyed a convivial evening before his nightmare ride home.

Off the High Street is the narrow cobbled 'Auld Brig', dating from the 15th century, which replaced an earlier wooden bridge of 1250, and was for several centuries the main way into the town. It is now used only as a footbridge. In his poem 'The Brigs of Ayr', Robert Burns has the Auld Brig trade insults with Robert Adam's smart new bridge of 1788 downstream. The New Bridge says of the Auld,

'. . . poor narrow footpath of a street,
where twa wheel-barrows tremble when they meet'

to which the Auld Brig replies,

Conceited gowk! puffed up wi' windy pride!
This mony a year I've stood the flood and tide . . .
. . . I'll be a brig when ye're a shapeless cairn.'

And, nearly a century later the New Bridge was indeed reduced to a shapeless cairn when it was swept away by floods. It had to be replaced in 1877 by the existing five-arched bridge. Twenty-five years later the town planners

wanted to knock the Auld Brig down, but Burns Club members from across the world joined the people of Ayr and raised the money to rescue and restore it.

Close to the New Bridge is Loudoun Hall, built in 1513 and SCOTLAND'S OLDEST MERCHANT'S HOUSE, now restored as an arts centre.

In a corner of handsome 19th-century Wellington Square there is a memorial to 'road builder' JOHN LOUDON MCADAM, who was born in 1756 at Lady Cathcart's House, a tenement block in the Sandgate.

Also in the Sandgate there is a bronze plate on a wall marking the site of MURDOCH'S LODGINGS, where Robert Burns went to school.

During the 18th century, when Ayr was a thriving port trading with America and Spain, the town was home to SCOTLAND'S LARGEST WINE MERCHANT, Oliphant & Co.

Ayr racecourse is SCOTLAND'S FOREMOST RACECOURSE and home to the SCOTTISH GRAND NATIONAL.

Robert Burns

Scotland's National Poet

It is impossible to travel about Ayrshire without coming across ROBERT BURNS. Everyone and everywhere in the county boasts a Burns quote, memorial, monument or story. Brilliant, handsome and funny, Burns was every bit the glamorous poet – a drinker, a womaniser, perpetually broke but a brilliant wordsmith who perfectly captured the Scottish spirit and whose

greatest achievement was to preserve and make respectable the Scots dialect and the Scottish traditional song.

Robert Burns was born in ALLOWAY, on 25 January 1759, the eldest of seven children. His father William was a tenant farmer who built, with his own hands, the low, thatched 'auld clay biggin' where Robert was born. It is set in three lovely acres, what his father called 'William Burnes's New Garden'. For much of the 19th century the cottage was an alehouse, but is now the most comprehensive of all the many Burns museums. It is also the oldest house in Alloway.

Although Alloway is now an affluent suburb of Ayr, and a Robert Burns theme park, it has somehow managed to remain a quiet and attractive place. There are cottage gardens, winding leafy lanes and many peaceful corners, particularly down by the river, where the 15th-century BRIG O' DOON elegantly spans the water, carrying pedestrians from a hotel garden into a field. In the poem 'Tam o' Shanter', Tam flees across the Brig o' Doon on his grey mare Meg, pursued by the witch, Nannie.

Just up the road is Alloway's AULD

KIRK, setting for the witches' dance in 'Tam o' Shanter', a scene only too easy to picture as you wander through the roofless old ruin, lurking under dark, spooky trees. Robert's father William is buried here, but not his mother Agnes. Although she is given a credit on William's headstone, she is actually buried in Bolton, East Lothian.

Across the road, surrounded by yet more gorgeous gardens, is the BURNS MONUMENT. Wherever you go in Scotland, when you see a towering, epic monument you can be sure it will commemorate either William Wallace or Robert Burns. And the people of Alloway have not skimped. Their monument to their famous son is colossal – it stands 60 ft (18 m) high, with a triangular base supporting a circle of Corinthian columns, topped with a cupola and a gilt tripod. It was designed by Thomas Hamilton, who put up the Wallace Tower in Ayr, and was built in 1820. There is a small museum inside the base.

Prestwick

The Visit of the King

PRESTWICK vies with Tain in Ross and Cromarty as the oldest burgh in Scotland, having been a free burgh of barony since 'beyond the memory of man' according to a charter of 1600. It is the only coastal town in Ayrshire that does not have a harbour.

THE FIRST EVER OPEN GOLF CHAMPIONSHIP was played at Prestwick in 1860, and it was held there for the next 11 years. Prestwick went on to host the tournament on 24 occasions, the last time in 1925.

Prestwick Airport was developed in 1935 by flying enthusiasts the Marquess of Clydesdale, later the 14th Duke of Hamilton celebrated as Rudolf Hess's putative host (see Eaglesham, Lanarkshire) and David McIntyre, THE FIRST MEN TO FLY OVER MOUNT EVEREST. It was SCOTLAND'S FIRST TRANSATLANTIC AIRPORT and for a long time was the only Scottish airport allowed to operate transatlantic flights, since it has a far lower incidence of fog than any other British airport – even today it IS THE ONLY GUARANTEED FOG-FREE AIRPORT IN BRITAIN. In terms of physical size, Prestwick is SCOTLAND'S LARGEST AIRPORT.

It is also THE ONLY PLACE IN BRITAIN WHERE ELVIS PRESLEY EVER SET FOOT. On 3 March 1960, 'The King' passed through on his way to America after being discharged from the US Army in Germany. While his plane was re-fuelling he spent an hour mixing with the American base staff and the lucky few fans who had somehow found out that he was coming. There is a plaque in the terminal building marking the occasion.

Bridges of Ayrshire

Ballochmyle Viaduct

You would think that BALLOCHMYLE VIADUCT, THE HIGHEST RAILWAY BRIDGE IN BRITAIN, would be easy to spot. It isn't. First, you have to turn left off the A76, just before it crosses the River Ayr south of Mauchline, wiggle down a tiny lane and park at the bottom. Then you climb a

stile and follow the footpath through deep woods along the top of a rocky gorge, with the River Ayr glinting far below to your left. Suddenly, shockingly, magnificently, there it is – a wondrous, soaring stone arch rising majestically into the heavens. Although the path is already high above the river, the bridge still seems impossibly tall. When a train crosses, seen from down here it looks like something from a miniature model railway.

The viaduct consists of three small arches at each end flanking the wide, graceful central arch, which stands 169 ft (51.5 m) above the river and has a span of 181 ft (55 m) – THE WORLD'S LONGEST MASONRY RAILWAY ARCH at the time of its completion in 1848.

The best view of the viaduct, not obscured by trees, is from the river. This necessitates a steep scramble down the side of the gorge and then a bare-foot paddle over mossy rocks along the riverbed. In the summer, when the leaves are full, it gets very dark and sinister down here. The bridge, when it comes into view around a rock promontory, seems to fill the heavens and the rippling water echoes coldly off the stonework. It is all wonderfully eerie.

Nearby, chiselled into the sheer rock face, hidden beneath hanging roots and lichens, are a collection of NEOLITHIC CUP AND RING MARKINGS, thought to be anything up to 3,500 years old.

In more modern times, Ballochmyle starred in the 1996 Tom Cruise movie *Mission Impossible*. Director Brian de Palma needed a stretch of railway free from overhead wires and bridges to double as the approach to the Channel Tunnel in Kent and the memorable scene with Cruise clinging to the top of a train while pursued by a helicopter was filmed as the train sped across the Ballochmyle viaduct.

During this scene, the town of CATRINE can be glimpsed in the background. Catrine was founded as a cotton mill town, in 1787, by Sir Claude Alexander, of Ballochmyle House, and David Dale the industrial reformer (*see* New Lanark, Lanarkshire). The mill which was destroyed by fire in 1963, was one of the finest industrial buildings in Scotland and was the only example in Scotland of a factory where all the processes of manufacture from yarn to the finished product were carried out. From 1828 until 1947, the mill was powered by THE TWO BIGGEST WATER-WHEELS IN BRITAIN, each 50 feet (15.2 m) in diameter, 12 feet (3.6 m) wide, with 120 buckets capable of lifting 120 tons of water per minute, generating 500 horsepower.

Between Ballochmyle Viaduct and Catrine is Howford Bridge, built in 1963 to take the A76 across the Ayr, and once THE LARGEST CONCRETE SPAN IN SCOTLAND.

Laigh Milton Viaduct

THE LAIGH MILTON VIADUCT, at Gatehead near Kilmarnock, is THE OLDEST SURVIVING PUBLIC RAILWAY VIADUCT IN THE WORLD. It was opened in 1812 to carry the Kilmarnock to Troon line, SCOTLAND'S FIRST PUBLIC RAILWAY, across the River Irvine. The viaduct is no longer in use but has been beautifully restored. The railway was engineered by William Jessop, for the 4th Duke of Portland, to carry coal and passengers in horse-drawn wagons from the coalfields of Kilmarnock to the harbour at Troon. In 1816, SCOTLAND'S FIRST RAILWAY ENGINE, George Stephenson's 'The Duke', named after the Duke of Portland, was used to haul coal along the line, giving the Kilmarnock to Troon railway line a claim to be THE OLDEST STEAM RAILWAY IN THE WORLD.

John Loudon McAdam

Jolly Tar

JOHN LOUDON MCADAM (1756–1836) was born in Ayr. Having made his fortune in America as a prize agent, he returned in 1783 and bought Sauchrie House on the southern slope of Brown Carrick Hill outside Ayr. It was here that he first experimented with the road-building technique that was to make his name famous around the world. The modern side-road at the bottom of the driveway to Sauchrie House runs along the line of that very first stretch of 'macadam' for about one mile (1.6 km). McAdam's system involved laying down a layer of small stones and gravel covering a layer of larger stones, so that the weight of traffic compacts the material into a hard-wearing surface. The road was raised above the level of the surrounding terrain and cambered so that water would drain away.

One of the very first practical stretches of road that McAdam constructed was FURNACE ROAD, an access road for McAdam's tar pits, located in bleak moorland at Muirkirk, in the far east of Ayrshire. Parts of the road still exist, as do the remains of Springhill House where 'Tar' McAdam, as he became known, lived. The word 'tarmacadam' or 'tarmac' comes from the use of tar as a binding agent for a McAdam-type road. Ironically, McAdam never thought of using tar in this way himself. It was an idea that other engineers developed and it did not become commonplace until the 20th century. The tar from 'Tar' McAdam's pits was used for weatherproofing ropes. There is a cairn, built with stones from his tar kilns, marking the site, right at the end of the bumpy track that is all that remains of Furnace Road.

Culzean Castle

A President's Holiday Home

CULZEAN CASTLE, perched dramatically on a cliff above the wild Firth of Clyde, was fashioned out of a 12th-century tower house by Robert Adam between 1777 and 1792 for the 10th Earl of Cassillis, head of the Kennedy family later Marquesses of Ailsa. The spectacular OVAL STAIRCASE inside is considered by many to be Robert Adam's masterpiece.

The armoury display in the entrance hall at Culzean is the largest display of

Culzean Castle

its kind in the world after the Queen's display at Windsor Castle. Suspended from the ceiling and used as a fan is the propeller from the aeroplane that shot down the first Zeppelin. It was presented to the 3rd Marquess of Ailsa, in 1919, by No. 1 Fighting School from nearby Turnberry Airfield .

In 1945, Culzean was donated to the National Trust for Scotland, who presented lifetime tenure of the top-floor apartment to US President Dwight D. Eisenhower, in recognition of his wartime achievements. Eisenhower who relished the nearby golf courses stayed there four times, once while he was in office. Today the apartment is available for rent – at a price. In 1969, the estate surrounding the castle was opened as SCOTLAND'S FIRST COUNTRY PARK.

Penkill Castle

Protected by a Curse?

Hidden deep in a fold of the Carrick Hills, just east of Girvan, perched above the Penwhapple glen, is the fairy-tale 16th-century castle of PENKILL, described by the Pre-Raphaelite poet William Bell Scott as 'The Palace of Sleeping Beauty, in its enchanted and limitless response'.

The castle was home of the Boyds, at one time the most important family in Scotland. Sir Robert Boyd became Regent of Scotland in 1460 and later the family became Earls of Kilmarnock. Their main home was Dean Castle in Kilmarnock. The 4th Earl was beheaded in London for 4th part in the Jacobite rebellion of 1745.

William Bell Scott stayed at Penkill on many occasions, as a guest of the owner Spencer Boyd and his sister Alice, whose family had been lairds of Penkill for 300 years. With the occasional help of his Pre-Raphaelite friends William Holman Hunt, William Morris, Edward Burne-Jones and Dante Gabriel Rossetti, Scott refurbished and refashioned the castle and gardens with a dazzling array of murals, paintings, furniture, tapestries, carvings and china.

Even though married, Scott was obviously in love with Alice and spent his happiest days with her at the romantic and bewitching Penkill. His favourite work was his portrait of Spencer and Alice on top of the round tower with Ailsa Craig in the distance. This was hung in the Rossetti room over the fireplace under an inscription in gold leaf by Bell that read, 'Move not this picture, let it be, for love of those in effigy'. Not long afterwards a potential burglar fell from the castle wall and was impaled on a tree in the glen below.

Scott died of angina at Penkill in 1890 and is buried in the churchyard at Old Dailly. The castle descended eventually to Evelyn May Courtney-Boyd, a kindly, generous old lady who was taken advantage of by various antiques dealers and con men who slowly divested the castle of many of its treasures.

A particular rogue was the local milkman, who inveigled himself and his wife into living in the castle and then proceeded to sell or auction off various paintings and other articles. His downfall came when he tried to prise the portrait of Spencer and Alice off the wall of the Rossetti room with a poker: he started choking violently and fell writhing to the floor. Later that night he died horribly – of angina.

Was he the victim of the Penkill Curse, which promises certain death to anyone trying to bring harm to Penkill?

In 1978, Penkill and its contents were sold to a private American buyer, who has restored the castle and opens it occasionally to visitors by appointment. It is a mystical, timeless place, this ancient turreted castle set in a secret sylvan valley, blessed with a priceless collection of Pre-Raphaelite treasures – and protected by a curse.

Loudoun Castle

Windsor of Scotland

Five miles (8 km) east of Kilmarnock is the impressive shell of LOUDOUN CASTLE, a 19th-century mansion built around a 15th-century tower house, gutted by fire in 1941. The house was so grand that it was known as the 'Windsor of Scotland'. It had 12 towers, one for every month, and 365 windows, one for every day of the year. At one time some of the windows were boarded up to avoid window tax – the tax that gave rise to the expression 'daylight robbery'.

Sir Hugh de Crauford of Loudoun was the grandfather of William Wallace, whose sword once hung in the hallway of Loudoun Castle. The sword was sold at auction in 1930.

Against the south wall of the castle is the magnificent AULD YEW TREE, thought to be over 700 years old. In 1707, in the shade of this tree, articles of the Act of Union between England,

Wales and Scotland were discussed and drawn up.

LOUDOUN GOWF CLUB has been in existence since the early 16th century, and the club's golf course can make a claim to being in possession of THE OLDEST GOLF TURF STILL IN USE FOR GOLF IN SCOTLAND. It was once the private gowf field of the Campbells of Loudoun Castle, 'gowf' being the old Scottish word for golf, and the turf has not been replaced or dug up for over 400 years. In 1920, some of the roadside rough was used to re-turf Scotland's National Stadium at Hampden Park in Glasgow.

The grounds of Loudoun Castle are now home to SCOTLAND'S LARGEST LEISURE PARK. Attractions include BRITAIN'S BIGGEST CAROUSEL and SCOTLAND'S HIGHEST ROLLER-COASTER.

Kilmarnock

Whisky Town

In 1786, the first edition of Robert Burns's poems was published in KILMARNOCK at Star Inn Close. An original Kilmarnock edition is very rare and much sought after today. A stone marks the site, which is now a shopping mall.

JOHNNIE WALKER was born near Kilmarnock in 1805, and in 1820, aged just 15, he opened a grocery shop in Kilmarnock's King Street. Using his tea-blending skills, Johnnie became known for his own special blended whisky, Walker's Kilmarnock Whisky. When his son Alexander took over, in 1859, the firm expanded to become THE LARGEST WHISKY FIRM IN THE WORLD. The famous 'striding man' logo was drawn, in 1908, by a leading black-and-white line artist, Tom Browne. Today Kilmarnock is still the centre for Johnnie Walker Red and Black Label blending and bottling. Johnnie Walker himself is buried in the churchyard of the disused St Andrew's Glencairn church, south of the town centre, and there is a statue of him in the Strand. Johnnie Walker Red Label is THE BEST SELLING WHISKY IN THE WORLD.

The Eglinton Tournament

Knights of Old

In 1839, steeplechasing was first introduced to Scotland at Irvine's Bogside racecourse, owned by the Earls of Eglinton. In that same year, Irvine was the setting for the great EGLINTON TOURNAMENT, organised in the grounds of Eglinton Castle on the outskirts of the town, by Archibald Montgomerie, 13th Earl of Eglinton. Disappointed by having been denied the chance to officiate at Queen Victoria's coronation, in his position as Knight Marshal of the Royal Household, due to the Whig government's insistence on holding a simple ceremony without expensive pageantry, Archibald decided to re-create medieval pageantry at a tournament of his own, with jousting, feasting, sword fights and other knightly pursuits. Thousands came, but the heavens opened and the event, which cost £4 million in today's money, was a washout.

The Eglinton family subsequently lost all their fortune building docks at Ardrossan, and there is nothing left of the castle. However, the ornamental tournament bridge, built by the 13th Earl to convey his guests over the River Lugton, still stands in Eglinton Country Park.

Well, I never knew this ABOUT AYRSHIRE

Ayrshire is the only county in Britain to have three golf courses that have hosted the Open Championship: ROYAL TROON, TURNBERRY and PRESTWICK.

Travellers on the A719 between Culzean and Ayr should be extra vigilant as they come to a sloping stretch of road just south of Dunure, as they may suddenly come across a car with no driver, free wheeling up the hill. At least that's what it looks like at ELECTRIC BRAE. The configuration of the land here causes an optical illusion, making it look as though the road is sloping in the opposite direction to that which it actually is. Hence a stationary car left with the brakes off appears to begin to roll uphill. It is an experience that many find diverting and, since there is no sufficient lay-by, many drivers just stop in the middle of the road and get out of their cars to experiment. In the past it was thought that the phenomenon was caused by an electric attraction from within the hillside, or brae, which explains the use of the term 'electric'.

CROSSRAGUEL ABBEY, just outside Maybole, is the best preserved of all the ruined abbeys in Ayrshire. Of particular merit are the imposing four-storey gatehouse, with a fine viewing platform at the top, and the chapter house, renowned for its acoustic qualities.

Robert the Bruce was baptised at Crossraguel. The simple stone font at which he was christened can be found locked behind an iron grill in the roofless old kirk at KIRKOSWALD, just down the road, where it was taken for safety during the Reformation.

JAMES BOSWELL (1740–95), whose *Life of Samuel Johnson*, published in 1791, is

generally considered to be the greatest biography in the English language, is buried in the family vaults beneath AUCHINLECK church. An avenue of trees leads 3 miles (4.8 km) from the church to his ancestral home AUCHINLECK HOUSE, which is now owned by the Landmark Trust.

Towering spectacularly over the Doon valley near Auchinleck, like something out of *The War of the Worlds*, is a restored 'A' frame winding-gear tower, THE ONLY ONE OF ITS KIND LEFT IN BRITAIN. It stands on the site of the BARONY COLLIERY and is a striking landmark for miles around. The effect is unexpectedly moving. At the foot of the massive structure, by the side of the road, there is a landscaped memorial stone that reads: 'Erected in memory of those who worked and lost their lives in the Barony Colliery 1908–1989'.

WILLIAM MURDOCK (1754–1839), the engineer who built the first house in the world to be lit by gas, at Redruth in Cornwall, was born at Bello Mill in Lugar. He carried out many of his early experiments with gas lighting in a nearby cave, overlooking the River Lugar, which can still be explored today.

SIR ALEXANDER FLEMING, the inventor of penicillin, was born in Lochfield near Darvel on 6 August 1881. In 1928, while researching the flu virus, he noticed that mould had developed on a staphylococcus culture plate he had left lying around the laboratory and that the mould had killed off the bacteria around it. He christened the active substance produced by the mould 'penicillin'.

The 12th-century church at SYMINGTON, south of Kilmarnock, is noted for its three lancet windows in the east wall

and the open-work timber roof of worn black beams – ONE OF ONLY TWO SURVIVING EXAMPLES IN SCOTLAND, the other being in the Church of the Holy Rood in Stirling.

JOHN BOYD DUNLOP (1840–1921), inventor of THE FIRST PRACTICAL PNEUMATIC TYRE, was born in the village of Dreghorn, just outside Irvine.

MAUCHLINE has THE ONLY WORKING CURLING STONE FACTORY IN BRITAIN.

It was in a field at MOSSGIEL FARM, near Mauchline, that Robert Burns's plough turned up the 'wee, sleekit, cow'rin, tim'rous beastie' of a mouse. Burns and his brother were renting the farm.

MUIRKIRK, on the eastern border of Ayrshire, was THE FIRST TOWN IN BRITAIN TO BE LIT BY GAS, in 1859. This was due to the opening of the Muirkirk Coke and Gaslight Company, which remained in operation at Muirkirk until 1977.

In 1815, the American horror writer EDGAR ALLAN POE spent some months attending the local school in IRVINE. His writing lessons consisted of copying the epitaphs from the tombstones in the parish churchyard, no doubt providing food for thought in his later career.

Sometime in 1271, the recently widowed MARGARET, COUNTESS of CARRICK became infatuated with a handsome knight who rode past her castle at Turnberry. She had him kidnapped and brought to her, then seduced him into marrying her. In 1274 they had a son, born here or at Lochmaben, or possibly even in Essex (see *I Never Knew That About England*). The handsome knight turned out to be Robert de Brus and their son grew up to be Robert the Bruce, Earl of Carrick and, eventually, Robert I of Scotland. Earl of Carrick became a royal title – the present Earl of Carrick is Prince Charles.

SIR THOMAS BRISBANE (1773–1860), soldier and astonomer, was born in LARGS, and is buried in the family vault in Douglas Park. He was Governor of New South Wales and set up Australia's first significant observatory. The state capital of Queensland is named after him, as well as a crater on the moon. He was born and died in the same bed, at his family seat, Brisbane House in Largs. The house was demolished in World War Two.

BANFFSHIRE

COUNTY TOWN: BANFF

Boineffe – 'Land of the stream or Boyn' (Gaelic name for River Deveron)

Cullen House, seat of the Earls of Seafield and celebarted for its art collection. Robert the Bruce's Queen, Elizabeth, died in an earlier building here

Banff

Time to Go

BANFF is an ancient royal burgh and county town that once boasted a massive castle, now vanished, and a busy harbour, now mostly silted up. Many of the local grandees built winter homes in Banff, however, and the town possesses a superb collection of fine 17th- and 18th-century buildings, making it one of Scotland's most elegant towns. Lord Byron and his mother would occasionally stay in Banff, at the townhouse of the poet's grandmother, Mrs Gordon of Gight.

The Biggar Fountain in the town centre stands on the site of the old gallows whose most famous victim, in 1701, was the 'Banff Freebooter', fiddler James Macpherson, 'knave, vagabond and oppressor'. In fact he is thought to have been something of a Robin Hood figure, robbing the rich to give to the poor. As he waited for his execution, Macpherson entertained the crowd with an impromptu performance on his fiddle of an original composition, now known as 'Macpherson's Rant'. He appealed to the crowd for their support, promising his violin to anyone who would speak up for him, but no one came forward. Dismayed, he smashed the instrument in two and flung it into the open grave awaiting him at his feet. As it turned out, the local people had petitioned for his reprieve, and a pardon was on its way, but the Sheriff of Banff, Lord Braco, who was no doubt one of the rich, wanted blood, and he moved the town clock forward an hour, so that the hanging could be carried out before the messenger arrived. The offending clock was later sent to Dufftown.

Duff House

Jewel of the North-East

Banff's great treasure lies just outside the town to the south-west in its own extensive grounds. DUFF HOUSE is the jewel of north-east Scotland, a breathtaking baroque pile built by William Adam in the 1730s for William Duff, later the 1st Earl of Fife, and almost as big as the town of Banff itself. It was intended to have colonnaded wings, but Duff fell out with Adam over costs and they were never built. So bitter was the quarrel that Duff swore he would never set foot in Duff House, or even look at it, and would draw down the blinds of his carriage whenever he passed. He missed a splendid sight.

In the 19th century, Duff's descendent, the 6th Earl of Fife, married Princess Louise, eldest daughter of the Prince of Wales (later Edward VII), and became the Duke of Fife. Finding it diplomatic to move across the mountains to Mar Lodge, close to his grandmother-in-law at Balmoral, the new Duke turned his back on Duff House and finally handed it over to the burgh of Banff in 1906. Since then it has led a rather spotty existence as a palm court hotel, a sanitarium for sufferers from constipation or, if you prefer, 'disorders of nutrition, excluding inebriation', a prisoner-of-war camp and a billet house for troops.

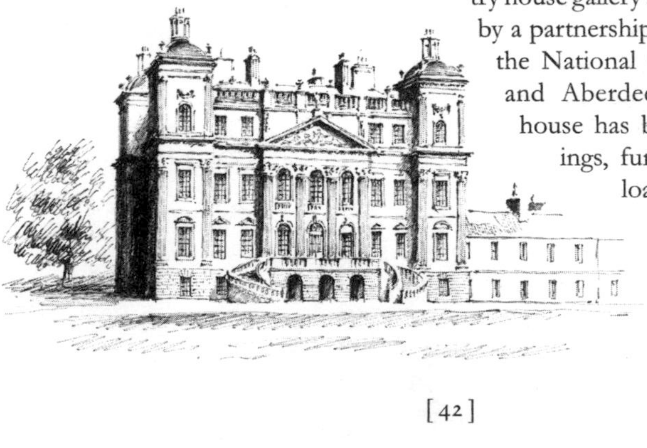

Since 1995 it has been run as a country house gallery and cultural arts centre, by a partnership of Historic Scotland, the National Galleries of Scotland and Aberdeenshire council. The house has been filled with paintings, furniture and *objets d'art*, loaned by various institutions and individuals from around Scotland, and is now a peaceful place to shelter from the bleak north wind and linger awhile. Unloved from the beginning, hopelessly out of place, hugely over the top, Duff House is nonetheless, magical – an unexpected treat.

Craigellachie Bridge

'The bridge is of iron, beautifully light, in a situation where the utility of lightness is instantly perceived'
ROBERT SOUTHEY

Below the village of CRAIGELLACHIE, perched on its terrace of rock above the junction of the Fiddich and Spey rivers, you can find SCOTLAND'S OLDEST IRON BRIDGE. Soaring above a deep brown, swirling Spey pool is a graceful silver arch of delicate tracery, suspended between battlemented stone towers, seemingly hewn from the living rock. The poet Southey wrote his words in 1819, five years after the bridge was completed, and Craigellachie is unarguably one of Scotland's most handsome pieces of engineering.

It was built by Thomas Telford, with the 150 ft (46 m) main span being cast in Wales by William Hazeldine, nicknamed by Telford 'the arch conjuror'. This was a difficult site to build a bridge, with low-lying water-meadows on one side, and a vertical cliff on the other. Telford blasted a 100 ft (30 m) approach road on the north side, 70 ft (21 m) above the water, which required a sharp left-hand turn on to the bridge itself. Stone arches were included to bring the bridge level with the road, and these proved invaluable during floods in 1829, when the Spey rose 20 ft (6 m) above its normal level. The bridge was restored in 1964 and by-passed not long after that, by a new bridge downstream. In 1994 the commanding officers and regimental colour parties of the Queen's Own Highlanders from Morayshire, and the Gordon Highlanders from Banffshire, met on the bridge to show unity, before being merged into a new regiment called the Highlanders.

The Spey and the Fiddich are two of

the most renowned rivers on the whisky trail, and Craigellachie, ranked by many as the most beautiful village in Banffshire, boasts two distilleries, the Craigellachie and the Macallan.

Dufftown

Rome was built on seven hills
Dufftown stands on seven stills
(ANON)

Founded in 1817 by James Duff, 4th Earl of Fife, as a means of giving employment after the Napoleonic Wars, DUFFTOWN is to be found in GLEN FIDDICH – the valley of the deer. Styled 'The Whisky Capital of the World', it is a quietly prosperous, attractive stone village, built around a central square, at the heart of which stands a sturdy, pink granite baronial tower, completed in 1839 and built originally as a jail. The splendid tower clock came from Banff, and is known as 'The Clock that Hanged Macpherson' (*see* Banff).

Probably the best known of Dufftown's seven distilleries is Glenfiddich, which has been owned and managed by the Grant family since the day it opened in 1887. In 1963, Glenfiddich became THE FIRST DISTILLERY TO MARKET SINGLE-MALT WHISKY (AS OPPOSED TO BLENDED WHISKY) OUTSIDE SCOTLAND and, later, THE FIRST DISTILLERY TO SET UP A VISITOR CENTRE. Glenfiddich is THE ONLY HIGHLAND SINGLE MALT THAT IS DISTILLED, MATURED AND BOTTLED AT ITS OWN DISTILLERY, and is now THE BIGGEST SELLING SINGLE-MALT WHISKY IN THE WORLD.

Thanks to its position at the centre of so many productive distilleries, Dufftown, for its size, is one of THE TOP FOUR FOREIGN CURRENCY EARNERS IN THE WHOLE OF BRITAIN.

Tomintoul

Highest Village in the Highlands

Actually, TOMINTOUL is not quite the highest village in the Highlands. That accolade goes to Dalwhinnie in Inverness-shire, which is 12 ft (3.6 m) higher, depending, of course, on where you take the measurement. Then again, the good people of Tomintoul could justifiably claim that Dalwhinnie is actually more of a hamlet than a village. Whatever your preference, Tomintoul is certainly very high up, 1,160 ft (354 m) above sea level, and the first place to get cut off by the winter snows.

Tomintoul is a pleasant place with one long, gently rising street and splendid views in all directions. It was founded in 1750 by the 4th Duke of Gordon so that all his widely dispersed tenants could live in one comfortable spot, with the purely coincidental added benefit of making it easier for him to keep an eye on their cattle rustling and illegal whisky stills.

There is something seductive about Tomintoul. It may be the mountain air or the presence of so many whisky distilleries nearby but, whatever it is, in 1988 Tomintoul cast its spell on a gentle fellow from Surrey, one Tony Williams. He fell in love with the village during a visit with his wife, while they were on holiday in Ballater, and they bought a dilapidated cottage on the village green. Then he gradually began to buy up the village, starting with the Gordon Arms Hotel in the square and the Clockhouse restaurant nearby. Through a holding company, Tomintoul Enterprises, he poured money into the village, restoring run-down cottages, supporting local businesses and generally behaving like an old-fashioned and gratifyingly generous laird.

Quite naturally, he became immensely popular with the locals, which made the blow, when it came, all the more traumatic. Tony Williams was not, in fact, a rich English philanthropist, but a finance director at Scotland Yard, the Metropolitan police headquarters in London. And the £2 million or more that he lavished on Tomintoul was not from stock options but from the funds of the Metropolitan Police. From under the very noses of the Fraud Squad he had embezzled some £5 million, not to live the life of Riley, but to live the life of the Laird of Tomintoul.

Williams was arrested in 1994 and jailed for seven years at the Old Bailey in London in 1995.

Tomintoul declined for a while after this affair, but the development of the LECHT SKI CENTRE 5 miles (8 km) away has helped to revive the village's fortunes.

A little to the north of Tomintoul is STRATH AVON, where a winding road runs above the river to the Glenlivet distillery, past lush meadows full of highland cattle, and through scented woods, teeming with wildlife, along one of the most ravishing river valleys in Scotland.

Scotch Whisky

Scotland's Greatest Export

The word whisky is derived from the Gaelic 'uisge beatha', meaning 'water of life', and is recorded even earlier in Latin as 'aqua vitae'.

Banffshire, and particularly SPEYSIDE, is the spiritual home of Scotch whisky, which has been distilled here, legally or illegally, for probably 600 years or more. The first record of whisky in Scotland was in 1494. Whether the Scots took it to Ireland, or the Irish 'Scots' brought it with them to Scotland in the 6th or 7th century, is not clear, but whisky was first distilled by monks who brought the art home with them from their travels in Europe and Asia, and adapted it to their own environment in the monasteries. Excavations on the island of Rum suggest that some sort of alcoholic drink was distilled here some 6,000 years ago.

Scotland's pure, clear, peaty water is the magic ingredient that makes Scotch so special. Scotch whisky is made by malting barley, extracting the sugars with hot water, fermenting the sweet worts to form wash, and distilling this into a spirit that must then be matured for at least three years before it can be called Scotch.

Malt whisky comes from malted barley. Grain whisky comes from maize, with a little malted barley. Most Scotch whisky is a blend of the two, but single malts, though more expensive, are becoming increasingly popular (*see* Glenfiddich).

Well, I never knew this ABOUT BANFFSHIRE

KATHERINE, DUCHESS OF ATHOLL (1874–1960), known as 'Kitty' or the Red Duchess, was born in Banff. She was THE FIRST SCOTTISH WOMAN MEMBER OF PARLIAMENT, and THE FIRST CONSERVATIVE WOMAN CABINET MINISTER.

BEN MACDHUI, at the southwest extremity of Banffshire, rises to 4,296 ft (1,309 m), and is THE SECOND HIGHEST MOUNTAIN IN BRITAIN.

BALLINDALLOCH CASTLE dates from the 16th century and has been lived in by the Macpherson-Grants since its construction. The herd of Aberdeen Angus cattle at Ballindaloch Castle, introduced by the 3rd Baronet, Sir George Macpherson-Grant, in 1878, IS THE OLDEST HERD OF THIS BREED IN THE WORLD.

The MACDUFF boatyard is THE LAST PRIVATE YARD IN EUROPE STILL BUILDING TRADITIONAL WOODEN FISHING BOATS.

MACDUFF MARINE AQUARIUM displays many of the marine species found in the Moray Firth in a deep tank complete with living kelp reef and wave machine, unique in Britain. The tank is THE DEEPEST OF ANY AQUARIUM IN BRITAIN.

The ninth tee at DUFFTOWN GOLF CLUB stands 1,294 ft (394 m) above the sea, making it THE HIGHEST GOLF HOLE IN BRITAIN.

BALVENIE CASTLE near Dufftown dates from the 12th century and lays claim to being SCOTLAND'S OLDEST STONE CASTLE.

CULLEN is a pretty seaside town divided into two by three spectacular railway viaducts, now disused. A walk along the railway provides, on the seaward side, glorious views over the red and grey roofs of brightly painted fishermen's cottages. On the inland side, Seafield Street heads uphill, away from the viaducts, and is home to The Ice Cream Shop, in many people's opinion the best ice cream shop in Scotland. Cullen is also famous for Cullen Skink – an unfortunate name for a delicious soup of smoked haddock, potato and onion. 'Skink' comes from the Gaelic word for 'essence'.

KEITH is the second largest town in Banffshire after Buckie, and home to the Keith Kilt School, THE ONLY SCHOOL IN THE WORLD THAT TEACHES THE ART OF KILT MAKING.

Operating since 1786, Keith's Strathisla distillery is THE OLDEST LEGAL DISTILLERY IN THE HIGHLANDS.

KEITH was the birthplace, in 1795, of journalist and newspaper publisher JAMES GORDON BENNETT. Having emigrated to America in 1819, he founded the *New York Herald* in 1835 and became a joint founder of The Associated Press in 1848. His son, James Gordon Bennett Jnr, financed Stanley's expedition to Africa to find Dr Livingston, and instigated the Gordon Bennett motor races, forerunners of Grand Prix racing. Something of a playboy, and always in some newsworthy scrape or another, his name has become an expletive, 'Gordon Bennett!' – which derives from the exasperated question, 'What on earth has Gordon Bennett been up to this time . . . ?'

BERWICKSHIRE

COUNTY TOWN: DUNS

Bere wic – 'bare place' (Old English)

Ayton Castle, an outstanding example of Scottish baronial architecture

Duns

Dunce

DUNS was originally built on the 713 ft (217 m) high dun, or Iron Age fort, to the north of the present-day settlement, and takes its name from the same. In 1903, Duns was finally established as county town of Berwickshire, at the end of a bruising 300-year tussle with neighbouring Greenlaw for the privilege. Berwick-upon-Tweed, the original county town, had ended up in England in 1482, after changing hands between Scotland and England 14 times.

JOHN DUNS 'SCOTUS' (c.1265–1308) was born in Duns, as hinted at by his surname, and was also a Scot, as suggested by his nickname Scotus. He was a Franciscan monk, the greatest philosopher and theologian of his time, and his works had a profound effect on schools of thought throughout Europe in the Middle Ages. Known as Dr Subtilis, or the 'subtle doctor', his works ranged across metaphysics, morality,

psychology, language and religious beliefs, but his claim that religion was based on faith, not reason, was a deeply unpopular view, and it is from the detractors of John Duns that we derive the word 'dunce', meaning dim-wit.

Six hundred years later Duns contributed another son to a slightly different branch of the philosophical profession. George Allardice Riddell, born here in 1865, went on to become long-standing chairman of the *News of the World*.

Manderston

Family Silver

In a county full to the brim with stately houses, MANDERSTON deserves a special mention as Britain's purest expression of Edwardian architecture and way of life, encapsulating the very best of that brief but glamorous era between the Victorian age and the First World War. Sometimes called the swan-song of the great classical house, Manderston was built between 1901 and 1905 for Sir James Miller, known as 'Lucky Jim', whose father had made his fortune selling herring and hemp to the Russians. Every aspect of Manderston, from the furniture and Adam-style interiors to the Alpine boat-house and baronial gardener's cottage, was designed on Lucky Jim's premise that the costs 'simply didn't matter'. The dairy is in the form of a vaulted, marble Roman cloister, while the stables, with their polished brass posts, tiled troughs and stalls of teak were described by *Horse and Hound* as 'probably THE FINEST STABLING IN ALL THE WORLD'.

The most glittering of the treasures inside the house is the world's only silver staircase. In November 1905, Sir James and his wife Eveline, a sister of the 1st Marquess Curzon of Kedleston, gave an unforgettable house-warming ball at Manderston, but within three months Sir James was dead from pneumonia, brought on by going out hunting in January.

A display of biscuit tins in the basement celebrates the fact that the present laird, Lord Palmer, is a Palmer of Huntley & Palmer biscuit fame.

Manderston has remained virtually unchanged since it was built, and in 2002 was chosen by Channel 4 as the setting for their reality television series *The Edwardian Country House*, in which a family of five and a staff of 14 attempted to re-create everyday life in the Edwardian era.

Dryburgh Abbey

A Writer and a Soldier

DRYBURGH ABBEY was founded in 1150 by Sir Hugh de Moreville on the site of a 6th-century Celtic monastery. Sir Hugh's son was one of the four knights who murdered Thomas à Becket in Canterbury Cathedral in 1170.

The abbey's romantic ruins are set amongst the trees on a lazy loop of the River Tweed. While not so grand as Kelso or Melrose, the abbey's remote location is wonderfully peaceful and atmospheric and, as such, was chosen by Sir Walter Scott as the last resting-place of him and his wife. Scott's great-grandfather, Sir Thomas Haliburton, had owned the ruins in 1700 but, much to Scott's later dismay, he sold them, although retaining 'the right of stretching our bones here'. High above the abbey on Bemersyde Hill is Scott's View, looking west over the Tweed to the Eildon Hills. Scott cherished the Borders more than anywhere and he would always stop to look at the marvellous view from here. During his funeral procession from Abbotsford to Dryburgh the horses pulling his coffin halted at this spot of their own accord, almost as if to give their master a last look at his beloved native land.

Breathes there the man with soul so dead,
Who never to himself hath said,
This is my own, my native land!
from *The Lay of the Last Minstrel*

Also buried within the north transept of Dryburgh Abbey is FIELD MARSHAL 1ST EARL HAIG (1861–1928), Commander-in-Chief of British forces in France during the First World War. Haig's reputation has suffered as a result of the horrific slaughter at Mons and Ypres, although he hastened the end of the conflict by introducing the first tanks at the Somme in 1916, and his assault on the Hindenburg Line in 1918 brought about the end of the war. His memory is held in high esteem at Dryburgh for his tireless work in caring for the wounded and bereaved after the war. In 1921, Haig founded the British Legion to provide financial, social and emotional support to ex-servicemen and their dependants, and every year, on the Sunday nearest the anniversary of his birth, 19 June, the British Legion hold a commemoration service in the abbey. At his own request, Lord Haig lies beneath the same kind of simple headstone as those buried on the battlefields of France.

Chirnside

World Champion

The village of CHIRNSIDE is renowned for its fantastic views across the Berwickshire plain of the Merse, for the exquisite Norman doorway at the west end of the parish church, for the Ninewells estate, family home of philosopher David Hume, and for the Jim Clark Memorial Clock, complete with Lotus racing car silhouette, that stands in the middle of the village.

JIM CLARK (1936–68), was born in Fife, and moved as a boy to Chirnside, where his family had a farm. He was one of the best-loved and most dominant racing drivers of his time. He raced almost exclusively for Lotus and was responsible for bringing Colin Chapman's Grand Prix team to world prominence. Brilliant and unflappable inside the car, he was shy and indecisive out of it. He had no technical ability at all and relied on Chapman to translate his observations into mechanical solutions, but he is still regarded by many as the most naturally gifted racing driver of them all. He won the Formula One World Championship in 1963 and 1965. In 1965 he became the first Briton to win the Indianapolis 500 and the first non-American in nearly 50 years. His victory in the first race of 1968 brought his total to 25 Grand Prix wins, beating the previous record held by Fangio. Later that year, while practising at Hockenheim, a tyre burst, and his car was catapulted into a tree. He died before reaching hospital. His grave in the churchyard at Chirnside is still visited by fans, and every summer THE ONLY 'CLOSED ROADS' RACE IN BRITAIN, the Jim Clark Rally, is run on the roads around the village. There is a Jim Clark Room in Duns where many of his trophies and other memorabilia can be seen.

Well, I never knew this ABOUT BERWICKSHIRE

One mile (1.6 km) north of Cockburnspath is a deep, precipitous, tree-lined gorge spanned by three fine bridges. The oldest of these, dating from 1786, is 130 ft (40 m) high, and was THE HIGHEST BRIDGE IN THE WORLD WHEN IT WAS CONSTRUCTED.

AYTON CASTLE is regarded by many as perhaps the finest example of Scottish baronial architecture in the country, and is the first example of it that travellers on the London to Edinburgh train from England see once they are north of the border.

PAXTON HOUSE, on the north bank of the River Tweed some 4 miles (6.4 km) from Berwick, is an elegant Palladian house. It was built by John and James Adam in 1758, for Patrick Hume. An outstation of the National Galleries of Scotland, Paxton has THE LARGEST PURPOSE-BUILT PICTURE GALLERY OF ANY SCOTTISH COUNTRY HOUSE.

Linking Scotland and England across the Tweed, not far from Paxton House, is the UNION CHAIN BRIDGE, BRITAIN'S FIRST SUSPENSION BRIDGE FOR ROAD TRAFFIC. It was built in 1820 by Sir Samuel Brown, who devised a new kind of link for chain cables that made possible the development of bigger and heavier suspension bridges. The Union Bridge has a span of 360 ft (110 m).

The medieval, two-storey, crow-stepped tithe barn at FOULDEN, east of Duns, is regarded as THE FINEST TITHE BARN IN SCOTLAND.

COLDSTREAM sits on the north bank of the River Tweed, the first town in Scotland across John Smeaton's fine bridge

of 1766. In 1659, General Monck, Cromwell's military commander in Scotland, marched his Regiment of Foot across the ford from Coldstream at the start of their march to London to restore Charles II to the throne. They became known as the Coldstream Guards, THE ONLY BRITISH REGIMENT TO TAKE THEIR NAME FROM A TOWN. Nearby is The Hirsel, seat since 1611 of the Earls of Home, inlcuding the 14th Earl who disclaimed the title in 1963 to become Prime Minsiter as Sir Alec Douglas-Home. The house is private but the grounds can be visited.

BUTESHIRE

COUNTY TOWN: ROTHESAY

Ey bhiod – 'Island of Corn' (Gaelic)

Mount Stuart, the grandest Gothic-style private house in Britain

Island of Bute

Lovely to a Fault

The island of BUTE sits at the mouth of the Firth of Clyde and is separated from the Argyll mainland by the glorious Kyles of Bute. The island scenery is gentle and unspoilt, hilly in the north, flatter and more fertile in the south, with many small beaches and coves. Bute sits astride the Highland Boundary Fault which passes through Loch Fad near the centre of the island, placing the northern part in the Highlands and the southern section in the Lowlands. Two routes connect the island to the mainland. A small ferry runs between Rhubodach in the north and Ardentaive on the Cowal Peninsula, a crossing that cattle were once made to swim, while the main ferry links

Wemyss Bay in Renfrewshire to the island's main town, Rothesay.

On the southern end of the island is ST BLANE'S CHAPEL, with Norman ruins on the site of a Celtic monastery founded in the 6th century by St Blane, who was born on Bute and was a contemporary of St Columba.

Rothesay

Madeira of the Clyde

ROTHESAY, old county town of Buteshire, and attractively sited on the east coast of the Isle of Bute, has grown up around one of the oldest and most remarkable castles in Scotland. Built in the early 13th century, the castle consists of a very high curtain wall, protected by four drum towers, enclosing a circular courtyard, all within a deep moat. THE DESIGN IS UNIQUE IN SCOTLAND.

The castle was occupied by King Hakon of Norway before his defeat at the Battle of Largs in 1263 (*see* Ayrshire).

Rothesay became a favourite residence of the Stewart kings, particularly Robert III, who died there in 1406. He created Scotland's oldest Dukedom when he made his son Duke of Rothesay, a title held ever since by the eldest son of the King of Scotland. Prince Charles, heir to the British throne, is often referred to as the Duke of Rothesay when he is in Scotland.

With its sandy beach and mild climate, Rothesay has long been one of the most popular of the Firth of Clyde resorts, and the holiday villas of wealthy 19th-century Glasgow merchants jostle together along the sea front. A useful remnant from those days is the block of flamboyant Victorian lavatories at the end of the pier. Commissioned in 1899, they are THE FINEST SURVIVORS OF THEIR KIND IN BRITAIN, with the interior walls covered in decorative ceramic tiles and mosaic designs on the floors, incorporating the Royal Burgh of Rothesay crest.

Mount Stuart

Gothic Fantasy

Five miles (8 km) south of Rothesay is MOUNT STUART, family seat of the Crichton-Stuarts, Marquesses of Bute, and the grandest Gothic-style private house in Britain, an extraordinary extravaganza of red sandstone, marble and stained glass, surrounded by 300 acres (121 ha) of beautiful gardens.

The family have held the hereditary title of Steward of Bute since 1157 and are direct descendants of Robert the Bruce, whose daughter Marjorie married Walter, 'Steward of Bute', in 1315. Their son became Robert II, first of the 'Steward' or 'Stewart' kings. The spelling was changed to 'Stuart' by Mary, Queen of Scots.

John Stuart, 3rd Earl of Bute (1713–92), was a friend of George III and THE FIRST SCOT TO BECOME PRIME MINISTER, in 1762. He was unpopular with the English, who were distrustful of the Scots after the recent Jacobite Rebellion of 1745–6, and Bute resigned in 1763. He was a founder of Kew Gardens.

The 2nd Marquess (1793–1848) inherited the title Earl of Dumfries from his maternal grandfather, and so added Crichton to the Stuart name. It was he who enhanced the family fortune, risking it all on building the Bute docks at Cardiff, an investment that paid off handsomely when Cardiff became the biggest coal port in the world.

The 3rd Marquess (1847–1900) was only six months old when his father died, and he enjoyed a noble inheritance. We know exactly when he was born, as Mount Stuart's Horoscope Room is crowned with a decorative ceiling, showing the exact position of the stars and planets at the time of his birth, on 12 September 1847.

The 3rd Marquess was somewhat eccentric and wore a monk's habit for most of his life, but he was a brilliant scholar and a great patron of the arts and architecture. His first love was Mount Stuart, and when much of the old house burned down in 1877, he set about creating his exhilarating fantasy palace, giving the commission to Sir Robert Anderson from Edinburgh, who later designed the Scottish National Portrait Gallery.

'The dark and mysterious heart of Mount Stuart' is the stupendous 80 ft (24 m) high MARBLE HALL, like something from *The Arabian Nights*, created out of Italian marble, lit by richly coloured, zodiacal, stained-glass windows, and with a ceiling of glittering painted stars.

The Marble Chapel, lined with pure white Carrara Marble, is considered to be THE FINEST PRIVATE CHAPEL IN SCOTLAND. The windows are of crimson glass, and on a sunny day the walls of the chapel turn blood red. The effect is amazing.

The 3rd Marquess died of a stroke in 1900, aged 53, and in 1920 Mount Stuart was threatened with demolition when the 4th Marquess, influenced by his generation's distaste for Victorian Gothic, put the house up for sale. Luckily it proved too expensive for anyone to take on. Sixty years later, in 1980, the 6th Marquess embarked on a full-scale restoration programme, inside and out, a project being continued by his son the present Marquess, one-time racing driver Johnny Dumfries.

In August 2003, fashion designer Stella McCartney, daughter of former Beatle Sir Paul McCartney, married publisher Alasdhair Willis at Mount Stuart. Amongst those who attended were former James Bond Pierce Brosnan, Sharleen Spiteri of pop group Texas, actress Liv Tyler and model Kate Moss.

Arran

Scotland in Miniature

ARRAN is one of Scotland's best-kept secrets, a special place that combines the wild remoteness of an island with the mountain scenery of the Highlands and the soft moorland countryside of the Lowlands. Although it only covers an area of 165 square miles (42,735 ha), the island's title of 'Scotland in miniature' is a bit misleading, for the mountains are majestic, rising to over 2,500 ft (762 m), the highest being Goat Fell which rises to 2,866 ft (874 m). It is an easy climb to the summit, where the views are amongst the most spectacular in Scotland.

Lying beneath Goat Fell is BRODICK, Arran's 'capital', main port and the terminal for the car ferry from Ardrossan. Brodick Castle, now in the hands of the National Trust for Scotland, used to belong to the Dukes of Hamilton, as did most of Arran.

In the summer months a small ferry leaves for Claonaig, on the Mull of Kintyre, from

LOCHRANZA, a straggling village on the north coast of the island, surrounded by high moors. The Isle of Arran distillery, the first legal distillery on Arran for 150 years, opened at Lochranza in 1995.

On a shingle spit in the sea loch are the imposing ruins of Lochranza Castle, said to have been the model for the castle in *The Black Island*, one of the Tintin adventure stories by Hergé.

LAMLASH BAY is where King Hakon of Norway reassembled his shattered fleet after defeat at the Battle of Largs in 1263. It also served as an important naval anchorage during the First World War.

HOLY ISLAND, sitting at the mouth of Lamlash Bay, is 2 miles (3.2 km) long and reaches a height of 1,030 ft (314 m) at Mullach Mor. It takes its name from St Molaise, who lived here in a cave and died in 639 at the age of 120, after bearing 30 diseases at one time, in order to avoid purgatory. His cave contains some interesting runic inscriptions referring to those who fell at Largs. In 1991, Holy Island was bought for £400,000 as a Bhuddist retreat and can be visited.

CORRIE, 5 miles (8 km) north of Brodick beyond Goat Fell, is not much more than a picturesque row of whitewashed fishermen's cottages. Prime Minister Herbert Asquith called it 'one of the prettiest villages in Europe'. DANIEL MACMILLAN, the grandfather of another Prime Minister, Harold Macmillan, was born at HIGH CORRIE, a hamlet in the hills above Corrie, in 1813. One of ten children, he eventually left Arran and went on to found the Macmillan publishing house in 1843.

The Cumbraes

Britain's Smallest Cathedral

A 19th-century minister on Cumbrae, the Revd James Adam, used to pray for blessings on the Great and Little Cumbraes and for 'the adjacent islands of Great Britain and Ireland'.

LITTLE CUMBRAE is privately owned and consists of 684 acres (277 ha), a small farm, a lighthouse complex and Little Cumbrae House, which overlooks a ruined 13th-century castle keep on the minuscule Castle Island. It was recently for sale at £2.5 million.

GREAT CUMBRAE is a very pretty holiday island and can be visited by ferry from Largs. The first ferry to enter Millport, the island's only town, was THE WORLD'S FIRST STEAM BOAT, Henry Bell's *Comet*, in 1812.

Millport is home to THE SMALLEST CATHEDRAL IN BRITAIN, and THE SECOND SMALLEST IN EUROPE after a tiny cathedral in Greece. The Cathedral of the Isles, consecrated as such in 1876, was founded in 1851 as an Episcopal collegiate church by George Boyle, later 6th Earl of Glasgow. It was designed by William Butterfield, who also designed Keble College, Oxford. The nave of the cathedral measures 40 ft (12 m) by 20 ft (6 m) and seats a congregation of 100. Painted on the ceiling are all the wild flowers of Cumbrae.

Well, I never knew this

ABOUT

BUTESHIRE

In 1779, David Dale (*see* Lanarkshire) opened SCOTLAND'S FIRST COTTON MILL in Rothesay.

PORT BANNATYNE, a little to the north of Rothesay, stands at the north end of the West Island Way, SCOTLAND'S FIRST LONG-DISTANCE ISLAND FOOTPATH, 30 miles (48 km) long. The village was used as a base, during the Second World War, for midget submarines, which exercised in Rothesay Bay before setting off to engage the German battleship, *Tirpitz*.

LENA ZAVARONI, the singer, was born in Rothesay on 4 November 1963. She won fame by winning *Opportunity Knocks* and sang in front of US President Gerald Ford at the age of 12. After appearances on the *Morecambe and Wise Show* and at the Royal Variety Performance she soon had her own television series and was, at one time, SCOTLAND'S RICHEST TEENAGER. She died of anorexia nervosa in 1999.

Three miles (4.8 km) south of Rothesay, in the grounds of ASCOG HALL, is a rare sunken Victorian fernery built in 1879. Restored and reopened in 1997, it houses over 80 species of subtropical ferns, including a huge *Todea Barbara*, some 3 ft (0.9 m) in diameter and 9 ft (2.7 m) tall, the only survivor from the original collection and thought to be over 1,000 years old. The fernery, which was THE FIRST SCOTTISH GARDEN FEATURE EVER TO WIN AN AWARD FROM

THE Historic GARDENS FOUNDATION, can be visited, along with the surrounding gardens.

The churchyard at Ascog has only one occupant, Montague Stanley, an actor who gave up the stage, believing it to be sinful. He died in 1844.

Another thespian who lived on Bute was the legendary, hard-drinking Shakespearean actor EDMUND KEAN (1787–1833), credited with bringing a new kind of romantic and emotional style to classical acting. In the early stages of his career he was fêted and lauded, but later his reputation declined as he became more difficult and temperamental. He separated from his wife when accused of adultery in 1822 and built Woodend House on the northern shore of Loch Fad as a place to get away from the heckling crowds and his creditors.

MOUNT STUART was THE FIRST HOUSE IN SCOTLAND TO BE LIT BY ELECTRICITY and THE FIRST PRIVATE HOUSE IN SCOTLAND TO HAVE AN INDOOR HEATED SWIMMING POOL.

Caithness

County Town: Wick

Kataness – 'Nose of the Cat'
(Norse description of the shape of the county)

Thurso Castle, seat of the Sinclairs, before it burnt down

Wick

Herring and Paperweights

During the 19th century, WICK, the county town of Caithness, was the herring capital of Europe, processing more herring than all the other Scottish ports put together. The name comes from the Norse word 'vik', meaning 'bay', and Wick Bay has been used as a harbour for trading and fishing since Viking times. The Earls of Caithness, who once ruled their fiefdom from Wick, were also Norwegian Jarls of Orkney, and Wick has a distinctly foreign feel to it as though the town still thinks of itself as Norse. This, added to the dark stone of the buildings and the frequently dark skies, gives the town a slightly forbidding air.

The herring business sadly declined many years ago, although there is still a fleet of some 30 boats, but Wick has

found new employment in servicing the North Sea oil industry. In 1961 the Caithness glassworks opened and quickly gained a worldwide reputation for good quality and colourful design. Their speciality is unique engraved paperweights, with abstract designs and colours inspired by the Scottish landscape, which are highly sought after by collectors. There is no longer a Caithness glassworks in Wick, but in 2006 paperweights were still being made at Caithness Glass's studio at Perth, although the company was in administration.

John o' Groats

End of the Line

JOHN O' GROATS is not so much a place as an aspiration. It consists of a number of low buildings scattered across the bleak Caithness moorland, including a hotel, a craft centre and a small souvenir shop, and it has a car park and a harbour. Not much to look at but strangely exhilarating. It is not the northernmost point of mainland Britain but it is THE NORTHERNMOST VILLAGE and has THE NORTHERNMOST POST OFFICE IN BRITAIN. More important, it is at the northern end of THE GREATEST DISTANCE BETWEEN TWO POINTS ON THE BRITISH MAINLAND, being 873 miles (1,405 km) from Land's End. This is why people come here, to have their photographs taken under the famous mileage sign – but be warned: it is taken down at the end of the day. People also come to take the ferry for day trips to Orkney, 8 miles (13 km) away across the Pentland Firth.

John o' Groats is named after a Dutchman, JAN DE GROOT, who established the ferry to Orkney from here in the 15th century and set the fare at one 'groat'. He built an octagonal house on the site, with eight doors that opened on to an octagonal table. Some say that this was because he had eight sons, others that it avoided arguments about who sat at the head of table. Perhaps he wanted one side for every one of the eight miles to Orkney. Unromantic types think it was merely an effective design for combatting the elements. A flagpole now marks the mound where the house stood, and the octagonal shape is reflected in the John o' Groats House Hotel nearby.

In 1938, the Monte Carlo Rally started from John o' Groats.

The first person to walk from Land's End to John o' Groats was the eccentric pedestrian Barbara Moore in 1960 – because she 'didn't have anything better to do'.

Thurso

Most Northerly Town

THURSO IS THE MOST NORTHERLY TOWN ON THE MAINLAND OF BRITAIN and has BRITAIN'S MOST NORTHERLY RAILWAY STATION. In Norse times it was the main Viking gateway to Scotland. Such was the importance of Thurso as a trading centre between Scotland and Scandinavia, that David II decreed the Caithness pound weight should become the standard weight measure for all of Scotland.

During the 18th century Thurso, along with neighbouring Castletown, was an important outlet for the export of Caithness flagstone, a unique, virtually indestructible stone that paves the streets of cities as varied as Edinburgh, Paris, Boston, Bombay and Melbourne.

In the 12th century an earthwork fortress was constructed to the east of the town which was replaced by a stone castle in the 17th century. This was the birthplace of Sir John Sinclair of Ulbster (1754–1835), whose statue stands proudly in Sir John Square, at the heart of the smart Regency area of Thurso that he planned and laid out.

Sir John was MP for Caithness, a lawyer and an agricultural reformer, who proposed, and became the first president of, the Board of Agriculture, forerunner of the modern Ministry of Agriculture (now part of the Department of the Environment). He was also responsible for THE FIRST STATISTICAL ACCOUNT, OR CENSUS, OF SCOTLAND, which provides a fascinating record of Scottish life at the end of the 18th century. Thurso Castle was rebuilt as a grand baronial mansion in 1872 for John George Tollemache Sinclair, grandfather of the 1st Viscount Thurso, Secretary of State for Air during the Second World War. It burnt down at the start of the 20th century and is now just a ruin.

Castle of Mey

'Never! It's a part of Scotland's heritage. I'll save it'
QUEEN ELIZABETH, the Queen Mother, on being told that the castle was going to be abandoned

The exquisitely beautiful little CASTLE OF MEY IS THE MOST NORTHERLY CASTLE ON THE BRITISH MAINLAND. It stands, literally, on the edge of the kingdom, a tiny jewel of understated luxury set amongst the raw splendour of the northern wastes. You can spot where the castle is from miles off, as it is cloaked by the only trees worthy of the name in this whole stretch of Caithness. A long driveway through the trees takes you down to the miniature grey stone castle, set against a backdrop of wide green fields and a sea made impossibly blue, no doubt by royal decree.

The Castle of Mey was built in 1572 by the 4th Earl of Caithness and passed to his third son George, founding father of the Sinclairs of Mey, who succeeded to the Earldom of Caithness in 1789. At this point the name was changed to Barrogill. The castle then changed hands several times and slowly fell into disrepair until the Queen Mother saw it in 1952, while staying in Caithness, in mourning for her husband George VI. Curiosity took her down the drive and up to the castle, where she found the family living in one room and their sheep in the next room. She instantly fell in love with the place and bought it from the owner, Captain F.B. Imbert-Terry, then straight away set about restoring and upgrading both house and garden.

She came to stay every year for three weeks in August, and a week in October, and in 1996 she put the castle into a trust to secure its future. Since the Queen Mother's death in 2002, her grandson Prince Charles has usually gone there with his wife for at least a week in August; otherwise the castle is now open for visitors.

The joy of the Castle of Mey is that it was the Queen Mother's personal home, the only one she ever owned. Personal effects and belongings, such as jigsaw puzzles and copies of her favourite *Dad's Army* videos, are strewn about as though she has just gone for a walk, and the rooms are intimate and comfortable. A visit here is much more like being a guest than a tourist.

The walled garden is planted with rows of delicious, old-fashioned British favourites such as gooseberries, blackcurrants and rhubarb, and if you walk up through the tiny front garden, you can gaze at the Queen Mother's award-winning herd of black Aberdeen Angus cattle, THE MOST NORTHERLY SUCH HERD IN THE WORLD.

Well, I never knew this ABOUT CAITHNESS

The EARLDOM OF CAITHNESS IS one of the most ancient earldoms of Britain.

Wick airport is THE NORTHERNMOST COMMERCIAL AIRPORT ON THE BRITISH MAINLAND.

The famous WHALIGOE STEPS are extremely hard to find. Turn east off the A9 by the phone box at Ulbster, opposite the Historic Scotland sign to Cairn of Get. Follow the road until you reach the car park, park and then take the driveway on the left down towards a house. Go round the right side of the house, and there are the steps. They were cut in 1790 to link the tiny little harbour of Whaligoe at the foot of the cliff with the curing house and fishermen's cottages at the top.

DUNCANSBY HEAD, 2 miles (3.2 km) further on from John o' Groats, is at THE ACTUAL EXTREME NORTHEASTERN TIP OF MAINLAND BRITAIN. A short walk brings into sight the amazing

DUNCANSBY STACKS, two jagged sea stacks that thrust up from the ocean like great molars.

DUNNET HEAD, about 10 miles (16 km) west of John o' Groats, and 2 miles (3.2 km) closer to the Arctic Circle, is THE MOST NORTHERLY POINT ON THE BRITISH MAINLAND. On a clear day the views from the lighthouse are magnificent, ranging from Cape Wrath in the west to Duncansby Head in the east and the Old Man of Hoy on Orkney to the north. Such is the power of the wind here that pebbles are sometimes thrown up by the stormy waters of the Pentland Firth, 300 ft (90 m) below, to smash against the windows of the lighthouse.

Down a mile or two of winding moorland lane, to the east of Dunnet Head, is HAM, once a bustling harbour for shipping corn and oatmeal. Today there is just a fine house, a stream tumbling down shallow steps from a reed-filled mill-pond, and the romantic ruin of a corn mill. With high sheltering cliffs on either side, the wind goes quiet here and the sunshine lingers, seals bask on the beach, oystercatchers bob and weave and all is peaceful. It could almost be a Cornish hamlet. Then, all too soon, the road rises and turns a corner, the harsh north wind begins to buffet and roar once more, and the tiny haven is lost behind. Ham is like a dream.

ALEXANDER BAIN (1811–77), clockmaker and inventor of the chemical telegraph, forerunner of the fax machine, was born in Watten, a small village half-way between Wick and Thurso.

DOUNREAY NUCLEAR POWER STATION west of Thurso is home to THE WORLD'S FIRST OPERATIONAL FAST BREEDER REACTOR, which came on line on 14 November 1959. It is housed in a vast, white sphere, like a ping-pong ball, with a diameter 3 ft (1 m) wider than the dome of St Paul's. It dominates the flat Caithness coastline for miles around, making it look more than ever like some barren moonscape. The first reactor closed in 1977 and was replaced by the even bigger prototype fast reactor, but this was closed down in 1994 when Britain began to lose interest in fast reactor development. The Dounreay site is now being decommissioned, a task that it is reckoned will take about 35 years.

The writer NEIL M. GUNN (1891–1973) was born, the son of a fisherman, in

DUNBEATH. His novels, of which *Highland River* (1937) and *The Silver Darlings* (1941) are perhaps the best known, paint a portrait of highland living, often harsh, based on the communities he knew from his childhood. He was a great champion of the highland culture and way of life, which he thought should be preserved and supported, and was active in the Scottish National Party, or SNP.

CLACKMANNANSHIRE

COUNTY TOWN: ALLOA

Clach Mannau – 'Stone of the god Mannau's land' (Welsh)

Alloa Tower, the largest surviving keep in Scotland

Alloa

Cheers!

County town and the largest town in Britain's smallest county, ALLOA was once Scotland's premier brewing town, with no fewer than nine major breweries. Surrounded by barley fields, with a constant supply of hard water from the Ochil Hills, in easy reach of coalfields for feeding the boilers, and handily located on the River Forth for distribution to Edinburgh, London and the east of England, Alloa had plenty of natural advantages.

George Younger established the first big brewery in 1764, producing over the years such brews as Younger's Milk Stout and Revolver Ale. In 1810, the Alloa Brewery opened and became known for Graham's Golden Lager, later renamed Skol. This brewery was finally closed by Carlsberg Tetley in 1998.

SCOTLAND'S OLDEST FAMILY BREWERY was started by local boy James Maclay, born in Alloa around 1810. In 1870, after 40 years as the lessee of Mills Brewery, Maclay built the huge Thistle Brewery which still dominates the town, although brewing ceased here in 2001.

Today, there is just one brewery left in Alloa, Williams Brothers, noted for their secret recipe Fraoch Heather Ale.

Alloa Tower, now in the care of the National Trust for Scotland, was built in the 14th century for the Erskine family, later Earls of Mar. John, the 3rd Lord Erskine, was guardian to Mary, Queen of Scots and she spent much of her childhood at Alloa. As Queen, Mary brought her infant son, the future James VI, to Alloa so they could both recover in safety after a difficult birth. Some believe that James actually died here and was secretly replaced by the Earl of Mar's own baby son.

In the 17th century the tower was enlarged and refurbished as the centre-piece of a large mansion house. Throughout these alterations the magnificent original oak roof beams were preserved, and can still be seen today. An extraordinary, elaborate Italianate staircase was added in 1700.

In 1800, the house, with the exception of the original stone tower, burned to the ground. The chief loss was a rare authentic portrait of Mary, Queen of Scots, given to one of her attendants on the eve of Mary's execution at Fotheringay Castle in 1587.

In 2006, an oil portrait of Queen Mary, painted on wood, and originally thought to have been 18th-century, was re-dated using modern techniques, and found to have actually been executed during Mary's lifetime – which means it is THE ONLY KNOWN CONTEMPORARY PORTRAIT OF MARY AS QUEEN. It is on display at the National Portrait Gallery in London.

Clackmannan

High and Dry

CLACKMANNAN exudes a rather forgotten feel as it slumbers astride a high ridge, just outside Alloa. Once a busy port on the River Devon where it meets the Forth, Clackmannan lost its trade, and eventually its role as county town, to Alloa when the river silted up, leaving it, literally, 'high and dry'. It is hard to imagine that this pleasant, quiet town was once important enough to give its name to the county, and today it is quite possible to drive through Clackmannan without realising it. This would be a shame, for the gently rising main street possesses several fine buildings and points of interest.

One of these is the picturesque bell tower of the old Tolbooth, built by town sheriff William Menteith in 1592. Beside it can be found the mysterious 'clach mannan', or 'Stone of the sea god Mannau', from which the town gets its name. The Stone is mounted on a plinth quarried from the same place the 'clach' itself is thought to have come from, Abbey Craig near Stirling, now crowned by the Wallace Monument.

There is another theory as to how the

Stone got its name, which is that Robert the Bruce, while resting on the 'clach', removed his glove or 'mannan' and left it behind there. Bruce is believed to have had a hand in building Clackmannan Tower, which sits on King's Seat Hill to the west of the town. The tower is well preserved, but suffers from mining subsidence and can only be viewed from the outside at present – work is being done to stabilise the structure so that visitors can one day see inside.

A huge stone mansion was put up next to the tower, and was lived in by Bruces right up until the end of the 18th century.

In 1787, the poet Robert Burns was fortunate enough to be 'knighted' by Mrs Bruce of Clackmannan, a direct descendent of Robert the Bruce, using her kinsman's actual two-handed sword. Mrs Bruce told Burns that she had more of a right to bestow this honour on those she thought fit than 'some others she might mention', like those unspeakable Hanoverians . . . She was in her nineties at the time and the last member of the family to live in the house at Clackmannan before it was demolished in 1791.

Dollar

Gloom, Sorrow and Care

DOLLAR lies at the foot of the Ochils and is home to the famous DOLLAR ACADEMY founded in 1818 by a local boy called John McNabb (1732–1802). McNabb, whose childhood was spent as a herdsman in the hills, eventually made his way to London and amassed a fortune in shipping. He left a large chunk of the money, some £70,000, to build a school for the children of the local poor, and such was his

generosity that the good people of Dollar were able to erect for themselves a vast, imposing, neo-classical Temple of Learning, designed by the eminent architect William Playfair. While the Academy, in keeping with its founder's wishes, has always striven to provide good facilities and the opportunity of a sound education for the children of less well-off local families, its reputation has attracted the sons and daughters of the wealthy from far and wide. Coeducational from the start, Dollar Academy is now one of Scotland's most sought-after fee-paying independent schools.

Dollar's High Street leads north to the mouth of the beautiful, wooded Dollar Glen, at the top of which stands CASTLE CAMPBELL, once the lowland home of the Dukes of Argyll. The lofty setting of the ruined castle is spectacular, with views over all of Clackmannanshire and beyond to the Kingdom of Fife. It was once called Castle Gloom and lies between two burns, the Burn of Sorrow and the Burn of Care – strange names for such an exhilarating place.

BORN IN CLACKMANNANSHIRE

SIR WILLIAM ALEXANDER (1567–1640), 1st Earl of Stirling, born in MENSTRIE CASTLE. Poet and tutor to James VI's son Prince Henry. In 1621, he was granted land in the New World by James VI, and founded the province of Nova Scotia where he attempted, unsuccessfully, to establish a Scottish colony. In 1632, Charles I handed Nova Scotia over to the French as part of a peace settlement, but in 1713 it was ceded back to Britain, and many Scots emigrated there, taking their Scottish culture with them.

GENERAL SIR RALPH ABERCROMBY (1734–1801), born in Menstrie. In 1801 he commanded the army which defeated the French forces in Egypt at Aboukir Bay and the Battle of Alexandria, the first British military victories in the Napoleonic Wars. Later that year he died of wounds received in battle.

ROBERT DICK (1811–66), botanist and geologist, born in TULLIBODY. Dick worked most of his life as a baker in Thurso, and spent all his spare time collecting fossils and plants from the Caithness landscape. Never one to seek publicity, he sent much of what he collected to Hugh Miller (*see* Ross and Cromarty) and other noted geologists. His herbarium, a unique collection of 200 mosses, flowers and ferns, can be seen in Thurso museum.

Well, I never knew this
ABOUT
CLACKMANNANSHIRE

Clackmannanshire is THE SMALLEST COUNTY IN THE BRITISH ISLES, covering an area of just 55 square miles (14,245 ha).

In the late 18th century A THIRD OF SCOTLAND'S TOTAL COAL PRODUCTION was exported through Alloa.

The United Glass bottle factory in Alloa is THE LARGEST PRODUCER OF BOTTLES IN BRITAIN.

DOLLAR WAS THE FIRST TOWN TO HAVE A LADY PROVOST, Lavinia Malcolm in 1913.

THE STERLING WAREHOUSE, which occupies a former woollen mill in TILLICOULTRY, is BRITAIN'S LARGEST FURNITURE STORE.

GARTMORN DAM COUNTRY PARK, east of Sauchie, is THE OLDEST MAN-MADE RESERVOIR IN SCOTLAND STILL IN USE. It was created in 1713 by the Earl of Mar to provide water power for the pumps in his coal-mines.

Clackmannanshire possesses THE HIGHEST MOUNTAIN IN THE OCHIL HILLS, BEN CLACH at 2,363 ft (720 m).

DUMFRIESSHIRE

COUNTY TOWN: DUMFRIES

Dum phrys – 'Fort of the Copse' (Gaelic)

Drumlanrig Castle – before a robbery in 2003, Drumlanrig was the only place in the world where you could see, simultaneously, a Rembrandt, a Holbein and a Leonardo da Vinci

Dumfries

'Maggie by the banks o' Nith – a dame with pride eneuch'
ROBERT BURNS

The old county town of DUMFRIES is a pleasant, bustling place of warm red sandstone, rising from the banks of the River Nith. It is affectionately known as the 'Queen of the South', the name by which the town's football team is also known.

In 1306, Dumfries was the setting for an event that changed the fate of Scotland. It was here, before the high altar of the Greyfriars monastery, that Robert the Bruce murdered his rival for the Scottish throne, 'Red' John Comyn, Earl of Badenoch. There is nothing left of the monastery, but the site of the altar is shown by a plaque on the wall of a shop in Castle Street, opposite Greyfriars Church.

After disposing of Comyn, Bruce marched along the river to secure

Dumfries Castle, now just a mound at the centre of Castledykes Park. An inscription on a stone slab reads, 'King Robert the Bruce, on 10th February, 1306, captured the castle of Dumfries which occupied this site, and so began the War which vindicated Scotland's Independence'.

The original Greyfriars monastery was founded by Devorgilla, wife of John Balliol (*see* New Abbey, Kirkcudbrightshire). She also put the first bridge across the River Nith, a wooden affair of 13 arches, replaced in 1431 by the present stone 'Auld Brig', itself restored in the 17th century after a flood. It is THE LONGEST MEDIEVAL BRIDGE and THE OLDEST SURVIVING MULTIPLE ARCH STONE BRIDGE IN SCOTLAND.

In the middle of the wide, handsome Georgian High Street stands red-stoned Mid Steeple, erected in 1707 as a place for the town council to meet, and used also as a gaol and courtroom.

Scotland's national poet, Robert Burns, lived in Dumfries for the last five years of his life, working as an exciseman. He and his family lived in a stone cottage in Mill Vennel, now Burns Street. The poet died from rheumatic fever on 21 July 1796, the same day his ninth child, Maxwell, was born. His wife, Jean Armour, lived on in the house until her own death in 1834. In 1851, Burns's son Colonel William Nicol Burns, bought it and set up a trust to preserve the house as a museum to his father's memory.

Burns was buried in the churchyard of St Michael's, originally under a plain stone slab paid for by his widow. In 1815 his body was moved to its present resting-place, beneath a marble statue of Burns being invested with the mantle of the poetic muse, enclosed in a vast, Grecian mausoleum, all paid for by public subscription at the behest of George IV. Burns's wife, Jean, and their five sons are buried with him.

Inside St Michael's church there is a plaque on the pew used by Burns and his family at Sunday service.

Burns's favourite haunts were both in the High Street: the Hole in the Wa' tavern and, hidden down an alleyway, the Globe Inn, whose 'hearty, gay and lavish Scottish barmaid', Anna Park, the landlord's niece, presented Burns with Elizabeth, one of his many illegitimate children. Patrons of the snug, wood-panelled Globe can still sit in Burns's chair, provided they correctly quote a snatch of his poetry, while on one of the upstairs windows are some words from 'Lovely Polly Stewart' and 'Coming through the Rye', etched by Burns himself.

The Murder of John Comyn

In 1292, John Balliol, son of John Balliol and Devorgilla of Galloway, was chosen by Edward I to be his puppet King of Scotland, in preference to Robert the Bruce's grandfather, Robert the Competitor. Balliol was a mere vassal of Edward, and when the English king demanded that Balliol help him wage war against France, the Scots rebelled, having no quarrel with the French themselves. Instead, they negotiated the famous 'Auld Alliance' with the French, to protect themselves from Edward.

King Edward was furious. He had Balliol thrown into the Tower of London and proceeded to invade Scotland, only to be defeated by William Wallace at the Battle of Stirling Bridge in 1297. In 1298 Wallace's army was routed at the Battle of Falkirk, largely because many of the Scottish nobles fled the battlefield with their men – notably 'Black' John Comyn, father of 'Red' John Comyn.

After Wallace's demise Robert the Bruce and 'Red' John Comyn, who was a nephew of King John Balliol, became rivals for the vacant Scottish throne, and agreed to meet at the Greyfriars Monastery in Dumfries to resolve their differences. They quarrelled, Bruce lost his temper and ran Comyn through with his dagger. After this violence, for which he was excommunicated, Bruce had no choice but to assume the crown and set out upon the march to victory at Bannockburn in 1314, and eventually, in 1328, to independence for Scotland.

Ellisland Farm

'A poet's choice but not a farmer's'
ROBERT BURNS

Robert Burns leased ELLISLAND FARM from Patrick Millar of Dalswinton House and moved his family down from Ayrshire in 1788, keen to establish himself under his own roof and as a farmer. The soil proved barren and unworkable, however, and Burns quickly found that he couldn't make farming pay so, in 1791, they moved to Dumfries.

These years were far from wasted, though, for the long, low farmhouse rests in a beautiful setting by the Nith and it was while walking by the river that Burns conceived what many regard as his masterpiece, 'Tam o' Shanter'. Today, visitors to Ellisland can retrace the poet's walk, and the farmhouse is open to visitors as a small museum.

Burns also wrote the words to 'Auld Lang Syne' while living at Ellisland, and it has become a tradition in Britain to sing his words, to the music of an old Scottish song, on New

Year's Eve. Visitors from Japan are often surprised that the music originates in Scotland, for it is well known to every Japanese child as the tune for a traditional song called 'Light of the Fireflies', sung at the conclusion of school graduation ceremonies. The tune is also played at supermarkets and in village high streets in Japan, to indicate closing time. A lot of Japanese people are shocked to learn that what they believe to be an old Japanese folk tune is, in fact, Scottish. It was possibly taken to Japan by the 'Scottish Samurai', Thomas Blake Glover from Fraserburgh (*see* Aberdeenshire).

Caerlaverock Castle

Triangles

CAERLAVEROCK CASTLE, standing proud but forgotten where the River Nith meets the Solway Firth, IS SCOTLAND'S ONLY TRIANGULAR CASTLE. 'So strong a castle that it feared no siege . . . in shape it was like a shield for it has but three sides round it, with a tower at each corner . . . and I think that you will never see a more finely situated castle.' So wrote one of Edward I's men when the English king laid siege to the castle in July 1300 – it took 3,000 of his troops two days to overcome 60 Scottish defenders. One of the features of Caerlaverock, a stronghold of the Maxwells, is the striking contrast between the purely defensive 14th-century outer walls and the Renaissance interior, begun in 1638. Built around the triangular inner courtyard, what remains is exquisite and sumptuous with large windows and decorated fireplaces.

In Caerlaverock churchyard lies ROBERT PATERSON (1715–1801), Scott's 'Old Mortality', a stonemason who left his wife and family at home in Balmaclellan, and spent 40 years wandering Scotland with his old grey pony, restoring the neglected tombstones of Covenanters. Strathaven Ales of Lanarkshire have a beer named Old Mortality in his honour.

The Covenanters

Covenanters were Scots Presbyterians who signed the National Covenant of 1638, at Greyfriars churchyard in Edinburgh. They refused to accept the Book of Common Prayer, which they saw as an attempt to anglicise the Scottish Church. Nor did they recognise the Divine Right of the Monarch as head of the Church, as claimed by the Stuart kings. Covenanters believed that only Jesus was the head of the Church. While loyal to the king they resented the Stuarts' attempts to impose their authority through bishops. Until 1688 Covenanters were persecuted with torture, transportation and execution, hence the huge number of graves and memorials dedicated to them throughout Scotland.

Ruthwell

Ancient Artistry and Scottish Thrift

Motorists passing through RUTHWELL on the road from Annan to Bankend little suspect that this small, scattered village in the flatlands of the Solway Firth hides, on one side, Scotland's most valuable ancient treasure and, on the other side, the origins of a great movement given to the world by a Scotsman.

At the crossroads turn north, along a lane to nowhere, and after quarter of a mile there appears a copse with a nondescript church inside it. The breeze off the Solway rustles the trees. The peace of centuries is here. Open the creaking church door and there, bathed in a halo of sunlight, stands what the *Guinness Book of Records* describes as 'THE GREATEST DARK AGE MONUMENT IN EUROPE' – THE RUTHWELL CROSS.

The first impression is of how tall it is – 18 ft (5.5 m) high and sunk into the floor of the apse, specially built for it in 1886. The curve of the apse seems to project the cross into the body of the church, while skylights in the roof admit sunbeams that dapple and highlight its rough beauty. The whole vision is breathtaking.

The Ruthwell Cross was carved in the late 7th century by Northumbrian craftsmen, this area being part of the kingdom of Northumbria at the time. It is a preaching cross, which uses carvings as pictures for those who can't read. The broad faces show stories from the New Testament along with the Holy Trinity and the four writers of the gospels – Matthew, Mark, Luke and John. Latin inscriptions tell the stories for the learned. The sides are carved with foliage interlaced with animals and birds feasting on fruits, while on the raised margins is THE LONGEST RUNIC INSCRIPTION IN BRITAIN. This is THE EARLIEST KNOWN EXAMPLE OF WRITTEN ENGLISH and consists of extracts from the Anglo-Saxon poem *The Dream of the Rood*, which tells the story of the Crucifixion from the perspective of the Cross and is THE OLDEST POEM IN THE ENGLISH LANGUAGE.

The Ruthwell Cross was almost destroyed in the aftermath of the Reformation, when the Church of Scotland General Assembly passed an act to demolish all 'idolatrous monuments'. The minister at Ruthwell, the Revd Gavin Young, managed to protect the cross by carefully breaking it up and hiding it in the churchyard and under the floor, where it remained until the REVD HENRY DUNCAN arrived in 1799. He realised the significance of all the fragments scattered about and spent the next 24 years piecing them together, finally raising the completed cross in the garden of the manse in 1823. It was moved into the church in 1886.

If you can tear yourself away from this glorious antiquity, make your way back to the main road and cross straight over, going south. You will soon come to the picturesque main street of Ruthwell, lined on either side by typical Scottish crofts, gaily painted and covered in garden flowers. Turn left and a little way down on the right is the Savings Banks Museum. In 1810, in this humble cottage, the Revd Henry Duncan (1774–1846), the man who restored the Ruthwell Cross, set up THE WORLD'S FIRST COMMERCIAL SAVINGS BANK. This was the direct forerunner of the Trustee Savings Bank, now part of Lloyds TSB, one of the world's biggest banks. The movement he began here blossomed into 109 organisations in 92 countries.

Henry Duncan was a remarkable man who devoted his life to finding ways for the poor to improve their lives, while keeping their dignity and self-respect. He thought the Poor Law subsidies degrading and he set up his savings bank as a way of helping his parishioners gain some financial independence. The minimum deposit required was sixpence (as opposed to £10 for established banks) and deposits earned 5 per cent interest – 4 per cent to the customer and 1 per cent to a charity fund. This tradition is maintained by Lloyds TSB to this day, with the bank giving Lloyds TSB charity foundations 1 per cent of pre-tax profits each year.

Just west of Ruthwell is BROW WELL, where Robert Burns came in 1796, in the last week of his life, to try and find a cure for his illness. Three days after he returned to Dumfries from here, he was dead. Brow Well is now a place of mournful pilgrimage for his admirers. The Revd Henry Duncan and Burns had met when Duncan was 18. His father said at the time, 'Look well at Mr Burns, for you'll never again see so great a genius.'

Darien

An Expensive Gamble

Banker WILLIAM PATERSON (1658–1719) was born in Skipmyre, near Lockerbie. He went to London and made a fortune in trade with the West

Indies and, in 1691, proposed the idea for a Bank of England, which he co-founded in 1694, becoming one of its first directors. In 1695 the Scottish Parliament passed an act for the establishment of a Company of Scotland, trading with Africa and the West Indies, along the lines of the hugely successful East India Company. The East India Company, fearing a rival, ensured that London refused to invest in the company, so William Paterson raised the huge capital sum of £400,000 himself, entirely from within Scotland. He then chose the Darien peninsula in Panama as the location for the first Scottish trading colony. In 1698 he set out from Leith, with his wife and son and 1,200 other Scots, on the Darien Expedition. Less than half of them returned.

Darien was a failure for many reasons. The English in the West Indies refused to trade with Darien, on the orders of King William who was being pressured by the East India Company. The Spanish resented the Darien colonists as a threat to their own trade in the area, and when they attacked the settlement King William refused to help. He was about to embark on a war with France and didn't wish to antagonise Spain. Worst of all, yellow fever decimated the colony. Paterson's wife and son were among those who died, and Paterson himself only just made it back to Scotland, impoverished, his health broken.

Scotland was almost bankrupted by the fiasco, and the disaster brought to the fore the much-debated idea of a Treaty of Union with England, of which Paterson had long been an enthusiastic supporter. He set about drafting the trade and finance articles of the Union so that Scottish investors in the Darien Scheme received compensation from London for their losses – in fact they got back every penny of their subscriptions plus 5 per cent interest. Much of this money was later invested in founding The Royal Bank of Scotland. Paterson became MP for Dumfries in the first Union parliament in 1707.

Moffat

A Scottish Iliad

MOFFAT is a handsome place with a wealth of beautiful buildings and lime trees down the middle of the main street, THE WIDEST HIGH STREET IN SCOTLAND.

A remarkable building in the High Street is the Star Hotel: only 20 ft (6 m) wide, it is THE NARROWEST HOTEL IN BRITAIN.

JOHN LOUDON MCADAM, the road builder (*see* Ayrshire), lived for a time at Dumcrieff House, just outside the town, and is buried in the old churchyard at the south end of the High Street.

In Station Park there is a statue of AIR CHIEF MARSHAL 1st LORD DOWDING, head of Fighter Command during the Battle of Britain in 1940 and described by Winston Churchill as 'a genius in the art of war'. Dowding was born in Moffat in 1882 and buried in Westminster Abbey in 1970.

A resident of Moffat for 30 years was the author of the popular 'Mrs Tim' and 'Miss Buncle' books, D.E. STEVENSON (1892–1973), a cousin of Robert Louis Stevenson. She is buried in the cemetery in the hills above Moffat.

The architectural delight of Moffat is MOFFAT HOUSE, built in 1751 by John Adam for the 2nd Earl of Hopetoun. It is now a hotel but, in the 18th century, it was at the centre of one of the great scandals of the age – the mystery of the Ossian Papers.

Tutoring at Moffat House in 1759 was JAMES MACPHERSON from Kingussie in Inverness-shire. Taking the waters in Moffat, at the same time, were a couple of distinguished worthies, John Home, author of the successful play *Douglas*, and Alexander 'Jupiter' Carlyle, the minister from Inveresk (*see* Midlothian). Keen to impress, Macpherson showed the two men some verses which he claimed to have discovered in the Highlands, and translated from the original Gaelic. He convinced them that they had been written 1,000 years ago by Prince Ossian, the son of Fingal.

The good fellows were mightily impressed, and so keen to think that they might have stumbled upon a Scottish epic to rival Homer's *Iliad*, that they didn't think to check the poems' authenticity. Instead, they persuaded Macpherson to have them published. *Fragments of Ancient Poetry, Collected in the Highlands of Scotland* came out in Edinburgh in 1760, quickly followed by *Fingal, an Ancient Poem* (1762) and *Temora* (1765) and, later, *The Collected Poems of Ossian*. They caused a sensation, were translated into all the European languages, helped to initiate the Romantic movement in Europe and drew people to the Highlands from all over the world.

However, no less a critic than Dr Johnson pronounced them a fraud, and when challenged by Macpherson to a duel, Johnson bought himself a big stick and declared, 'I will not desist from detecting what I think to be a cheat, from any fears of the menaces of a ruffian.' Indeed, Macpherson never did produce the Gaelic originals, and the controversy raged on well after his death.

The general belief is that Macpherson had himself embellished the poems, weaving his own words into genuine fragments of Gaelic poetry. Whatever the true origins of the Ossian Papers, they were a powerful piece of work. They were carried into battle by Napoleon, inspired the paintings of Ingres, influenced Byron and Sir Walter Scott and lured Felix Mendelssohn to Scotland in 1829, on a trip that resulted in the *Hebrides Overture*. And it all began in Moffat.

Wanlockhead

Scotland's Highest Village

WANLOCKHEAD, 'God's Treasure House in Scotland', is situated in the Lowther Hills and is THE HIGHEST VILLAGE IN SCOTLAND, 1,531 ft (467 m) above sea level. Although the village is bleak and somewhat dishevelled, with cottages and bungalows scattered haphazardly about the rocky landscape, the views are breathtaking.

The community grew up to serve the local mines, and although Wanlockhead was known mainly for lead, the Lowther Hills possess a greater variety of minerals than anywhere else in Britain, producing zinc, copper, silver and some of the purest gold in the world – 22.8 carats. Gold from Wanlockhead was used in the regalia of the Scottish Crown.

The lead mines, the first of which opened in 1680, finally closed in the 1950s and Wanlockhead is now best known as the home of the Museum of Lead Mining – THE ONLY FORMER LEAD-MINE OPEN TO THE PUBLIC IN SCOTLAND. The museum also contains THE ONLY WATER-POWERED BEAM ENGINE OF ITS KIND STILL *IN SITU*, AND WORKING, IN BRITAIN today.

The engineer William Symington (1763–1831) lived and worked for most of his life in Wanlockhead. He invented BRITAIN'S FIRST STEAM-POWERED BOAT, which made its first outing on Dalswinton Loch in 1788 (*see* Dalswinton Loch). Symington built the engine for the boat at the Old Manse in Wanlockhead.

The telecommunications station on nearby Green Lowther mountain is THE HIGHEST IN BRITAIN.

Drumlanrig

Brave Heart

DRUMLANRIG CASTLE near Thornhill is one of Scotland's grandest houses. Designed by Sir William Bruce for William Douglas, 1st Duke of Queensberry, the house was begun in 1679 on the site of a former castle, and completed in 1689. On his first night there the Duke felt unwell and next morning he went back to his doctors in Edinburgh, never to return to Drumlanrig.

Throughout the castle are depictions in stone, wood and iron of the Douglas crest, a winged heart surmounted by a crown. The story of this emblem dates back to the early 14th century, and the death of Robert the Bruce. Bruce had always dreamed of going on a crusade to the Holy Land, but he died in 1329 before his ambition could be realised. His great friend Sir James Douglas was entrusted with the task of taking the King's heart, contained in a silver casket, to Jerusalem, when he himself went off to fight the Muslims. But Douglas fell in battle against the Moors in Spain, and as he lay dying he flung the heart into the air crying, 'Forward, brave heart!'

Keir Mill

'Birthplace of the Bicycle'

Keir is a tiny hamlet lost in the hills some 14 miles (23 km) north of Dumfries. It is a quiet, sleepy place, with a small church, a mill and a few cottages. Oh, and COURTHILL SMITHY, where the local blacksmith built a machine that changed the world.

KIRKPATRICK MACMILLAN was born at Courthill Smithy in 1813, one of the many sons of the village blacksmith. He worked for a while as a blacksmith's apprentice, at Drumlanrig just up the road, and then returned to work with his father. One day he spotted a 'hobby horse' being ridden through the village. A hobby horse consisted of two wheels in line, joined by a wooden plank, with handle bars and a saddle. It was a popular contraption at the time and Macmillan decided he wanted to build one of his own. However, it proved very difficult to ride, as you had to propel the machine along by pushing on the ground with your feet – not easy on the hilly local roads. So Macmillan set about devising a system of pedals to turn the back wheel, with power transmitted to a crank on the wheel, via a connecting rod, rather like the drive shaft on a steam locomotive.

Eventually, on one momentous morning in 1839, Kirkpatrick Macmillan, beaming proudly, wheeled his pedal bike out of Courthill Smithy, into the sunlight and into history – he had invented THE WORLD'S FIRST TRUE BICYCLE, one of the greatest British inventions of the Victorian or any other age. The local people thought he was dotty – 'daft pate', they called him – but that day this shy village blacksmith spawned a mighty industry – today there are over one billion bicycles in the world.

Macmillan made frequent trips into Dumfries on his machine, and in June 1842, he set off on what, at that time, would be THE LONGEST BICYCLE RIDE IN HISTORY, 68 miles to Glasgow. The trip took him two days and he was mobbed when he arrived in the Gorbals. In the mêlée he knocked down a little girl who ran out in front of him and, although she was only slightly injured, he was fined for speeding at 8 mph (13 kph) – THE FIRST TIME A CYCLIST HAD EVER BEEN FINED FOR A TRAFFIC OFFENCE. In the end the magistrate paid the fine for him, in return for a go on the bicycle.

When the excitement was over and Macmillan got back to Keir Mill, he dismounted, rather stiffly, and leaned the machine against the wall of the smithy, before going off to rest from his exertions. His niece, Mary Marchbank, disobeying her parents who thought cycling not a suitable pastime for a young lady, sneaked away with the bicycle and took it through the village for a spin – THE FIRST-EVER LADY CYCLIST.

Despite the interest shown in his bicycle – even Queen Victoria and Prince Albert owned one – Macmillan was happy with his life as a blacksmith, and never bothered to patent his invention. It was soon copied and exploited by others. It wasn't until well after his death in 1878 that Kirkpatrick Macmillan was acknowledged as the true inventor of the bicycle.

He married Elizabeth Goldie in 1854, and they had several children of whom only two lived to be adults. He died on 26 January 1878 and is buried beneath a simple grey stone in the old graveyard near the river.

Every year, on the last weekend in May, the Kirkpatrick Macmillan Cycle Race is held in his memory, and on the wall of his smithy there is a plaque inscribed with the words, 'He Builded Better than He Knew'. Indeed.

Dalswinton Loch

The First Steam Boat

Dalswinton, a few miles north of Dumfries, is a pretty hamlet, consisting of two short rows of cottages, Dalswinton Tower, a former stronghold of the Comyns, and Dalswinton House, home of banker and entrepreneur PATRICK MILLER (1731–1815), who introduced a yellow-fleshed turnip into Scotland. It was sent to him by King Gustav of Sweden – which is why turnips of this sort are sometimes called swedes.

Miller was a partner in the Carron Iron Company (*see* Stirlingshire), for which he invented a small, light cannon called a carronade, but his greatest claim to fame was as the owner of BRITAIN'S FIRST STEAM BOAT, launched on DALSWINTON LOCH in the grounds of his house, in 1788. Miller commissioned WILLIAM SYMINGTON, an engineer from Wanlockhead, to build a small boat, 25 ft (7.6 m) long, powered by an experimental twin-cylinder, atmospheric steam engine. Two paddle wheels, set one behind the other between twin hulls, drove the boat forward at 5 mph (8 kph), during successful trials on the loch on 14 October 1788. Among the passengers on the world's first steamboat journey were Miller himself, the artist Alexander Nasmyth, who painted the scene, and Miller's tenant at Ellisland Farm, the poet Robert Burns.

Well, I never knew this ABOUT DUMFRIESSHIRE

The author JAMES BARRIE attended Dumfries Academy and is said to have dreamed up the characters of Peter Pan and Captain Hook while playing in the gardens leading down to the river behind the school.

In 1753, Dumfries Burgh School held THE FIRST RECORDED SCHOOL COOKERY CLASS IN BRITAIN.

In 1912, the Arrol-Johnston Motor Car Company erected THE FIRST FERRO-CONCRETE FACTORY IN BRITAIN, at Heathall on the outskirts of DUMFRIES. Arrol-Johnston was founded by locomotive engineer George Johnston and the engineer of the Forth Bridge, Sir William Arrol (*see* Renfrewshire). Under a variety of names, the company manufactured cars from 1896 until 1931. An Arrol-Johnston won the inaugural Tourist Trophy (TT) race on the Isle of Man in 1905, beating a Rolls-Royce into second place.

At Eskdalemuir, in a bleak, high Scottish moorland setting, is THE LARGEST TIBETAN BUDDHIST MONASTERY IN WESTERN EUROPE. THE SAMYE LING CENTRE was founded by two refugee Tibetan monks in 1967.

THOMAS TELFORD (1757–1834), Scotland's greatest engineer, was born the son of a shepherd in WESTERKIRK, near Moffat. He designed and built countless bridges, roads and canals throughout Britain and is buried in Westminster Abbey. Amongst his most famous works are the Dean Bridge in Edinburgh, the Pontcysyllte Aqueduct over the River Dee in Wales, Britain's longest and highest aqueduct, the Menai Suspension Bridge, the world's first large suspension bridge, also in Wales, the Caledonian Canal and the A5 road between London and Holyhead.

SANQUHAR, a small town on the River Nith, is home to THE WORLD'S OLDEST POST OFFICE. It was established in 1763 and ran a horseback service to Edinburgh.

AE, a tiny village 8 miles (13 km) north of Dumfries, founded in 1947 to house forestry workers, has THE SHORTEST NAME OF ANY VILLAGE OR TOWN IN BRITAIN. It is also the only place name in Britain without a consonant.

The actor JOHN LAURIE (1897–1980), best known for playing the part of Private Fraser in BBC TV's *Dad's Army*, was born in Dumfries.

Inside the church at DUNSCORE there is a plaque commemorating JANE HAINING, the most famous of the seven Scots-born men and women who died at Auschwitz during the Second World War. She was born in 1897 at Lochenhead Farm just outside Dunscore, and attended Dumfries Academy with the actor John Laurie. She was arrested while serving the Church of Scotland's Jewish Mission in Hungary, for refusing to give up the Jewish children in her care.

The historian THOMAS CARLYLE (1795–1881), the 'Sage of Chelsea', was born in the small village of ECCLEFECHAN, in 1795. His birthplace was a big room above the kitchen of the Arched House on the main street, built by his father and uncle. It now houses a small collection of his memorabilia. He is buried in the village churchyard.

DUNBARTONSHIRE

COUNTY TOWN: DUMBARTON

Dun Breaton; 'Fort of the Britons' (Gaelic)

Dumbarton Castle, one of three remaining royal Scottish fortresses

Dumbarton

Shipping Firsts

DUMBARTON, the old county town of Dunbartonshire is, for some reason unknown, spelt with an 'm' rather than an 'n'. The rather functional concrete town is dominated to the south by DUMBARTON ROCK, a 240 ft (73 m) high volcanic plug which has been fortified for longer than anywhere else in Britain. Capital of the Kingdom of Strathclyde until 1018, Dumbarton was described by the Venerable Bede as 'the best fortified city the Britons had'. It was the last Briton stronghold to succumb to the Saxons, finally surrendering to King Edbert of Northumberland in 756.

Strathclyde eventually merged into

the Kingdom of Scotland, and Dumbarton became a royal burgh in 1222. It is one of three remaining royal Scottish fortresses, the others being Edinburgh and Stirling.

In 1305, the governor of DUMBARTON CASTLE, Sir John Menteith, having captured William Wallace by treachery, brought him to Dumbarton before he was sent to London for execution. The small stone building beside the long flight of steps leading up to the top of the rock is known as 'Wallace's Guardhouse' and has a gable end representing the head of Sir John Menteith, with his finger in his cheek, the sign of betrayal.

In 1548, Mary, Queen of Scots, then a child of five, sailed secretly from Dumbarton Castle to France, accompanied by the famous 'four Marys'. She was promised in marriage to the Dauphin, son of Henry II of France, a union that did not meet with the approval of the English king Henry VIII, who wanted her to marry his own son. In 1568, Mary was again headed for Dumbarton Castle, after her escape from Loch Leven, but before she could get there she was defeated at the Battle of Langside and forced to flee Scotland for ever. Dumbarton then held out for Mary longer than anywhere except Edinburgh. The sundial at the foot of the rock was a gift from Queen Mary.

The town of Dumbarton, which spreads northwards from the foot of the Rock, sits at the confluence of the Clyde and Leven rivers. Before the Clyde was dredged this was the river's highest navigable point, and Dumbarton became an important shipbuilding centre.

Denny's Shipyard

Cutty Sark and Hoverbus

Most famous of all the shipyards was that of WILLIAM DENNY AND BROTHERS, which notched up a remarkable number of firsts. In 1818, Denny's built the *Rob Roy*, THE FIRST STEAM-POWERED FERRY USED FOR THE ENGLISH CHANNEL CROSSING, and in 1869 they completed THE SECOND FASTEST CLIPPER OF ALL TIME, the *Cutty Sark*, named after the young witch in Robert Burns's 'Tam o' Shanter'.

Subsequently Denny's shipyard built THE WORLD'S FIRST OCEAN-GOING VESSEL MADE OF MILD STEEL, THE FIRST ALL-WELDED SHIP and, in 1901, they launched the King Edward, THE FIRST PASSENGER STEAMER IN THE WORLD DRIVEN BY TURBINES.

THE FIRST HELICOPTER IN THE WORLD CAPABLE OF VERTICAL FLIGHT WHILE CARRYING A MAN was built by Denny's in 1905. Designed by E.R. Mumford, it achieved tethered flights of up to 10 ft (3 m) from the ground during trials. Apparently it took a whole team of men hanging on to prevent the machine from taking off and disappearing into the skies above Dumbarton along with its intrepid test pilot.

In 1949 the P&O ship *Chusan* was THE FIRST OCEAN LINER TO BE FITTED WITH THE NEW REVOLUTIONARY DENNY-BROWN STABILISERS, which were subsequently fitted to the *Queen Mary*, the *Queen Elizabeth* and the *QE2*.

In 1963, the year before it closed, Denny's launched the Denny D2

Cutty Sark

Hoverbus, THE WORLD'S FIRST COMMERCIAL HOVERBUS.

All that is left of Denny's shipyard today is the Denny Ship Model Experiment Tank, THE FIRST COMMERCIAL SHIP MODEL TESTING TANK IN THE THE WORLD, designed in 1882 by the same E.R. Mumford who would later design the world's first helicopter (*see* opposite). It is dedicated to William Froude, who invented the original experiment tank for warships in Plymouth.

Clydebank

The World's Shipyard

In 1870, it was a little village called Barns of Clyde surrounded by acres of farmland. Thirty years later it was CLYDEBANK, the heart of the greatest shipbuilding centre in the world, and home to Singer, the largest sewing machine factory in the world.

In 1871, J. and G. Thompson moved their shipyard from Govan to a site at the mouth of the River Cart. In 1882 Singer opened their factory nearby at Kilbowie.

In 1899, JOHN BROWN & CO., armour plate makers from Sheffield, took over Thompson's yard and created the most famous shipbuilding yard in the world.

'There is not a Briton anywhere who ought not to feel proud that this launch has placed Great Britain firmly at the forefront of marine architecture.' So said Sir Charles McLaren, Chairman of John Brown & Co., at the launching of the Cunard liner *Lusitania* from the Clydebank yard in 1906. *Lusitania* was THE FASTEST SHIP OF ITS TIME, holder of the Blue Riband in 1907. In 1915, she was torpedoed by a German submarine off the southeast coast of Ireland, with the loss of 1,198 lives, including that of American railroad millionaire Alfred Vanderbilt.

In 1920 John Brown launched what was then THE BIGGEST WARSHIP IN THE WORLD, the battle cruiser HMS *Hood*.

The Cunard Queens

Royal Liners

In 1934 the *Queen Mary*, FIRST BRITISH SHIP OVER 1,000 FT (305 M) IN LENGTH, and the first of the famous Cunard Queens, was launched from the John Brown shipyard by Queen Mary herself. It was THE FIRST TIME A SHIP HAD BEEN CHRISTENED BY THE CONSORT OF A REIGNING MONARCH and THE FIRST SUCH OCCASION TO BE REPORTED LIVE ON BBC RADIO.

Previously, when the directors of Cunard met with King George V, they told him that they were going to name their magnificent new ship 'after the greatest Queen in our nation's history'. The King smiled and replied, 'Thank you, gentlemen, Queen Mary will be most pleased.' The directors were far too embarrassed to admit that Mary was not actually the Queen they had in mind, and so the *Queen Victoria* became the *Queen Mary*. In 1967, after long service, the *Queen Mary* sailed to Long Beach, California, where she became a floating hotel. The company that owns her went bankrupt in 2005 and her future is uncertain.

In 1938, John Brown launched the *Queen Elizabeth*, then THE BIGGEST PASSENGER LINER EVER BUILT. In 1972, fire broke out on the ship while she was being refitted as a floating university in Hong Kong harbour. She capsized on to her starboard side and remained as a notable landmark for several years, featuring in the 1974 James Bond film *The Man with the Golden Gun* as MI6 field headquarters. She finally rolled over and sank in 1975.

In 1941, the town of Clydebank was virtually destroyed by a series of German bombing raids known as the Clydebank Blitz, which left the shipyard miraculously almost untouched. That same year HMS *Hood* was sunk by the German battleship *Bismarck*.

In 1953, the Royal Yacht *Britannia* was launched by the new young Queen, Elizabeth II. *Britannia* is now preserved as a tourist attraction at Leith docks.

In 1967, Queen Elizabeth II returned to Clydebank to launch her own namesake, affectionately known as the *QE2*. The *QE2* is still in service as a cruise liner.

In the same year that the *QE2* was launched, the John Brown shipyard was incorporated into the government-sponsored Upper Clyde Shipbuilders, and the yard ceased to build ships in 1972, after 101 years.

Alexandria

World's Greatest Car Factory

Dominating the town of ALEXANDRIA is a vast, ornate, red sandstone edifice, with ornamental gates and a glittering dome that would not look out of place in Vienna or St Petersburg. This is not, however, the domain of some municipal grandee or foreign potentate but a palace of industry, THE FIRST PURPOSE-BUILT CAR FACTORY IN BRITAIN and, in its day, THE LARGEST CAR PRODUCTION PLANT IN EUROPE, the ARGYLL MOTOR WORKS.

Opened in 1906 by the 2nd Lord Montagu of Beaulieu, it took just under a year to build and is still, quite simply, magnificent, redolent of an era of immense confidence and grandeur. Argyll cars were originally built in Glasgow, but demand was such that new premises were needed and Alexander Govan, chief designer and managing director of Argyll Motors, wanted the very best. He got it.

The breathtaking façade is 540 ft (165 m) long, with hand-carved stonework and an entrance porch crowned by a huge baroque clock tower with a gold-leafed dome.

Inside there are hand-painted tiles lining the corridors which stretch 300 ft (90 m) in each direction, and a grand Italian marble staircase based on that of the Paris Opera House. The workers were not neglected – there were cloakrooms with hot and cold running water, sports clubs, restaurants and musical entertainments.

The site covers 60 acres (24 ha) and it was envisaged that up to 2,500 cars per year would be produced here. This figure was never reached, but in its opening years the factory was THE MOST PRODUCTIVE IN ALL OF EUROPE, managing 800 cars per year, second only to Ford in Detroit.

Argyll Motors finally went out of business in 1914. In their time, Argyll cars had a reputation for being well built, reliable and innovative. In 1910 they brought out THE FIRST CAR IN THE WORLD TO HAVE FOUR-WHEEL BRAKES and in 1913 a 15/30 Argyll single-seater broke a number of speed and endurance records at Brooklands.

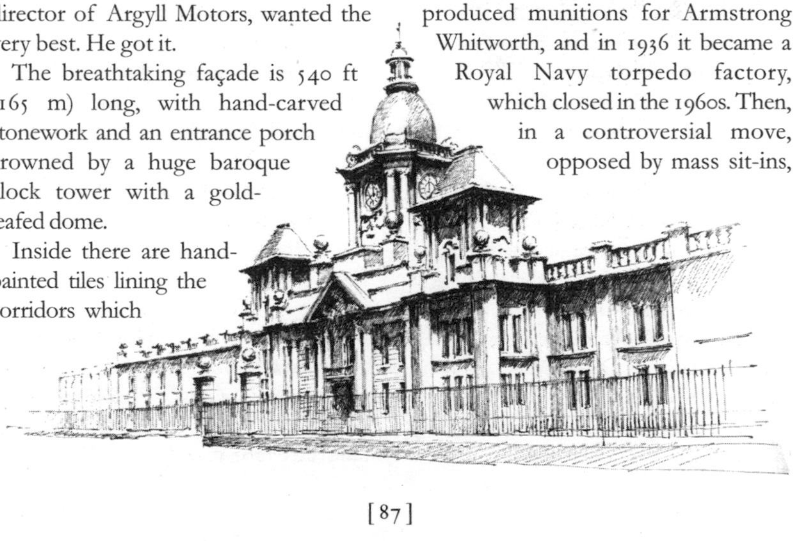

Since Argyll Motors ceased, the factory has been through a number of incarnations. During the First World War it produced munitions for Armstrong Whitworth, and in 1936 it became a Royal Navy torpedo factory, which closed in the 1960s. Then, in a controversial move, opposed by mass sit-ins, the electronics firm Plessey moved in and stripped out the machinery.

Today the Argyll Motor Works is home to the Lomond Factory Outlets and it houses, in the original building, a restaurant, some 24 small discount retail units and a motor museum. The grand façade, the entrance hall and the marble staircase all remain, and the world's oldest and most opulent car factory still stands as a proud monument to Scotland's once-thriving motor industry.

Helensburgh

Steam TV

HELENSBURGH was laid out in 1776, on a grid pattern, by Sir James Colquhoun of Luss, 1st Bt who named the town after his wife Helen, sister of the 17th Earl of Sutherland. Since then it has grown into an attractive residential resort of wide, handsome streets lined with Victorian and Edwardian villas.

In the early 19th century Helensburgh benefited greatly from being at one end of Europe's very first passenger steamboat service, inaugurated in 1812 by the engineer HENRY BELL. He moved to Helensburgh in 1808 with his wife and bought the public baths and a hotel. To bring guests and holidaymakers out from Glasgow to his hotel, he designed the *Comet*, THE WORLD'S FIRST SEA-GOING STEAMBOAT, built in Port Glasgow by John Wood and powered by a 4-horsepower, single-cylinder steam engine. *Comet* sailed three times a week between Glasgow's Broomielaw Quay, Greenock and Helensburgh.

Down on the waterfront there is a tall obelisk dedicated to Henry Bell's memory, and the flywheel from *Comet* is preserved as a monument in the town's Hermitage Park, along with the anvil Bell used while building the boat.

Like so many inventors, Henry Bell was not good with money and he died broke in 1830, at the age of 63. He is buried in the cemetery at Rhu, just along the coast.

Today Helensburgh is a summer port of call for the PS *Waverley*, THE WORLD'S LAST SEA-GOING PADDLE STEAMER, LAST OPERATING EXAMPLE OF A 'CLYDE STEAMER' and LAST IN A LONG LINE OF PADDLE STEAMERS that began with the *Comet* in 1812.

Also down by the water is a memorial to JOHN LOGIE BAIRD (1888–1946), the pioneer of television, who was born in Helensburgh.

Set in the hills above Helensburgh and commanding spectacular views across the town and the River Clyde, is HILL HOUSE, Charles Rennie Mackintosh's finest domestic creation, commissioned in 1902 for the Glasgow publisher W.W. Blackie. Modern, simple and distinctive, the house echoes the Scottish baronial style, but tailored to the needs and wishes of the

Blackie family. The interiors were designed by Mackintosh with the help of his wife Margaret MacDonald, and even the garden shows Mackintosh touches, with the trees clipped into typical Mackintosh shapes. The house is now run by the National Trust for Scotland.

Loch Lomond

By yon bonnie banks, and by yon bonnie braes,
Where the sun shines bright on Loch Lomond,
Where me and my true love were ever wont to gae,
On the bonnie, bonnie banks of Loch Lomond

Oh ye'll tak' the high road, and I'll tak' the low road,
An' I'll be in Scotland afore ye,
But me and my true love will never meet again,
On the bonnie, bonnie banks of Loch Lomond

These words were written by a homesick Jacobite prisoner, languishing in Carlisle gaol on the eve of his execution, in conversation with a pardoned man who would be taking the high road back to Scotland while he, the condemned man, took the low road, or death.

LOCH LOMOND, considered by many to be the loveliest of all Scotland's lochs, seems to conjure up romantic visions in even the most hardbitten of Scottish souls. TOBIAS SMOLLETT, the 18th-century novelist born near Loch Lomond at Renton, travelled widely throughout Europe, but was still inspired to write, 'I have seen Lake Garda, Albana, de Visco, Bolsetta and Geneva. Upon my honour I prefer Loch Lomond to them all.'

Smollett's grandfather was Sir James Smollett, a commissary judge who helped draw up the Act of Union in 1707, and lived at Cameron House on the banks of Loch Lomond. Cameron House was the Smollett family home for 300 years, until sold by Major Patrick Telfer Smollett in 1986. It is now a luxury hotel.

Loch Lomond is THE LARGEST LAKE IN BRITAIN. It is 23 miles (37 km) long but rarely more than 1 mile (1.6 km) wide, covers 27 square miles (6,993 ha) and contains 30 islands. St Mirren founded a monastery on the largest island, Inchmurrin, which is 284 acres (115 ha) in size, THE BIGGEST LAKE ISLAND IN BRITAIN.

As it funnels northwards the loch reaches a depth of 623 ft (190 m), which makes it THE THIRD DEEPEST LOCH IN SCOTLAND.

MORE VARIETIES OF FISH ARE FOUND

IN LOCH LOMOND THAN IN ANY OTHER SCOTTISH LOCH, including salmon, brown trout, sea trout, pike and a fresh water herring thought to have been marooned here when the sea receded after the Ice Age, and found in only one other loch, Loch Eck.

The loveliest village on Loch Lomond is LUSS, a tiny estate village built by the Colquhouns. The beautifully kept rows of flower-covered cottages and basking cats make a perfect film set, and Luss was the setting for Glendarroch, in the Scottish television soap opera *High Road*.

On the shores of Loch Lomond at Inveruglas is the Loch Sloy hydroelectric power station, which opened in 1950 and is THE LARGEST OF ITS KIND IN BRITAIN. The Loch Sloy dam, 177 ft (54 m) high, was THE FIRST DAM OF ITS KIND IN THE WORLD. A smaller dam in the scheme, in Glen Fyne, WAS THE FIRST PRE-STRESSED DAM IN EUROPE, that is a dam secured to the rock foundations by steel bolts. The line of huge pipes sweeping down the hillside towards Loch Lomond is an impressive sight. Water stored in Loch Sloy high up on the slopes of Ben Vorlich rushes down through 2 miles (3.2 km) of tunnel, turning the turbines and generating electricity, before being vented into Loch Lomond. It is THE SECOND LARGEST HYDRO POWER GENERATOR IN SCOTLAND.

Well, I never knew this
ABOUT
DUNBARTONSHIRE

The LOCH LOMOND and Trossachs National Park opened in 2002 and was SCOTLAND'S FIRST NATIONAL PARK.

LOCH LOMOND GOLF CLUB is laid out on the ancestral lands of Clan Colquhoun and is the home of the Scottish Open. The 625-yard sixth is THE LONGEST GOLF HOLE IN SCOTLAND.

Britain's oldest regiment, the Royal Scots, formed in 1633 for Charles I, has 'Dumbarton's Drums' as its regimental march.

Three miles (4.8 km) west of Dumbarton is the site of CARDROSS CASTLE, where Robert the Bruce died in 1329.

Novelist A.J.CRONIN was born in CARDROSS in 1896. Trained as a doctor, he began writing in 1930 when ill health forced him to spend some time convalescing in the Highlands. His most influential work was *The Citadel*, published in 1937, which attacked the practices of Harley Street doctors, and kindled the debate which led to the establishing of the National Health Service. *Dr Finlay's Casebook*, based on Cronin's experiences as a doctor, became a popular radio and television series.

World Champion racing driver JACKIE STEWART was born in MILTON, just east of Dumbarton, on 11 June 1939. He finished third in the World Championship in his first season in Formula One in 1965, and then moved on to Ken Tyrell's team, with whom he won three World Championships in 1969, 1971 and 1973. Altogether he won 27 Grand Prix, a record that would not be equalled for 20 years.

To the west of Helensburgh is GLENFRUIN, the Glen of Sorrow. Here, in 1603, the Colquhouns were ambushed by the Macgregors and, in the bloody slaughter that followed, over 100 Colquhouns died for the loss of only two Macgregors. The victors went on to plunder Colquhoun properties in an act of savagery that so angered King James VI that he had the Macgregor lands confiscated and the clan made outlaws. Their story is told in Sir Walter Scott's novel *Rob Roy*.

FASLANE, lying on the eastern shore of Gareloch, is the home of Britain's Trident (formerly Polaris) submarine fleet and is frequently the scene of anti-nuclear protests. In a nearby cemetery, there is a memorial and some graves, shaped in the form of a submarine, commemorating a tragedy that happened here in 1917.

During trials, a submarine named *K13* sank to the bottom of the loch, when the boiler room flooded after the air inlets were left open. Thirty-two of the 80 crew were drowned almost instantly – the others were rescued after nearly three days.

The ANTONINE WALL reaches its western extremity at OLD KILPATRICK, a little to the east of Dumbarton. St Patrick was allegedly born here around AD 387, and it was from here that he was taken by pirates to be sold as a slave in Ireland.

The actor JACK BUCHANAN (1891–1957), known for his portrayal of the quintessential Englishman, on stage and screen, was born in HELENSBURGH. He starred alongside Fred Astaire in the MGM musical comedy *The Bandwagon* in 1953. Buchanan also financially backed the work of fellow Helensburgh native John Logie Baird in his efforts to develop his television system.

DEBORAH KERR, the actress, was born in HELENSBURGH in 1921. She is best remembered for her roles in such Hollywood epics as *The King and I* and *From Here to Eternity*. In 1994 she was given a Lifetime Achievement Oscar.

Designated as the third of Scotland's 'new towns' in 1956, CUMBERNAULD found fame as the setting for Bill Forsyth's cult 1981 film *Gregory's Girl*.

KIRKINTILLOCH was one of the last places in Scotland to remain totally dry – alcohol was prohibited in the town until the 1970s.

MARTI PELLOW, lead singer of pop group Wet Wet Wet, was born Mark McLachlan, in CLYDEBANK, in 1965.

East Lothian

County Town: Haddington

East territory of *Loth*, grandfather of St Mungo

Seton Castle, site of the first recorded game of golf by a monarch and a woman

Haddington

Birthplace of John Knox and Self Help

HADDINGTON, capital of East Lothian and ancient royal burgh, is one of Scotland's most attractive and unspoiled towns, and was once Scotland's fourth largest city. Burned and sacked many times, like most towns near the border, Haddington endured THE LONGEST SIEGE IN SCOTTISH HISTORY, for 16 months in 1548–49, when the English garrison was trapped in the town by a combined force of French and Scots. The elegant Georgian town centre is evidence of the prosperous times when Haddington was Scotland's premier corn market. The two wide, tree-lined main streets converge, following the V shape of the original town, while intriguing narrow passageways and alleys lead off to crafts shops and rows of old cottages. Some 130 buildings are listed, including the imposing TOWN HOUSE, built in 1748 by William Adam.

In 1143 WILLIAM THE LION was born here, as was his son Alexander II in 1198, in a royal palace that stood where the County Buildings are now. In Giffordgate, historian Thomas Carlyle planted a tree to mark the site of the cottage where JOHN KNOX (1514–72), the fiery Protestant reformer, was born. Carlyle's wife, JANE WELSH, was born in an old, porticoed mansion house behind the County Buildings, in 1801.

Across the High Street a plaque indicates the house where the author SAMUEL SMILES (1812–1904) was born. He is best remembered for his hugely popular book *Self Help*, published in 1859, from which comes the quote 'Heaven helps those who help themselves'.

The main route into Haddington used to be over the 16th-century Nungate Bridge across the Tyne, one of the oldest Scottish bridges on record and now just for pedestrian use. It takes its name from the old nunnery that stood in Nungate, which has been turned into St Martin's Church. In 1543, the Scottish parliament met here to sanction the marriage of Mary Stuart to the Dauphin of France.

Further along the river is ST MARY'S CHURCH, THE LONGEST PARISH CHURCH IN SCOTLAND. This is a restored 14th-century church that replaced a Franciscan monastery known as 'The Lamp of Lothian', sacked in 1355 by Edward III. Several of the Earls and the Duke of Lauderdale from Lennoxlove, their grand seat nearby, are buried here, in the Lauderdale Aisle, which is unique in being THE ONLY EPISCOPALIAN CHAPEL IN A PRESBYTERIAN CHURCH IN SCOTLAND. Jane Welsh Carlyle is also buried in St Mary's, under the choir. Thomas Carlyle, who outlived his wife by 15 years, made a pilgrimage to this spot every year until he died.

Between the church and Nungate Bridge is SCOTLAND'S OLDEST BOWLING GREEN.

Athelstaneford

Birthplace of the Saltire

ATHELSTANEFORD, set on a ridge north of Haddington, occupies a very special place in Scottish history. Indeed, some think of Athelstaneford as the birthplace of the Scottish nation. In AD 832, a combined army of Picts and Scots, led by King Angus, made a foray into Lothian, then under Northumbrian rule. As evening approached, they were ambushed and surrounded by a much larger force led by the Northumbrian King Athelstan, and a battle on the morrow, against overwhelming odds, was inevitable. As darkness fell King Angus knelt down and prayed for deliverance. Later that night St Andrew, the patron saint of Scotland, appeared to the king and assured him of victory. As battle was joined the next morning, a diagonal white cross, like the one on which St Andrew had been martyred, was seen marked out by clouds against the blue sky, and the sight spurred the Picts and Scots on to victory. King Athelstan was caught at the river crossing and killed, hence the name Athelstaneford. From that day, the diagonal white cross of St Andrew, on a blue background, was adopted as the flag of Scotland, the Saltire, OLDEST NATIONAL FLAG IN EUROPE.

The story of the Saltaire is told at the National Flag Centre in Athelstaneford.

Whittinghame

Of Plots and Declarations

Deep in the woods of WHITTINGHAME PARK, not far from Dunbar, a huge ancient yew tree, 12 ft (4 m) in girth, dark and menacing, has spread its gnarled boughs across the centuries to form a green, vaulted chamber, bereft of sun or sky, echoing to the drip of stale rain, damp and musty. Under this black tree, in the winter of 1567, a group of furtive men met to possibly plot the murder of Lord Darnley, husband of their Queen. Amongst their number were the Earl of Bothwell, who had his eyes upon the Queen, and her crown, for himself, Secretary of State Lethington, Lord High Chancellor the 4th Earl of Morton, and Archibald Douglas. Not long afterwards, on the night of 9 February 1567, the house in Edinburgh where Darnley was staying blew up and Darnley's body was found lying in the garden. He had been strangled. The yew tree has kept its secret well, for no one knows if these men were really behind the plot, although they are the prime suspects.

The tree stands in the grounds of Whittinghame Tower, a massive, square, 15th-century fortified tower house that was, at that time, a home of the Douglas family. In 1817, Whittinghame was purchased by James Balfour, a wealthy merchant who had made his money in India. He commissioned Sir Robert Smirke to build a new house in the valley below the tower, and it was in this house, in 1848, that ARTHUR JAMES BALFOUR, the future Prime Minister, was born. Although Prime Minister from 1902 to 1906, he is best remembered for the Balfour Declaration of 1917, enacted when he was Foreign Secretary under Lloyd George. This declared that the British Government supported the idea of establishing a Jewish 'national home' in Palestine, and played a crucial part in the founding of the modern state of Israel. Balfour, who became the 1st Earl of Balfour, is buried in the grounds at Whittinghame.

Whittinghame House is now apartments, and the present Earl of Balfour lives, as his ancestors did, in Whittinghame Tower.

Dunbar

Green and Pleasant

The seaside resort and port of DUNBAR grew up around one of Scotland's mightiest castles, now a precarious ruin. Mary, Queen of Scots was brought here in April 1567, after her abduction by the 4th Earl of Bothwell.

Dunbar claims to have less rain and more sunshine than anywhere else in Scotland.

Opposite the attractive 17th-century Town House, at 128 High Street, is the birthplace of Dunbar's most famous son, the conservationist JOHN MUIR (1838–1914). He emigrated to America at the age of ten and travelled extensively throughout California, where he fell in love with the natural beauties of the Yosemite valley, eventually persuading Congress to declare it a National Park in 1890. Regarded as 'THE FATHER OF WORLD CONSERVATION', Muir was one of the first 'greens', and his ideas inspired national park schemes in America and around the world. Nearby John Muir Country Park, THE FIRST OF ITS TYPE IN SCOTLAND, is named after him, as is Muirfield golf course.

Prestonpans

First for Golf and First for Railways

The distinctive name reminds us that salt was panned here, by the monks from Newbattle and Holyrood abbeys, as far back as the 12th century. PRESTONPANS is also renowned for its oysters.

From the early 17th century, much of the land in this part of East Lothian was owned by the powerful Seton family, whose palace at nearby Seton was one of the grandest in Scotland. The 2nd Lord Seton was one of the 'flowers of Scotland' killed at Flodden Field in 1513. Mary, Queen of Scots stayed at Seton after the murder of her secretary Rizzio, and again after the murder of her husband Darnley, this time accompanied by the 4th Earl of Bothwell. It is recorded that, on this occasion, she played golf at Seton, against her friend Mary Seton, one of the 'four Marys' who accompanied her to France as a child. This is THE FIRST KNOWN RECORD OF EITHER A MONARCH OR A WOMAN PLAYING GOLF. In the grounds of the magnificent Robert Adam designed Seton House, which replaced the palace after it burned down in 1715, is the beautiful SETON COLLEGIATE CHURCH. Begun in the 13th century, it dates mostly from the 15th century, and is a wonderful oasis of peace and calm just off the busy A1. This little-known gem is now cared for by Historic Scotland and is open during the summer months.

The Setons forfeited their lands after backing the first Jacobite uprising of 1715, and the estates were bought by the York Building Company. They developed the local coal mines at Tranent and, in 1722, built the TRANENT WAGGONWAY, to transport coal from Tranent to Port Seton. It was a single-track line with wooden rails and two passing places, and was SCOTLAND'S FIRST-EVER RAILWAY. In 1745, the Hanoverian leader Sir John Cope commandeered the railway to haul his cannons to the battlefield at Prestonpans, THE FIRST TIME A RAILWAY HAD EVER BEEN USED IN BATTLE.

The Battle of Prestonpans of 1745 was an easy victory for Bonnie Prince Charlie's army. It was all over in 15 minutes, and the result more or less secured Scotland for the Jacobites. There is a cairn marking the site of the battlefield, which now lies under the power lines from Cockenzie Power Station.

In 1749, THE WORLD'S FIRST FACTORY FOR THE PRODUCTION OF SULPHURIC ACID was set up at Prestonpans, by the inventor and entrepreneur Dr John Roebuck (1718–94), of Kinneil House (*see* West Lothian).

There are some fine buildings left in Prestonpans itself, including the impressive 15th-century PRESTON TOWER. This was the home of the Hamiltons, before it burned down in 1663, after which they moved to Hamilton House just up the road, now run by the National Trust for Scotland. The magnificent Preston Mercat Cross, dating from 1617, is THE OLDEST MERCAT CROSS IN SCOTLAND, and still stands in its original location. Unfortunately, it is now surrounded by modern bungalows.

Well, I never knew this ABOUT EAST LOTHIAN

After Robert Burns died in 1796, his brother Gilbert, sister Annabel and mother Agnes moved to BOLTON, a little village just south of Haddington. They are all three buried in the church which Gilbert built there.

GIFFORD, south of Haddington, was the birthplace in 1722 of the REVD JOHN WITHERSPOON, a brilliant preacher who became a minister at Paisley Abbey. In 1768 he was persuaded by Benjamin Franklin to go to America as president of the College of New Jersey, later Princeton University. He became a member of the Continental Congress and was THE ONLY CLERGYMAN TO SIGN THE DECLARATION OF INDEPENDENCE in 1776, a document he was instrumental in drafting. He died in 1794. The actress REESE WITHERSPOON is his direct descendant.

In the gardens of 12th-century DIRLETON CASTLE, near North Berwick, is THE LONGEST HERBACEOUS BORDER IN THE WORLD.

On 2 July 1919, the *R34* airship left the First World War airfield at EAST FORTUNE and made THE FIRST-EVER EAST TO WEST ATLANTIC CROSSING, landing at Mineola on Long Island 108 HOURS LATER, A WORLD ENDURANCE RECORD. East Fortune is now the home of the Scottish Museum of Flight.

Picturesque PRESTON MILL near East Linton is THE OLDEST WORKING WATER-MILL IN SCOTLAND. The present buildings date from the 17th century but there has been a mill here since the 12th century. The mill is cared for by the National Trust for Scotland, as is the nearby PHANTASSIE DOOCOT, once the property of Phantassie House, birthplace of the prolific engineer JOHN RENNIE (1761–1821). Amongst his achievements are the breakwaters at Plymouth, Grimsby and London docks, Waterloo and Southwark bridges in London, and the London Bridge that now resides at Lake Havasu in Arizona. His best-known works in Scotland are the Crinan Canal, Kelso Bridge and Leith Docks.

Sixteenth-century FENTON TOWER near North Berwick, now a hotel, is the model for Archie's Castle from the BBC television children's show *Balamory* (*see* Mull).

The whalebone arch on the top of the 613 ft (187 m) high volcanic plug NORTH

BERWICK LAW, placed there in 1933, collapsed in 2005. There has been an arch there since 1709, and local people hope that a new one will be erected soon.

The distinctive landmark of BASS ROCK, off the coast at North Berwick, is THE LARGEST SINGLE-ROCK GANNET COLONY IN THE WORLD, home to some 40,000 pairs of birds. Its correct name is the Island of the Bass, and the earliest recorded owners were the Lauders of the Bass whose family crest is a gannet standing on a rock.

JOHN BROADWOOD (1732–1812), founder of the piano makers John Broadwood and Sons, was born in the village of OLDHAMSTOCKS, near the coast south of Dunbar, where his father was a carpenter.

MUIRFIELD, a links course in the lee of Gullane Hill, north of Haddington, is the headquarters of The Honourable Company of Edinburgh Golfers. They wrote the first 13 rules of golf in 1744, when they were founded, and are THE OLDEST GOLF CLUB IN THE WORLD. JACK NICKLAUS, who won the Open at Muirfield in 1966, announcing that the first hole was 'as tough an opening hole as there is anywhere in championship golf'. He so loved the course that when he built his own golf complex in Ohio, he named it Muirfield Village.

FIFE

COUNTY TOWN: CUPAR

Firth's kingdom or territory

Dunfermline

'Fortunate indeed the child who first sees the light of day in that romantic town'
ANDREW CARNEGIE

DUNFERMLINE, although industrial, is still a romantic town at its heart, clinging to the hillside, its narrow stone streets winding past clusters of baronial banks and crooked shop fronts. Until 1603, it was the capital of Scotland, and it is the burial place of numerous Scottish kings and queens, including the greatest of them all, Robert the Bruce.

Malcolm III (Canmore) had a palace here, to which he brought the beautiful Saxon Princess Margaret, rescued from a shipwreck on the rocks below Dunfermline, at the place that would one day be named Queensferry after her. In 1070, they were married at the church in Dunfermline and here Margaret founded SCOTLAND'S FIRST BENEDICTINE PRIORY, later transformed by her son David I into a great abbey. The nave of the abbey church, built around 1128, still stands and is magnificent with ranks of high, rounded arches on massive stone pillars carved with chevrons.

Queen Margaret was a saintly and educated woman, granddaughter of the English king Edmund Ironside, and she introduced culture and learning into the Scottish court. Hidden away in the corner of the town centre car park are some steps down into a cave where Margaret would go secretly to pray. Even today ST MARGARET'S CAVE is a place of remarkable peace and tranquillity.

Margaret was buried before the high altar in 1093, and when she was canonised in 1250 her relics, along with those of her husband Malcolm, were transported to a new shrine, the base of which can be seen against the east wall of the restored church. Margaret's bones were removed by Mary of Guise for safe keeping at the time of the Reformation and ended up in the Scots College of Douai in Northern France.

During the rebuilding of the abbey choir in the early 19th century, workmen came across a stone coffin containing a skeleton wrapped in gold cloth. The breastbone and ribs had been sawn away, and the body was identified straight away as that of ROBERT THE BRUCE, whose heart had been thus removed, so that it could be taken to the Holy Land. The body was reinterred in splendour beneath the pulpit and its presence emblazoned on the church tower, where the battlements depict in stone the words 'King Robert the Bruce'.

Just inside the west door of the great Norman nave is a monument to WILLIAM SCHAW, Master of Works for James VI, and the 'Father of Modern Freemasonry'. In 1598, he issued the Schaw Statutes, setting out the duties of lodge members and imposing penalties for unsatisfactory work. In a second statute of 1599 he makes the first known reference to the existence of an esoteric wisdom and knowledge within the craft of masonry.

In 1394, James I was born in a small residence carved out of the abbey guesthouse. All that remains of the lavish palace that replaced it in 1589, built for James VI's wife Anne of Denmark, is an impressive 200 ft (61 m) stretch of buttressed wall. Charles I was born in this palace in 1600 – THE LAST MONARCH TO BE BORN IN SCOTLAND and, in terms of height, BRITAIN'S SHORTEST KING.

Andrew Carnegie

Local Boy Makes Good

In stark contrast to this palatial birthplace but quite close by, on the corner of hilly Moodie Street to the south of the abbey, is a simple weaver's cottage where, on a November day in 1835, a boy was born who would become wealthy beyond the dreams of even kings. ANDREW CARNEGIE emigrated to Pennsylvania with his parents when he was 13 and built an empire out of coal and steel, becoming THE RICHEST MAN IN THE WORLD.

There is a statue to Carnegie in PITTENCRIEFF PARK, approached through handsome gates a short step from Dunfermline's central crossroads. As a boy, he had been barred from entering the grounds of Pittencrieff, so he came back in 1902 and bought the whole estate to give to the town and 'bring sweetness and light' to the people of Dunfermline. Despite all his achievements, this small triumph gave Carnegie more pleasure than any other: 'My new title beats all,' he said; 'I am Laird of Pittencrieff.'

In the 18th century, Pittencrieff Park was owned by John Forbes, the general who forced the French to withdraw from Fort Duquesne in America in 1758, and then rebuilt it and renamed it Fort Pitt, after William Pitt the Elder, the British Prime Minister of the day. Fort Pitt grew into Pittsburgh, the city where Andrew Carnegie was to make his fortune.

Andrew Carnegie once said, 'The man who dies rich, dies disgraced,' and he spent the last years of his life giving away $350 million to numerous charities and, of course, to the 3,000 Carnegie Libraries for which he is best known. THE VERY FIRST CARNEGIE LIBRARY was opened in Dunfermline in 1883. America's most famous theatre, Carnegie Hall in New York, is named for this son of Dunfermline.

MOIRA SHEARER (1926–2006), the ballerina and film star, was born in Dunfermline. She is best known for starring in the classic 1948 film, *The Red Shoes*. She was married to the writer and broadcaster Sir Ludovic Kennedy.

Singer BARBARA DICKSON was born in Dunfermline in 1947.

St Andrews

The Biggest Cathedral, the Oldest University and the Home of Golf

ST ANDREWS is a bright and breezy seaside resort that feels much bigger and busier than it really is. For somewhere so far away from anywhere it somehow manages to be right at the centre of things. The three main streets are lined with medieval shop fronts, churches and dignified college buildings, and converge in front of the great cathedral on the point.

St Andrews began in the 4th century, when a monk by the name of St Rule had a dream in which he was instructed to rescue the relics of St Andrew and deliver them to 'the utmost ends of the earth', i.e. Scotland, to prevent them from falling into the hands of the Emperor Constantine. St Andrew was the brother of Simon Peter and one of the twelve Apostles of Jesus. He was put to death on a diagonal cross at Patras in Greece by the Romans, and it was from there that St Rule set off on his mission. His ship was wrecked off the coast of Fife, and St Rule came ashore at what was then the Pictish village of Kinrymont. He put up a small chapel here, to house the relics, and Kinrymont became a place of pilgrimage, eventually changing its name to St Andrews. The truth of this story may be uncertain, but miraculous cures ascribed to the relics gave credence to the legend.

St Andrew became the patron saint of Scotland, his cross the national flag (*see* East Lothian), and St Andrews the ecclesiastical capital. The relics of St Andrew have sadly disappeared, probably destroyed during the Reformation.

The Cathedral

In 1130, the cathedral church of St Rule was built on the cliff top, its remarkable 110 ft (34 m) tower surviving as one of Scotland's finest antiquities, as well as a splendid observation platform for those with the energy to climb the narrow twisting staircase. The tower stands right at the heart of the majestic ruins of St Andrews Cathedral, begun in 1160 and, at 355 ft (108 m) long, THE LARGEST MEDIEVAL BUILDING IN SCOTLAND. The cathedral was consecrated in 1318 in front of Robert the Bruce, who rode down the aisle on his horse.

On a rock below the cathedral is the castle, residence of the archbishops. St Andrews's most unusual experience can be enjoyed here. Undulating through the rock from the outer castle wall to the street is a rough tunnel, remnant of a vicious conflict in 1546. In March that year the Protestant reformer George Wishart was burned at the stake in front of the castle, on the orders of Cardinal Beaton, the archbishop. In retaliation a group of local squires stormed the castle and murdered the Cardinal, hanging his body from a window. The Earl of Arran then besieged the castle and began digging a tunnel underneath the outer

defences in order to make them collapse. The men inside the castle got to learn of this and started a counter-tunnel, guided by the sounds of their attackers' digging. After three false attempts, the defenders finally met up with the attackers and forced them to flee. In 1879, these tunnels were rediscovered and can now be explored. It is great fun, but the tunnels are very narrow and tortuous, requiring some awkward contortions, and should not be tried by those prone to claustrophobia.

In July 1547 the castle fell to a bombardment from a French fleet, and the Protestants were taken prisoner, amongst them John Knox, who had joined those in the castle during the siege. Earlier that year Knox had preached his first-ever sermon from the pulpit of Holy Trinity. When he returned in 1559, his oratory incited the sacking of St Andrews Cathedral.

The University

ST ANDREWS UNIVERSITY was founded in 1410 and is SCOTLAND'S OLDEST UNIVERSITY. It was also home to BRITAIN'S FIRST FEMALE STUDENT in 1862, THE FIRST STUDENT UNION in 1864 and BRITAIN'S FIRST MARINE LABORATORY in 1882. In 1838, Sir David Brewster, inventor of the kaleidoscope, became Principal of the university. Famous alumni include Edward Jenner, pioneer of vaccinations, writer Fay Weldon, Alex Salmond, leader of the SNP, and Prince William. The students still sport red gowns, as worn by their medieval predecessors, so that the university proctors can spot where they are when out on the town.

Golf

Even though the relics of St Andrew have gone, the town that is his namesake still attracts pilgrims from all over the world, only now they come to worship at the shrine of the ROYAL AND ANCIENT GOLF CLUB, home of THE WORLD'S OLDEST AND MOST FAMOUS 18-HOLE GOLF COURSE, the Old Course. The earliest known reference to golf dates from 1457, when James II of Scotland banned golf and football because they were distracting his men from archery practice. In 1552 Archbishop Hamilton's Charter reserved the right of the people of St Andrews to use the linksland 'for golff, futball, schuteing and all gamis'. The five golf courses on the links turf behind the West Sands are still owned by a public trust, and an ancient right of way called Granny Clark's Wynd cuts right across the first and eighteenth fairways of the Old Course. Anyone can play the Old Course, by applying in advance. Tee times are decided by ballot, with the first match teeing off at 7 a.m. Before 1764 the course at St Andrews had 22 holes, four of which were then merged with others to make 18 holes. Since most golf clubs took the lead from St Andrews, 18 eventually became the accepted number of holes for a round of golf.

The Royal and Ancient Golf Club grew out of the Society of St Andrews Golfers, founded in 1754. Since 1897 it has been recognised as the governing body for the rules of golf in all countries except the USA and Mexico. The distinctive clubhouse is never open for visitors, and lady guests are only welcome on St Andrew's Day (30 November).

Two of golf's greatest names were born in St Andrews. OLD TOM MORRIS (1821–1908) competed in every Open Championship until 1896 – the first being held at Prestwick in 1860. He won four Opens and still holds the record as THE OLDEST WINNER – he was 46 when he won in 1867. His son, YOUNG TOM MORRIS (1851–75), recorded THE FIRST 'HOLE IN ONE' during the Open Championship at Prestwick in 1868. He won the Open a record four times in a row, but passed away of a broken heart at the age of just 24, a few months after his new bride had died in childbirth. There are memorials to both Tom Morrises in the grounds of the cathedral.

Culross

St Mungo's Birthplace

CULROSS, on the shores of the Forth, is one of Scotland's most perfect and unspoiled ancient burghs. The exquisite town centre appears to have been frozen in the mid-18th century, with smart pantiled mansions gathered around the town square and quaint little cottages piled up behind, along steep, narrow cobbled lanes. The streets around the Mercat Cross feature a 'crown o' the causie', or raised section down the middle, where only the grandees were allowed to walk, while the *hoi polloi* had to traipse along in the gutter with the slop and rubbish. There is only one other example of such a causeway in all Scotland, at Cromarty.

Poverty has preserved Culross as it is. In the 16th century it was a prosperous port trading with Europe, but the trade dried up and the wealthy merchants disappeared. Those left behind had no money to 'improve' their houses, which were allowed to fall into the genteel shabbiness we so love today. The pick of the grand houses, most of which are now cared for by the National Trust for Scotland, is CULROSS PALACE, built in 1597 for Sir George Bruce, who owned the local coal mines. Climbing the slope behind the palace are the old kitchen gardens, once again planted with the flowers and vegetables of the time.

On a shelf high above the village is the abbey, which stands on the site of the little wattle church where St Mungo was baptised in the 6th century. He went out as a missionary to the Strathclyde region now occupied by Glasgow and is buried there, in St Mungo's Cathedral.

Just up the road, in sharp contrast to the quiet beauty of Culross, is Longannet, SCOTLAND'S LARGEST COAL-FIRED POWER STATION.

Falkland

The Oldest Tennis Court

In 1970, FALKLAND was made SCOTLAND'S FIRST CONSERVATION AREA. It is a beautiful small town, and the stroll down Sharps Close, past a row of picturesque, low-roofed weavers' cottages, across a small green and down Mill Wynd beside the ancient Stag Inn to the Maspie Burn, is one of the loveliest town walks in Scotland.

At the other end of the town is the massive turreted façade of FALKLAND PALACE, impressive in its way but too vast and overpowering for these surroundings. This massive edifice grew out of a royal hunting lodge and is largely the vision of James V. The huge black oak four-poster bed in the King's Bedchamber is the bed in which James V died, broken and alone in 1542. News had been brought to him of the birth of his daughter Mary at Linlithgow, and his last words were, 'It cam' wi' a lass and it'll gang wi' a lass,' a mournful prophecy on the fate of the Stuart monarchy, which came in with Marjorie, the daughter of Robert the Bruce, and looked like ending with Mary, Queen of Scots. James was almost right: the last Stuart *was* a lass – not Mary but Queen Anne, in 1714.

Falkland Palace still belongs to the monarch but is actually the home of the Crichton Stuart family, Hereditary Keepers. The chapel is THE ONLY ROMAN CATHOLIC CHURCH IN BRITAIN ON ROYAL PROPERTY. Charles II raised the Scots Guards here in 1650.

In the grounds, and still in use, is the Royal Tennis Court, built in 1539 and THE OLDEST TENNIS COURT IN BRITAIN. Real tennis is played here, 'real' simply meaning 'royal'.

Scotstarvit

Mapping Scotland

A few miles south of Cupar, in the grounds of the Edwardian Hill of Tarvit Mansion House, stands SCOTSTARVIT TOWER, a handsome and well-preserved 14th-century tower house. In the 17th century this was the home of SIR JOHN SCOT (1585–1670), who sponsored and published the earliest topographical work on Scotland, the *Scotstarvit Maps* of 1654. These are maps of all the counties and islands of Scotland, drawn by master draughtsman Timothy Pont, with added descriptions written by Sir John. At Scotstarvit, Sir John hosted dinner parties and discussions with many of the most important and colourful characters of the day, occasions which no doubt provided material for his most famous work, *Scot of Scotstarvit's Staggering State of Scots Statesmen*. In this, Scot propounds the theory that the majority of Scottish statesmen had attained their status and wealth by fraudulent and underhand means, and the book was considered so libellous that no one would publish it until 1754, when Scot and all the people he referred to were long dead.

Well, I never knew this
ABOUT
FIFE

The little village of Wormit, at the southern bridgehead of the Tay Railway Bridge, was THE FIRST VILLAGE IN SCOTLAND TO BE LIT BY ELECTRICITY. Introduced by Alexander Stewart in the late 19th century, electric lighting for street lamps and householders was generated by a windmill on Wormit Hill, backed up by a steam engine.

LEUCHARS's proudest claim to fame is its extraordinary Norman church. The Norman work is only a fragment, a quite lovely semicircular apse and chancel with a Victorian Romanesque nave and 18th-century bell tower tacked on, but the rich arcading and the beautiful carvings are glorious.

Leuchars's other claim to fame is more modern. RAF Leuchars was established in 1908 and is THE OLDEST CONTINUOUSLY OPERATING MILITARY AIRFIELD IN THE WORLD. It is still THE RAF's BUSIEST FIGHTER BASE.

ST ANDREWS's LAMMAS FAIR, held in August, is SCOTLAND's OLDEST SURVIVING MARKET.

West Port, St Andrews

The WEST SANDS at St Andrews were used for the opening scenes of the

Oscar-winning 1981 film *Chariots of Fire*. Most of the runners in that scene were golf caddies from St Andrews.

A steep winding street descends into the dramatically situated village of NORTH QUEENSFERRY, squeezed on to a small peninsula that juts out into the Forth and cowering beneath the enormous creaking red girders of the Forth Railway Bridge. Sunk into a quarry dug out by the bridge works is the Deep World Centre, where you can walk through THE WORLD'S LONGEST UNDERWATER GLASS TUNNEL, while sharks, stingrays and other exotic sea creatures swim all around you.

KINCARDINE ON FORTH, at the north end of the Kincardine Bridge, is the birthplace of the inventor of the vacuum flask, SIR JAMES DEWAR (1842–1923).

A statue near the sea front in LARGO marks the site of the house where ALEXANDER SELKIRK, the model for Robinson Crusoe, was born in 1676. Selkirk was a foul-tempered man who was put ashore on the uninhabited Pacific island of Juan Fernandez in 1704, after quarrelling with the captain of his ship, the *Cinque Ports*. He lived there for four years before being rescued, and was alleged to have met Daniel Defoe, either in the Llantrodger Trow pub in Bristol, or in London's Wapping.

Buried in the church at Largo is SIR ANDREW WOOD, the Admiral who led a Scots fleet to victory over the English on the Forth in 1489. He had a canal dug from his castle, now a ruin, to the church, so that he could be rowed to Sunday service each week by his old shipmates.

SCOTLAND'S EARLIEST LIGHTHOUSE was a coal-fired beacon built in 1635 on the ISLAND OF MAY, 5 miles (8 km) off the coast of Fife at Anstruther.

BURNTISLAND is known as the BIRTHPLACE OF THE AUTHORISED BIBLE. King James VI of Scotland proposed an English translation of the Bible at a General Assembly of the Church of Scotland here in 1601. The idea was taken up once James had assumed the throne of England in 1603 and was published in 1611.

A tall monument by the side of the road at PETTYCUR CRAGS near Kinghorn marks the spot where SCOTLAND'S LAST CELTIC KING, ALEXANDER III, was thrown from his horse over the cliffs and killed in 1286. His heir was the three-year-old Margaret, 'the Maid of Norway'. Her death in Orkney plunged the Scottish monarchy into chaos and allowed Edward I of England to intercede and choose John Balliol as his puppet king.

KIRKCALDY was the birthplace of economic theory, for here was born the first economist, ADAM SMITH (1723–90). He wrote much of his seminal work *The Wealth of Nations* while living at his mother's house at 220 High Street, now gone, and was said to have been inspired by observing workers at the local nail factory.

THE HEBRIDES

Hebudes – the name given to Scotland's Western Isles by Pliny

Dunvegan Castle, on Skye, which is claimed to be the oldest castle in Scotland to have been lived in by the same family since it was built

Skye

The Misty Isle

SKYE is the largest and most northerly of the Inner Hebrides, a spectacular world of inlets and sea lochs, castles and misty landscapes. The distinctive, jagged shapes of the Cuillins, the highest mountains on Skye, form a striking backdrop to much of the western highlands and provide Britain's most dramatic mountain terrain. The highest peak is Sgurr Alasdair at 3,309 ft (1,009 m), and mountaineers come here from all over the world to test themselves against the challenging conditions.

Another of Skye's memorable landmarks is the OLD MAN OF STORR, a pencil-slim pillar of rock 160 feet (49 m) high, perched on the Storr plateau above Skye's capital, Portree.

Bonnie Prince Charlie spent some weeks in hiding on Skye after the Battle of Culloden in 1746. He left behind him something of inestimable value, the secret recipe for the liqueur Drambuie or 'an Dram Buidheach' – 'the drink that satisfies'. In 1746, as a thank-you for rowing him across to the mainland, the Prince gave the recipe to his loyal supporter John MacKinnon, whose family still guard the secret and run the Drambuie company to this day. DRAMBUIE WAS FIRST BREWED FOR PUBLIC CONSUMPTION, by the MacKinnons, at the Broadford Inn on southern Skye in 1893.

FLORA MACDONALD, who helped Bonnie Prince Charlie to escape to France after Culloden, is buried in a hill-top cemetery above KILMUIR, her tomb marked by a large Celtic cross. The original tombstone was chipped away by souvenir hunters, but Dr Johnson has added a few words of his own to the base of the cross: 'A name that will be mentioned in history, and if courage and fidelity be virtues, mentioned with honour.'

One of Skye's most romantic legends can be found on the northwest side of the island at DUNVEGAN, where the ancient castle on the crag, dating back to the 13th century, is the oldest castle in Scotland to have been lived in by the same family since it was built. On display inside the castle is the 'Fairy Flag' which, legend has it, will save the Macleod if waved in times of peril. Made of silk, it is thought to have been the flag of Harold Hardrada of Norway, defeated by Harold of England at Stamford Bridge in 1066. Twice it has been produced, at the Battle of Glendale in 1490 and at Trumpan in 1580, and on both occasions it brought victory. Another clan treasure is a bull's horn, cut from a mad bull slain at Glenelg by Malcolm, the third Clan Chief (1296–1370), in the 14th century. Every male heir of the Macleods must prove his manhood by draining the horn of claret in one go – no mean feat as it holds more than a litre.

Mull

Balamory

MULL is the second largest of the Inner Hebrides with over 300 miles (483 km) of coastline. The highest point is Ben More, at 3,140 ft (957 m) the only Munro in the Hebrides outside Skye. The capital of the island is TOBERMORY, better known to the outside world as Balamory from the BBC TV children's programme. It is a delightful town with colourful painted houses along the sea front and a bustling harbour.

At DERVAIG, on the west coast, is the MULL LITTLE THEATRE, which used to put on a summer season in a converted cowshed holding 43 seats, and was once

THE SMALLEST PROFESSIONAL THEATRE IN THE WORLD, but in 2007 moved to larger premises.

Just down the coast is CALGARY, a tiny fishing harbour on the silver sands of Calgary Bay, where Highlander Colonel J.F. Macleod spent many happy times as a boy. He emigrated to Canada and became Chief of the Mounted Police, and, in 1876, he named the city of Calgary in Alberta after this lovely Hebridean village.

On the centre of the island, at Gruline, is the Macquarie Mausoleum where the 'Father of Australia', MAJOR-GENERAL LACHLAN MACQUARIE (1761–1824), Governor-General of New South Wales from 1809 to 1820, lies with his wife and children. Born in Ulva, off the coast of Mull, he was sent to New South Wales to restore order after the colony had been in revolt against the rule of Governor William Bligh (of *Bounty* fame). Macquarie founded new towns, turned Sydney from a shanty town into an elegant Georgian city, oversaw the construction of churches, roads and public buildings, and transformed New South Wales from a penal camp into a free, thriving, self-governing colony, and a model for the other emerging Australian states.

Iona

Scotland's Sacred Place

The tiny island of IONA lies off the southwestern tip of Mull and is reached via a short ferry trip from Fionnphort. It comes as quite a surprise to find that the island is not empty, but home to a substantial community and a village which boasts a hotel, shops, a pub and a number of sturdy houses.

Iona, where ST COLUMBA founded his monastery in AD 563, is the most sacred place in Scotland. The saint settled here because it was the first island he reached from where he could not see the coastline of Ireland, whence he had sailed in disgrace following the Battle of the Books.

The Abbey, which sits on the site of the original wooden monastery of St Columba, was built in 1203, although the present building which has recently been restored dates from the 16th century. The nave slopes down to the wonderful altar

of Iona marble, which lies below the level of the west door – a rare configuration for Scotland, found only here and in St Mungo's Cathedral in Glasgow.

Iona is the birthplace of the Celtic cross. St John's Cross, THE ORIGINAL CELTIC CROSS, can be found in the Iona Heritage Centre beside the abbey. It was erected in AD 750 and the arms of the cross were so long that they collapsed soon after it was put up. It was then strengthened by adding a supporting circle of stone around the head, a design feature that was widely copied throughout Scotland and Ireland, as it allowed for much more elaborate and sumptuous carvings on the arms.

Beside the abbey is ST ORAN'S CEMETERY, containing the Ridge of Kings where some 60 Scottish, Norwegian and Irish kings are allegedly buried, including Macbeth. Definitely there is the simple granite tombstone of John Smith, the much respected leader of the Labour Party, who died of a heart attack in 1994. His inscription reads:

John Smith
Sept 1938 – May 1994
An Honest Man's
The Noblest
Work of God

Jura

Big Brother's Birthplace

The sparsely inhabited and spellbindingly beautiful island of JURA, possibly the largest expanse of wilderness left in Britain, was the birthplace in 1948 of Big Brother. In 1947, GEORGE ORWELL (Eric Blair) came here to write his prophetic novel *1984*. Orwell was a friend of David Astor, whose family owned the *Observer* newspaper for which Orwell wrote. The Astors also owned a large chunk of Jura and they asked their neighbours on the island, the Fletchers, if they knew of any quiet place where Orwell might go to write his book. He wanted somewhere 'ungetatable' and the Fletchers owned exactly the place, the cottage of BARNHILL, on the northern tip of the island, just as 'ungetatable' today as it was then.

There is only one road on Jura, and when that runs out there is still a 7-mile (11 km) walk to reach Barnhill. The walk is glorious, with views across the sound to the mainland, eagles soaring in the sky, seals and otters splashing around the shores and always the chance of spotting a magnificent stag – deer outnumber people by 100 to 1 on Jura. Barnhill, when you finally reach it, is exactly as it was when Orwell was living there with his son and nanny, 60 years ago. The views from the house are identical, much of the furniture remains, there is a pavement of sea shells at the back that were collected by Orwell and his son, and, most spine-tingling of all, upstairs in the bedroom is the battered typewriter on which he wrote *1984*.

George Orwell was to die shortly after his sojourn in this beautiful place. He had TB and spent much of his time in bed at the Fletchers' main house. The present owner, Charles Fletcher, then a small boy, remembers him as 'austere' and has vivid memories of his father burning Orwell's sheets, which was the only way of stopping the TB from spreading.

Between the northern tip of Jura and the island of Scarba is the fearsome CORRYVRECKAN, the SECOND LARGEST WHIRLPOOL IN THE WORLD and rated by the Royal Navy as THE MOST DANGEROUS STRETCH OF WATER IN THE BRITISH ISLES. A combination of undersea rock formations and strong tides forced through the narrow neck of water combine to create a terrifying maelstrom that can be heard from ten miles away and has claimed the lives of countless unwary sailors. In 1947 George Orwell took his son out in a small boat to look at Corryvreckan, and they were lucky to escape with their lives when the boat was caught in the whirlpool and capsized. They were swept up on to a tiny rock in the western approach and rescued after some hours by a fishing boat.

Harris

Home of Harris Tweed

HARRIS TWEED, hand-woven on Harris, Lewis, Uist and Barra, by weavers working from their own homes, is THE WORLD'S ONLY COMMERCIALLY PRODUCED HAND-WOVEN TWEED. Tweed has been made in the Outer Hebrides for hundreds of years, but the commercial Harris Tweed industry was initiated in 1846 by Lady Dunmore, widow of Charles Murray, the 7th Earl of Dunmore of Amhuinnsuidhe Castle, when she asked the local weavers to copy the Murray tartan for sale to her friends. All Harris Tweed must bear the orb trademark of the Harris Tweed Association.

On 28 July 1934, German rocket scientist Gerhardt Zucher posted 30,000 letters for the Hebrides by launching them from the tiny islet of Scarp, off North Harris, in a rocket. This attempt to persuade the British government that vital mail and medical supplies could be safely delivered to remote islands by rocket rather backfired when the wretched contraption exploded in mid-air, scattering the letters to the four winds. The idea was not pursued.

The rugged little church of St Clement's at RODEL on the tip of South Harris is the most beautiful building in the Hebrides. It was built in the 16th century by the Macleods of Dunvegan, and contains many fine Macleod tombs and monuments.

Eriskay

Whisky Galore!

On 23 July 1745, PRINCE CHARLES EDWARD STUART, or 'Bonnie Prince Charlie', stepped ashore from the French ship *Du Teillay* on to a beach on the west side of the tiny island of ERISKAY. This was THE FIRST TIME HE HAD EVER SET FOOT IN SCOTLAND. He was greeted by Alexander Macdonald, who urged him to go home. 'I am come home, Sir,' the Prince replied. A pink sea flower, not found anywhere else in the Hebrides, grows on this beach from seeds that fell from Prince Charles's pocket when he removed a handkerchief.

In 1941 the SS *Politician*, bound for New York with a cargo of 245,000 bottles of whisky, struck rocks off the north coast of Eriskay and foundered in the shallows. After rescuing the crew the islanders set about rescuing the whisky, managing to spirit away some 24,000 bottles before the authorities arrived. The incident gave Compton Mackenzie the idea for his novel *Whisky Galore*, which was later turned into a film.

Well, I never knew this ABOUT THE HEBRIDES

The most southerly and perhaps the most beautiful of all the Inner Hebrides, ISLAY is famed for its whisky and boasts no fewer than eight famous distilleries, of which the oldest is Bowmore, established in 1779. The church at Bowmore is ONE OF ONLY TWO ROUND CHURCHES IN SCOTLAND. It was built in 1797, with no corners for the Devil to hide in.

A visit to FINGAL'S CAVE on STAFFA off the coast of Mull in 1829 gave the composer FELIX MENDELSSOHN the inspiration for his *Hebrides Overture*. The cave is 227 ft (69 m) deep and 66 ft (20 m) high, and the surging of the waves against the basalt columns inside makes a strangely haunting musical sound. Turner painted a famous picture of Staffa in 1832. The island is owned by the National Trust for Scotland and can be reached by boat from Oban or Iona.

The stone circle at CALLANISH on LEWIS in the Outer Hebrides is THE SECOND LARGEST STONE CIRCLE IN BRITAIN, after Stonehenge.

The CLACH AN TRUSHAL standing stone on Lewis is 18 ft (5.5 m) high, and is THE TALLEST STANDING STONE IN SCOTLAND.

On Lewis the Free Church in STORNOWAY, capital of the Outer Hebrides, is reckoned to be THE BEST ATTENDED CHURCH IN BRITAIN, with a regular congregation of over 1,500.

The rocks of SOUTH UIST are thought to be THE OLDEST ROCKS IN BRITAIN. A tumble of stones at Mingary marks the birthplace of FLORA MACDONALD. The only significant castle on South Uist is Ormacleit Castle. Completed in 1708 for the Chief of the Clan Ranald, it was one of the last traditional castles to be built in

Scotland and the shortest lived – it burned down in 1715 and was never restored.

The daily air service to Glasgow from Barra takes off from the beach at Traigh Mhor and is THE ONLY SCHEDULED SERVICE IN BRITAIN TO BE 'SUBJECT TO TIDES'. Barra was used for the filming of *Whisky Galore!*, in 1949, and the author of the novel on which it was based, COMPTON MACKENZIE, is buried at Cillebharra on the northern tip of the island.

The now uninhabited island of ST KILDA, a World Heritage Site owned by the National Trust for Scotland, lies 45 miles (72 km) to the west of the Outer Hebrides and is THE MOST WESTERLY AND MOST REMOTE PART OF THE BRITISH Isles. The sea cliffs at Conachair are 1,300 ft (396 m) high, THE HIGHEST CLIFFS IN BRITAIN. St Kilda has THE LARGEST COLONY OF GUILLEMOTS IN THE WORLD and BRITAIN'S BIGGEST PUFFIN COLONY.

INVERNESS-SHIRE

COUNTY TOWN: INVERNESS

Inver Ness – 'at the mouth of the Ness' (Gaelic)

Ardverikie Castle; the choice for Queen Victoria was between Ardverikie and Balmoral

Inverness

Capital of the Highlands

INVERNESS, one of the fastest-growing towns in Europe, is Scotland's fifth city, having been granted that status in December 2000. It is also one of the oldest settlements in Scotland, lying in a strategic position on flat land between the head of the Great Glen and the Moray Firth.

Early signs of occupation can be found on Craig Phadrig, a wooded hill to the west of the River Ness, site of a Pictish capital. It was most likely here that St Columba came in 565 to convert Brude, King of the Northern Picts. The saint had the gates of the fortress slammed in his face so he drew a sign of the cross on them and the gates flew open of their own accord – Brude was so impressed he agreed to become a Christian there and then. Later, in the 11th century, Macbeth's castle occupied the site, and although this is yet another place where Duncan was probably *not* murdered (*see* Cawdor and Glamis), Duncan's avenging son

Malcolm Canmore nonetheless burned Macbeth's wooden stronghold to the ground.

Shortly after this, the first stone castle was built on a bluff to the east, and David I made Inverness a royal burgh. The castle that occupies the site today, and dominates views of Inverness, was built in 1830 and serves as a courthouse and council offices.

In the neo-Gothic Town House of 1882, THE FIRST BRITISH CABINET MEETING EVER HELD OUTSIDE LONDON took place, in 1921. David Lloyd George was on holiday at Gairloch, way up on the west coast in Ross and Cromarty, and had to call an emergency meeting to discuss the situation in Ireland. Amongst the ministers who attended were Winston Churchill and Stanley Baldwin, and the document that came out of the talks formed the basis of the Anglo-Irish Treaty of 1921.

ST ANDREW'S CATHEDRAL, consecrated in 1869, was THE FIRST CATHEDRAL TO BE BUILT IN BRITAIN AFTER THE REFORMATION.

Culloden

The Last Pitched Battle

THE BATTLE OF CULLODEN MOOR, on 16 April 1746, WAS THE LAST PITCHED BATTLE EVER TO BE FOUGHT ON BRITISH SOIL. It marked the end of the Jacobite struggle for the British throne that had begun in 1688, when James VII of Scotland and II of England was deposed by his brother-in-law, the Protestant William of Orange. James VII's son, James VIII, was mocked by his half-sister Queen Anne as 'he who pretends to the throne', hence his title of the 'Old Pretender'. After Anne died, and the Hanoverians took over, James made several attempts to restore the Stuart monarchy. His best opportunity was the uprising of 1715, but numerical advantage was wasted by his commander, the 6th Earl of Mar, at the indecisive Battle of Sherriffmuir, near Dunblane. In 1745 James VIII's son, 'Bonnie Prince Charlie', the 'Young Pretender', landed at Eriskay in the Western Isles, determined to reclaim the throne for his father. After gathering an army around him, Bonnie Prince Charlie marched as far south as Derby, in England, before realising that his cause was hopeless and returning home to ultimate defeat at Culloden.

Culloden is a bleak and melancholy spot 'where no birds ever sing', and although the area has been drained and planted with trees, the battlefield has been restored to more or less how it was. Flags show where the opposing forces were mustered, the graves of the various fallen clans are marked with slabs of stone and there is a massive memorial cairn at the centre. Humble LEANACH COTTAGE, around which the battle swirled, has been carefully preserved. The battlefield is now in the hands of the National Trust for Scotland.

Both BONNIE PRINCE CHARLIE and his opponent WILLIAM AUGUSTUS, DUKE OF CUMBERLAND, were 25 years old at Culloden. Hanoverian forces lost about 300 men, the Jacobites some 2,000. There were more Scots fighting on the Hanoverian side than on the Jacobite side.

After the battle the defeated Jacobites nicknamed the Hanoverian commander 'Butcher' Cumberland for his bloody reprisals, while the grateful House of Hanover named a flower after him, 'Sweet William'.

In the aftermath of the Battle of Culloden Moor, the Highland way of life and the clan system were brutally repressed, and the way was then opened for the Highland Clearances of the 18th and 19th centuries, when many crofters and farmers were moved from their Highland farms to the coast or sent to North America to make way for sheep. (see Sutherland)

Loch Ness

Here Be Monsters

LOCH NESS has an average depth of 427 feet (130 m) and is 22.6 miles (36.4 km) in length, making it THE LONGEST LAKE IN BRITAIN. Filling the northern half of the Great Glen which divides Scotland, it holds THE GREATEST VOLUME OF WATER OF ANY LAKE IN BRITAIN, more water than all the lakes and reservoirs in England put together. In fair weather the unrivalled beauty of Loch Ness and its setting can sometimes disappoint those who come seeking black, icy waters, lowering mists and monsters.

The first person to sight the infamous 'Nessie', or LOCH NESS MONSTER, was St Columba in 595 while he was travelling north to convert the Pictish King Brude at Craig Phadrig. According to Adamnan's *Life of St Columba*, the saint came across a monster attacking a man swimming in the loch, and quelled it with the power of prayer.

The modern legend began in 1933, when the Loch became more accessible thanks to the new road constructed long the northern bank. A local couple were driving home along the new road, when they were alarmed to see 'an enormous animal rolling and plunging on the surface'. The editor of the *Inverness Courier* chose to headline the story with the word 'monster'. Since then, despite hundreds of sightings and photographs, theories and scientific expeditions, no one has been able to prove the monster's existence. Most sightings seem to have been from the romantically sited Urquhart Castle, half-way along the loch on the northern side, close to where the loch is at its deepest. In the 1996 film *Loch Ness*, Ted Danson, star of *Cheers*, played a scientist attempting to disprove the legend.

Camusfearna

Heaven on Earth

CAMUSFEARNA was a name made up by the author GAVIN MAXWELL to disguise the lonely place where he came to get away from it all and write books about life with his otters, the best known of these being *Ring of Bright Water*, from which comes the passage:

It was early spring when I came to live at Camusfearna for the first time and the grass at the burn side was gay with thick clustering primroses and violets, though the snow was still heavy on the high peaks and lay like lace over the lower hills of Skye across the Sound . . .

It is not too hard to work out from this description that Camusfearna is, in fact, Sandaig, no more than a beach and archipelago of small islands on a fantastically remote part of Inverness-shire's west coast. It is extraordinarily hard to find. The journey begins with a hair-raising drive across the Mam Rattachan Pass to the little village of GLENELG, SCOTLAND'S ONLY PALINDROME. A couple of miles further on, off the single-track, no-through road to Corran, you have to locate and climb over a very un-romantic iron gate and then tramp for miles down a long, steep, twisting track, through dense and rather spooky woods, where all is very still, except for unexplained things rustling in the undergrowth.

If you have the courage and the stamina to carry on until the very end, there opens out before you what can only be described as a vision of paradise. Golden sands, rocky pools, fields of yellow irises, a turquoise sea, a waterfall, misty views across the Sound of Sleat to Skye and Rum and Eigg – just as Gavin Maxwell painted it. You can paddle in the water and clamber amongst the rock pools, just as he and his otter did, and for a while you can be in heaven. But, of course, there is no such thing as heaven on earth. In 1968 Maxwell's house burned to the ground, with his otter Edal inside it. Maxwell himself died a year later of cancer. His ashes are buried underneath a simple gravestone where his writing desk stood, and nearby, under a fir tree, there is Edal's stone, with an inscription which reads: 'Edal, the otter of Ring of Bright Water, 1958–1968.

Whatever joy she gave to you, give back to nature.'

It is a deeply moving spot, perhaps the loveliest place in all of Scotland.

'BONNIE PRINCE CHARLIE' IN INVERNESS-SHIRE

Loch Nan Uamh

Two days after landing on Eriskay, BONNIE PRINCE CHARLIE and a few companions came ashore on the Scottish mainland on the banks of Loch Nan Uamh. Ironically he was to leave Scotland for good, as a beaten man with a bounty of £30,000 on his head, from exactly the same place, barely one year later on 20 September 1746. THE PRINCE'S CAIRN marks the spot.

Seven Men of Moidart

In a watery meadow on the northern shore of Loch Moidart, near Kinlochmoidart, stand seven beech trees commemorating the seven companions of Bonnie Prince Charlie who came with him on the *Du Teillay* from France. These SEVEN MEN OF MOIDART were William Murray, recognised by Jacobites as the Duke of Atholl, Colonel Francis Strickland, the only Englishman, Aeneas Macdonald, the group's banker, and four Irishmen, Sir Thomas Sheridan, George Kelly, Sir John Macdonald and Colonel John William O'Sullivan. The original beech trees were badly damaged by a storm in 1988, and seven new trees have since been planted to maintain the memorial.

Glenfinnan

On the afternoon of Monday, 19 August 1745, Bonnie Prince Charlie stepped out of a small rowing boat at GLENFINNAN, at the head of Loch Shiel. A troop of 50 Macdonalds were awaiting him and, while the Prince took shelter in a barn, more Macdonalds, Camerons and Macdonnells arrived, swelling his ranks to some 1,300 men. Charles climbed to the top of one of the smaller hills and raised his father's standard, gave a brief rallying speech and distributed brandy all round. The GLENFINNAN MONUMENT, commemorating the event, was put up in 1815 and is now in the care of the National Trust for Scotland. The statue at the top is not of Bonnie Prince Charlie himself, but represents all the Highland clansmen who gathered there to fight in 1745.

Well, I never knew this
ABOUT
INVERNESS-SHIRE

Inverness-shire is THE LARGEST COUNTY IN SCOTLAND.

In 2006 Inverness-shire was voted SCOTLAND'S MOST BEAUTIFUL COUNTY.

At 4,406 ft (1,343 m), BEN NEVIS, above FORT WILLIAM, is THE HIGHEST MOUNTAIN IN THE BRITISH ISLES.

The CAIRNGORMS, shared with Aberdeenshire and Banffshire, covers 1,400 sq miles (3,800 sq km) and is BRITAIN'S LARGEST NATIONAL PARK.

The CAIRNGORM FUNICULAR RAILWAY, on the slopes of the 4,082 ft (1,244 m) Cairngorm Mountain, is THE HIGHEST RAILWAY IN BRITAIN. The Ptarmigan top station, which includes BRITAIN'S HIGHEST RESTAURANT AND SHOP, sits 3,608 ft (1,100 m) above sea level.

BRITAIN'S ONLY MOUNTAIN GONDOLA climbs the slopes of the 4006 ft (1,221 m) high Aonach Mor, a mile (1.6 km) east of Ben Nevis.

In the West Highland Museum at Fort William there is one of the most unusual portraits on show anywhere in Britain. The 'SECRET PORTRAIT OF PRINCE CHARLES EDWARD STUART' is a wooden board covered in random daubs of paint which, when reflected on to a polished metal cylinder, form a miniature portrait of the Prince.

BEAUFORT CASTLE, near Beauly, once the seat of the Frasers of Lovat, is now owned by ANN GLOAG, founder of Stagecoach, BRITAIN'S BIGGEST PRIVATE TRANSPORT BUSINESS.

TOMATIN DISTILLERY, 13 miles (21 km) southeast of Inverness, is 1,028 ft (313 m) above sea level, THE HIGHEST DISTILLERY IN SCOTLAND.

THE LAST WOLF IN SCOTLAND was killed at Slochd, near Tomatin, in 1743. Apparently.

The Fire Tower at the Landmark Forest Heritage Park near Carrbridge is THE TALLEST WOODEN TOWER IN SCOTLAND.

On a windswept plateau above SPEAN BRIDGE is the striking COMMANDO MEMORIAL, unveiled in 1952 by the late Queen Mother. In the summer of 1940, when Britain was at her lowest ebb, Winston Churchill called for the raising of an élite force of men to take on the enemy in Europe and regain the initiative for Britain. The new units, who were volunteers from throughout the regular army, were called 'Commandos' and their motto was 'United We Conquer'. Only the very best fighting men earned the right to wear the Commandos' green beret, and the enemy soon learned to fear them. Their training ground was right here in the rugged terrain of Inverness-shire.

ARDVERIKIE HOUSE, on the southeast bank of Loch Laggan, played the part of Glenbogle in the BBC television series *Monarch of the Glen*. The house also appeared in the 1997 film *Mrs Brown*, starring Judi Dench and Billy Connolly. Queen Victoria was staying at Ardverikie when she was invited to visit Balmoral for the first time, and when she decided to purchase a home in the Highlands the choice was between Ardverikie and Balmoral. She finally chose Balmoral because it always seemed to rain at Ardverikie, while the sky was always blue at Balmoral.

LOCH MORAR IS THE DEEPEST LAKE IN BRITAIN, reaching a depth of 1,017 ft (310 m).

The view from the top of the monument at Glenfinnan, now in the care of the National Trust for Scotland, is superb. Since 1901 it has included the spectacular 1,000 ft (305 m) curve of the GLENFINNAN VIADUCT which carries the Fort William to MALLAIG railway over the Finnan valley, across 21 arches, the tallest of which is 100 ft (30 m) high.

The viaduct is seen to great effect in the film *Harry Potter and the Chamber of Secrets* when the Hogwart's Express is seen steaming across it, chased by a flying Ford Anglia.

ARASAIG STATION, on the Fort William to Mallaig line, known as one of the great railway journeys of the world, is THE MOST WESTERLY MAINLAND RAILWAY STATION IN BRITAIN.

MALLAIG is BRITAIN'S MOST WESTERLY MAINLAND PORT.

KINCARDINESHIRE

COUNTY TOWN: STONEHAVEN

Cinnch ardain – 'at the end of the woods' (Gaelic)

Crathes Castle, home of the finest Jacobean painted ceilings in Scotland

Stonehaven

Birthplace of the Pneumatic Tyre and the Fountain Pen

STONEHAVEN, the county town of Kincardineshire since 1600, has one of the most picturesque and attractive harbours in Britain. What we see today was largely built in 1826 by Robert Stevenson, grandfather of the author Robert Louis Stevenson, to accommodate the town's large herring fleet.

The red sandstone, crow-stepped Tolbooth, down by the harbour, is the oldest building in Stonehaven and dates from the 16th century. In 1748 three ministers from the Episcopalian Church were imprisoned inside, but still managed to administer baptisms, by pouring water on to the heads of proffered infants through the bars in their cell window.

Stonehaven is now a resort town and the harbour, like that of many Scottish ports, is no longer home to a fishing fleet but, instead, provides shelter for pleasure craft and sailing yachts. A popular feature of the pretty town is SCOTLAND'S ONLY OLYMPIC-SIZED, ART DECO, HEATED, SALT-WATER SWIMMING POOL.

Robert William Thomson

Unsung Hero

In Stonehaven's Market Square, on the site of the house where he was born, there is a plaque to one of Scotland's least famous, but most brilliant and prolific inventors, ROBERT WILLIAM THOMSON (1822–73). The plaque was put there by the Scottish Royal Automobile Association in 1922, on the centenary of Thomson's birth.

His best-known invention, the pneumatic tyre, was patented in 1845, more than 40 years before his fellow Scotsman, John Boyd Dunlop, re-invented the tyre in a more practical form. Thomson's tyre consisted of an elasticated tubular ring of India rubber, encased in leather and inflated with air to the right degree of tightness. They were tested in Regent's Park in London and proved durable and quiet, hugely improving the traction of any vehicle to which they were attached. However, each tyre had to be hand made and took more than 70 bolts to fasten to the wheel, which made them somewhat cumbersome and rather too expensive for everyday use.

For several years between 1867 and 1873 Thomson's three-wheeled Road Steamers, shod with thick, corrugated rubber tyres, were a common sight on the roads of Edinburgh, hauling fully loaded coal wagons of up to 40 tons. Thomson's vehicles were popular with the authorities as the rubber tyres did not tear up the road surface as metal wheels did, and soon Thomson Steam Omnibuses were operating a regular passenger service between Edinburgh and Leith.

Thomson died in Edinburgh, at the age of just 50, little known, but having contributed a mass of ideas and inventions that have helped to shape today's world.

Stonehaven remembers him with a vintage car rally held every June in the Market Square.

Dunnottar

For the Honours of Scotland

DUNNOTTAR CASTLE is without doubt the most spectacularly sited castle on Scotland's east coast. It sits atop a rock promontory 160 ft (49 m) above the turbulent North Sea, connected to the mainland by a razor-thin ledge that requires a dizzying climb down, followed by an even steeper climb up again to the massive tunnelled entrance. Sea birds wheel in the sky, their harsh

cries cutting through the buffeting winds, as salt spray whips into your face.

Dunnottar's proud boast is that it was THE LAST CASTLE IN SCOTLAND TO HOLD OUT AGAINST OLIVER CROMWELL. The English Protector was particularly keen to take Dunnottar because he wanted to lay his hands on the Scottish Crown Jewels, the Honours of Scotland. They had been sent here, to Scotland's most impregnable fortress, from Scone, where they had been used for the coronation of Charles II on New Year's Day 1651, in what turned out to be the last-ever Scottish coronation.

On 26 May 1652, after eight long months of siege and deprivation, the garrison finally surrendered, but when Cromwell's eager men swept triumphantly into Dunnottar they found nothing there but hungry soldiers. The Crown Jewels were gone.

A few days beforehand, realising that they could not hold out for much longer, Lady Ogilvy, wife of the Governor of Dunnottar, had asked Cromwell's commander if she might invite Mrs Granger, the minister's wife from nearby Kinneff, to take tea with her in the castle. The commander saw no reason why two guileless Christian ladies should not console each other in these times of strife, and gave his permission. When she left after tea, Mrs Granger was full of more than just cake, and as the gallant English commander helped her up on to her horse, little did he realise that under her skirts she carried the King's private papers, and a daring plan to liberate the Crown Jewels from under his very nose. The next day Mrs Granger's serving girl was sent to gather seaweed on the beach below the castle and, while she was there, she also picked up the Honours of Scotland which had been lowered down the cliffs overnight at a pre-arranged spot. The maid hurried home with her stash, and the Crown Jewels were hidden away beneath the pulpit of Kinneff Church, until the Restoration of Charles II ten years later. Every three months the Revd Granger and his wife dug up the regalia and aired them in front of the fire at the Manse, so that they wouldn't rust or be damaged by the damp. Visitors to the church, which has

The Scottish Crown Jewels

The Honours of Scotland are THE OLDEST ROYAL REGALIA IN EUROPE. *Consisting of a Crown of Scottish gold, a Sceptre and a Sword of State with an elaborate sword belt, they date from the early 16th century, and were first used together for the coronation of the infant Mary, Queen of Scots at Stirling Castle on 9 September 1543. After being retrieved from Kinneff Church at the Restoration, they were locked away once more, in 1707, at Edinburgh Castle, following the Treaty of Union with England, and did not see the light of day again until Sir Walter Scott obtained permission from the Prince Regent to search for them in 1818. He found them, amidst much rejoicing, exactly as they had been left in 1707, covered in linen cloths and lying in a huge iron-bound chest, beyond the bricked-up doorway of the Crown Room. They are now on permanent display there.*

been rebuilt, can still see the pit where the treasures were concealed.

A quarter of a century later, in 1685, a group of 167 Covenanters, 45 of them women, were locked away for two months in a damp, dark, almost airless cellar beneath the main castle buildings, known as the Whig's Vault. Many of them died from starvation and disease, some fell from the cliffs on to the rocks below while trying to escape, and the survivors were transported to the colonies. They are commemorated by a stone in the churchyard at Dunnottar.

When Sir Walter Scott came to see the Covenanters' Stone in Dunnottar churchyard in 1793, he found ROBERT PATERSON busy cleaning it, an encounter which inspired Scott's novel *Old Mortality* (*see* Caerlaverock, Dumfriesshire).

Dunnottar Castle was the location for Franco Zeffirelli's 1991 film *Hamlet*, starring Mel Gibson and Glenn Close.

The castle is now owned by the Pearsons, Viscounts Cowdray, and is open to the public.

Fettercairn

The Golden Shot

FETTERCAIRN is a pretty village, set in the lush countryside of the Howe of Mearns and dominated by a turreted sandstone arch. This picturesque traffic bottleneck was built in 1864 to commemorate a visit by Queen Victoria and Prince Albert in September 1861. They were on an excursion from Balmoral and decided, as a wicked adventure, to stay for a night, incognito, at the Ramsay Arms in Fettercairn, even strolling through the village, apparently unrecognised. This must have been one of the last moments of carefree happiness they shared together – three months later Prince Albert was dead.

Finella's Castle

Not far from Fettercairn are the scant remains of FINELLA'S CASTLE, where Kenneth II met with an unusual end in AD 994. FINELLA, the daughter of the Earl of Angus, was thirsting for revenge after Kenneth had her son brutally put to death. Instead of allowing her anger to show, she pretended to be reconciled with the King and invited him to a lavish banquet at her castle. In honour of the occasion she had a statue of Kenneth constructed, representing him as a Greek god bearing a golden apple in his hand. The King was naturally flattered and when Finella invited him to take the apple as a gift, he reached out willingly and plucked it from the statue's outstretched hand. It was the last thing he ever did. What Finella had failed to tell him was that she had built in a booby trap, so that when the apple was removed, a golden arrow would shoot out and pierce the heart of whoever took it. Her 'infernal machine' worked to perfection, and so died King Kenneth II. Finella escaped but was

hunted down and killed at the Den of Finella at St Cyrus, a village on the coast.

Fettercairn House and Fasque

To the northwest of Fettercairn, their gates facing each other across the road, are the noble seats of Fettercairn House and Fasque. FETTERCAIRN HOUSE, built in the 17th century by the Earls of Middleton, was where the young Walter Scott came to woo the daughter of the house, Williamina Belsches. She turned down his proposal of marriage, and many people think that this traumatic rejection spurred Scott on to literary greatness. Williamina married the banking heir Sir William Forbes, and today the house is owned by their descendants the Somervells, via the Bowes Lyons.

FASQUE was built in 1809 by Sir Alexander Ramsay and bought in 1829 by John Gladstone, a wealthy merchant whose younger son William became Liberal Prime Minister four times in the 19th century. There are many souvenirs of the Prime Minister in the main house, including, in the main entrance hall, a variety of Gladstone Bags, a type of stiff leather travelling bag much favoured by the former Prime Minister and named in his honour. The Gladstone family still live at Fasque, in the West Wing, and rent out the property for weddings.

BORN IN KINCARDINESHIRE

JOHN ARBUTHNOTT (1667–1735), physician, humorist and writer, was born in the village of Arbuthnott near Inverbervie, son of an Episcopalian minister. He moved to London on the death of his father and became something of a star on the London literary scene, befriending the likes of Alexander Pope and Jonathan Swift. He is best remembered as the originator of that personification of the English character, John Bull, and as the author of a strangely prescient pamphlet entitled *The Art of Political Lying*.

RICHARD HENRY BRUNTON (1841–1901), civil engineer and 'Father of Japanese Lighthouses', was born in the coastal village of Muchalls, the son of a sea captain turned coastguard. In 1868, on the recommendation of the famous lighthouse builders David and Thomas Stevenson, Brunton went to Japan to supervise the foundation of the Japanese lighthouse service. After many years of isolation, Japan was rapidly opening up as a trading nation, and many western ships had foundered on the unfamiliar Japanese coast. Brunton supervised the building of some 50 lighthouses and set up a lighthouse system based on that of Stevenson's Northern Lighthouse Board of Scotland. He established his headquarters and training school in the small fishing village of Yokohama, near Tokyo, and oversaw the development of a major new harbour which would attract the bulk of Japan's foreign trade and emerging modern industries. It is largely thanks to the work of Kincardineshire's Richard Brunton that Yokohama is now Japan's largest port and second largest city. Along with his friend Thomas Blake Glover (*see* Aberdeenshire),

Brunton was one of the founding fathers of modern Japan and his memory is greatly revered in that country. In his native land of Scotland he remains almost unknown.

The 1st LORD REITH (1889–1971), first Director-General of the British Broadcasting Corporation. John Reith was born in Stonehaven on 20 July, fifth son of a Presbyterian minister. His strong, moral 'Reithian' principles permeated throughout the corporation and helped establish the BBC's worldwide reputation for impartial, informative and educational public service. He also initiated that proud BBC tradition, which still continues, of upsetting the government of the day, when he refused to allow Winston Churchill to commandeer the organisation for political propaganda during the General Strike of 1926.

Well, I never knew this ABOUT KINCARDINESHIRE

CRATHES CASTLE, near Banchory, a splendid example of a 16th-century tower house, has the finest original painted ceilings of any castle in Scotland.

Hidden deep in Dunnottar Woods, just outside Stonehaven, is A WONDROUS ALFRESCO BATHTUB built by a former laird's wife Lady Kennedy of Dunnottar. The large oval tub, 3 ft (1 m) deep and surrounded by a low stone wall, was created by damming the nearby Glasslaw Burn. While bathing, Lady Kennedy apparently posted handmaidens throughout the woods to look out for 'sightseers'.

Two fathers of famous sons were natives of Kincardineshire. In 1699, JOHN COUTTS, father of THOMAS COUTTS, who founded Coutts Bank, was born in Inverbervie. In 1721, WILLIAM BURNES, father of Scotland's national poet Robert Burns, was born at a farm called Clochnahill near Glenbervie. Although William Burnes left the area to try his hand at farming in Ayrshire, many of the poet's ancestors worked the hills around Glenbervie, and are buried in the churchyard there.

At INVERBERVIE there is a memorial and garden dedicated to HERCULES LINTON, designer of the world's fastest tea clipper, the *Cutty Sark*. He was born in the town in 1837 and buried in the churchyard in 1900.

GARVOCK HILL above Laurencekirk is crowned by a curious folly called JOHNSTON TOWER, built in 1812 by James Farquhar of Johnston Lodge. In 1420 the hill was the setting for a particularly gruesome murder reminiscent of that of Archbishop Thomas à Becket at Canterbury. James I of Scotland, in a fit of anger at the Sheriff of Mearns, let slip an incautious rant: 'A thousand pities that wretched Sheriff isn't boiled up and made into broth!' Five of the Sheriff's enemies took the King at his word and lured the Sheriff to GARVOCK HILL where they tossed him into a huge cauldron, boiling him to death and each supping on a spoonful of the human broth. The spot where this took place is known as THE SHERIFF'S KETTLE.

Whyte & Mackay's Fettercairn Distillery, founded in 1824, is claimed to be THE SECOND OLDEST LICENSED DISTILLERY IN SCOTLAND.

Johnston Tower

KINROSS-SHIRE

COUNTY TOWN: KINROSS

Kin ros – 'at the end of the moor' (Celtic)

Kinross House – Scotland's first great classical country house

Kinross

The Sleepy Hollow of Scotland

KINROSS, on the shores of Loch Leven, is the county town of Kinross-shire and the only burgh in the county. Known for a long time as a sleepy market town, Kinross is even sleepier now that it has been bypassed with the M90, although the motorway access has attracted commuters from Edinburgh and Glasgow who want a peaceful place to come home to every night.

In the town centre, next to the Town House, is a noble 18th-century steeple, cruelly abandoned by its parent church. In 1742 plans were submitted for a new church, without a steeple, an omission which outraged the town worthies. They formed a committee to raise money for building a steeple, but by the time this had been accomplished, the church had been erected elsewhere, leaving the steeple standing rather self-consciously on its own in the middle of the town.

Kinross House

'The most beautiful and regular piece of architecture in all Scotland'
DANIEL DEFOE

KINROSS HOUSE is a gorgeously untouched, late 17th-century Palladian mansion of pale brown stone, approached from the town of Kinross by a long, wide avenue. Kinross was SCOTLAND'S FIRST GREAT CLASSICAL COUNTRY HOUSE, the first house in Scotland not to be built or designed as either a castle or a fortified house. It is the creation of Sir William Bruce (1630–1710), architect and surveyor to Charles II, and was constructed between 1685 and 1691.

Sir William Bruce is credited with introducing the Palladian style to Scotland, and is best known for remodelling and extending the Palace of Holyroodhouse, as well as for his work at Thirlestane and Hopetoun. He rose to prominence at the court of Charles II, largely through his role as chief negotiator between General Monk and Charles in the lead-up to the Restoration in 1660.

Kinross House now the seat of the Montgomerys is open only by appointment, but the formal gardens surrounding the house, which were also created by Sir William Bruce, and are considered amongst the finest in Scotland, are regularly open. The house makes a splendid backdrop to numerous avenues and vistas, but perhaps the loveliest view of all is *from* the house, along green lawns to the elaborate Fish Gate, which frames romantic Loch Leven Castle on its island, across the blue ribbon of the loch. The Fish Gate is crowned by a stone carved basket of fish, representing the 11 species at one time caught in the loch.

Loch Leven

Elevenses

Eleven miles round, fed by eleven streams, has eleven islands, is surrounded by eleven hills and home to eleven kinds of fish. So runs the legend of LOCH LEVEN.

One of those eleven kinds of fish is a brown trout celebrated for its delicate pink flesh, the result of a diet of freshwater shellfish found only in Loch Leven. The brown trout has been exported across the world as far as America and New Zealand, and Loch Leven to this day is hugely popular with anglers. However, its position as the home of the Scottish National Fly-Fishing Championship, held on the loch since the 19th century, is under threat from large numbers of cormorants who have begun nesting around the loch and eating the trout stocks.

Lochleven Castle

The Great Escape

Crowning one of Loch Leven's 'eleven' islands (it actually has seven) is LOCHLEVEN CASTLE, associated with one of the most romantic tales of all Scotland's castles. There has been some form of fortification on the island since the King of the Picts built a wooden structure here in the 6th century. In the 13th century William Wallace captured the new stone castle from the English, with a force of just 18 men, by swimming the loch and surprising the garrison. Not long afterwards Robert the Bruce began using it as a prison.

Lochleven Castle's most celebrated prisoner was Mary, Queen of Scots. She was brought here in 1567 after being accused, along with her third husband the 4th Earl of Bothwell, of plotting the murder of her former husband Lord Darnley. While a prisoner at Lochleven, Mary was pressured to both abdicate the throne and divorce Bothwell, by whom she was heavily pregnant. She steadfastly refused to do either until, not long after her arrival on the island, she gave birth to twins that were stillborn. Her will finally broken by her grief, she agreed to sign the abdication papers in favour of her infant son James.

The owner of the castle, and Mary's gaoler, was the Dowager Lady Douglas, mother of Mary's half-brother and deadly enemy the Earl of Moray. Lady Douglas's other sons, Sir William and George, were detailed to keep an eye on Mary, but George, like so many before him, fell in love with the tragic Queen and made several attempts to help her escape.

On one occasion, acting on a plan thought up by George, Mary donned the clothes of her laundress, who every morning was rowed across to visit her and, thus disguised, took the boat back to shore. One of the oarsmen made a play at the 'laundress' and tried to strip the muffler from her face, at which Mary raised her arms defensively, revealing the fair white hands of one who had quite obviously never scrubbed laundry in her life. Her cover was blown and she was taken back to the castle, while George Douglas was sent away in disgrace.

On the evening of 25 March 1568, enter another lovesick Douglas, 16-year-old Willie Douglas, illegitimate son of Sir William, employed at the castle as a pageboy. Like his uncle George he had become besotted with the beautiful Mary and devised his own plan to rescue her. That night, while serving at dinner, he managed to pocket the keys to the castle's main door, which his father had left out on the dining table. He then guided Mary down from her room above the dining hall, out through the castle gates and into a waiting boat, locking the doors behind him and tossing the keys into the loch. Once ashore they were met by George Douglas and a troop of loyal soldiers, and taken to hide at Lord Seton's seat, Niddrie Castle in West Lothian.

Early in the 19th century the loch was partially drained and a rusty set of door keys was retrieved from an exposed mud bank near the island – the very keys dropped into the water during that dramatic escape. The keys are now kept in the Armoury at Abbotsford, Sir Walter Scott's home in Roxburghshire.

Well, I never knew this ABOUT KINROSS-SHIRE

Covering an area of 82 square miles (21,240 ha), Kinross-shire is THE SECOND SMALLEST COUNTY IN SCOTLAND.

Kinross's Sunday market is THE LARGEST INDOOR MARKET IN SCOTLAND.

Kinross has had two famous MPs, ROBERT ADAM the architect, from 1768 to 1774, and SIR ALEC DOUGLAS-HOME, when Prime Minister from 1963 to 1964. Douglas-Home renounced his title as 14th Earl of Home so that he could contest Kinross in a by-election. He remains THE ONLY PRIME MINISTER TO RESIGN FROM THE LORDS TO CONTEST A BY-ELECTION FOR THE COMMONS and was THE LAST PRIME MINISTER TO BE PERSONALLY CHOSEN BY THE MONARCH.

LOCH LEVEN is THE LARGEST LOCH IN THE SCOTTISH LOWLANDS.

VANE FARM NATURE RESERVE, on the south shore of Loch Leven, is administered by the Royal Society for the Protection of Birds and was THE FIRST EDUCATIONAL NATURE RESERVE IN EUROPE.

The annual 'T IN THE PARK' music festival, held in July on a disused Second World War airfield at BALADO, near Kinross, is SCOTLAND'S LARGEST OUTDOOR ROCK festival. Balado is also home to the 'Golfball', a futuristic NATO Communications Facility.

The village of RUMBLING BRIDGE takes its unusual name from an unusual double bridge across the River Devon. The first bridge, built in 1713, spans the narrow gorge at a height of 80 ft (24 m) above the river bed. The second bridge, of 1816, was constructed 40 ft (12 m) higher, directly above the older bridge. The river gorge contains a number of fine waterfalls.

KIRKCUDBRIGHTSHIRE

COUNTY TOWN: KIRKCUDBRIGHT

Kirk Cuthbert – 'Kirk of St Cuthbert'

Gatehouse of Fleet – the Murray Arms Hotel where Robert Burns wrote the words for 'Robert Bruce's March to Bannockburn' which begins 'Scots wha hae wi' Wallace bled'

Kirkcudbright

The Artist's Town

Kirkcudbrightshire (pronounced Kirk-coo-bree-shire) is sometimes referred to as The Stewartry, a name derived from the days when the area was ruled by a Royal Steward, having been taken away from the King, John Balliol.

The county town, KIRKCUDBRIGHT, 'Kirk of Cuthbert', is one of Scotland's least-known gems. Washed by the Gulf Stream, blessed with a mild climate and possessed of a special quality of light, it has become known as 'The Artist's Town' and supports a flourishing colony of painters and craftsmen. The streets are wide and breezy, with houses gaily painted in pastel colours, the High Street being perhaps the most lovely of them all.

No. 12, High Street is BROUGHTON House, home of the artist E.A. Hornel from 1901 to 1933. Hornel was one of the Glasgow Boys, a group of young artists who introduced their own highly colourful style of impressionism to Scottish art in the late 19th century. They used to travel throughout Scotland seeking characters and scenes of rural life to paint. Members included Sir James Guthrie, George Henry and Sir John Lavery.

E.A. Hornel sealed Kirkcudbright's reputation as an artist's colony when he settled here in 1901. He left Broughton House to the town and it is now a museum containing many of his works and memorabilia. He travelled extensively in Japan and the beautiful gardens at the back of the house, running down to the river, are full of Japanese plants and features.

A little further along, where the High Street turns sharply to the left, is the 17th-century Tolbooth, now a museum. John Paul Jones, father of the American Navy (*see* Kirkbean), was imprisoned here for a short time, accused of the murder of his ship's carpenter, who had died while being flogged.

While staying at the Selkirk Arms Hotel at the far end of the High Street, Robert Burns wrote the 'Selkirk Grace':

Some hae meat and canna eat,
And some wad eat that want it;
But we hae meat and we can eat,
Sae let the Lord be thankit.

Dominating views of the town from across the river is MacLellan's Castle, built in the 16th century by a Provost of Kirkcudbright, Sir Thomas MacLellan. Behind the fireplace in the Great Hall is a room where Sir Thomas would conceal himself and listen in to his guests' conversations, through a small hole in the wall known as 'the Laird's Lug'.

The village scenes from the cult 1973 horror film *The Wicker Man*, starring Edward Woodward and Christopher Lee, were filmed in Kirkcudbright.

Dundrennan

Queen Mary's Last Night

Kirkcudbrightshire's oldest ecclesiastical remains are those of the Cistercian Abbey at DUNDRENNAN, east of Kirkcudbright, founded in 1142 by David I. The lofty ruins, in their shady, velvet green setting, on a platform below the village street, are quietly impressive. Occupying a recess in a western wall is one of Scotland's most unusual stone effigies, remarkably well preserved. It represents the tall figure of an abbot, his heart pierced by a dagger, standing on a writhing creature, presumably his murderer, whose head is transfixed by the abbot's crook.

There is something mournful about this secluded place – it was here, on 15 May 1568, that Mary, Queen of Scots spent her last night in Scotland. She fled here after the Battle of Langside, and was received by one of her few remaining supporters, Edward Maxwell, Abbot of Dundrennan. Next morning she made her way down the burn to a creek on the Solway Firth, where she boarded a small fishing boat and sailed away, never to return. As she stepped on to a rock to climb into the boat, Mary left her last footprint on Scottish soil and local legend says that it is said that this footprint can still be seen when the rock is exposed at low tide. This lonely, desolate place is now called Port Mary, while the spot across the Solway where she landed in England is known as Maryport.

Dalbeattie

He Died a Hero

The once bustling town of DALBEATTIE gazes across the river Urr at what is left of Craignair Hill, from whence came the granite that built the town itself and many other places across Britain. Dalbeattie granite can be found in the Liverpool Docks, the Thames Embankment, the Eddystone Lighthouse, and as road chippings and railway ballast all over the world. In 1831, Dalbeattie became THE FIRST PLACE IN THE WORLD WHERE GRANITE WAS COMMERCIALLY POLISHED.

Craignair quarry is still working today but in a much reduced capacity, and the harbour, not so long ago thronging with ships and trade, is now silent and listless.

Close to Craignair Hill stood the castle home of John Balliol and his wife Devorguilla (*see* New Abbey). Their son, John Balliol, who became King of Scotland, was born here in 1249.

In the town centre, set into the granite wall of the town hall, is a memorial to LIEUTENANT WILLIAM MURDOCH, First Officer on the doomed liner *Titanic*, sunk by an iceberg in the North Atlantic on 14 April 1912. He was born in No. 3 'Sunnyside', Barr Hill, Dalbeattie, on 28 February 1873.

In the 1997 blockbuster film *Titanic*, Murdoch was portrayed as corrupt, a coward and a murderer who took bribes, shot passengers who tried to rush the boats, and then took his own life. In his home town he is a hero, for he was described in eyewitness accounts as calmly guiding passengers into the boats, helping people to climb overboard and throwing deck chairs for them to hold on to, saving countless lives and refusing to leave his post or save himself.

In April 1998, the Scots-born Vice-President of 20th Century-Fox, Scott Neeson, came to Dalbeattie to deliver an apology to Murdoch's 80-year-old nephew. Neeson insisted that the film-makers 'never intended to portray him as a coward', and that any implication otherwise was 'inadvertent'. Mr Neeson also presented £5,000 to the William Murdoch Memorial Prize which is competed for annually by fourth-year students at Dalbeattie's High School.

His attempts at an apology left the granite town of Dalbeattie unimpressed.

Kirkbean

Father of the American Navy

Down a maze of country lanes between lonely Criffell and the sea, on a windy promontory at the end of a rutted, bumpy track from Kirkbean, sits a simple, single-storey gamekeeper's cottage, birthplace in 1747 of JOHN PAUL JONES, 'FATHER OF THE AMERICAN NAVY'.

When he was just a boy John Paul sailed to Virginia, where his older brother was in business, and soon fell in love with America – 'my favourite country from the age of thirteen when I first saw it'.

A natural sailor, in 1775 Jones was assigned to the frigate USS *Alfred* and became THE FIRST-EVER 1ST LIEUTENANT IN THE CONTINENTAL NAVY, as well as THE FIRST MAN TO HOIST AN AMERICAN FLAG OVER AN AMERICAN NAVAL VESSEL – in this case the Grand Union flag, not the Stars and Stripes, which was introduced later.

In 1777, after the Declaration of Independence, he was given command of a sloop USS *Ranger*, one of the first naval vessels to fly the Stars and Stripes, and THE FIRST AMERICAN NAVY VESSEL TO BE SALUTED BY THE FRENCH, a nine-gun salute from Admiral Piquet's flagship at Brest. On 24 April 1778, Jones captured the HMS *Drake*, off Carrickfergus in Ireland, in THE FIRST-EVER VICTORY FOR AN AMERICAN VESSEL OVER A BRITISH SHIP OF WAR, a highly symbolic success.

He died on 18 July 1792 and is buried in the chapel of the US Naval Academy in Annapolis, Maryland. The inscription on his tomb reads: 'He Gave To Our Navy Its Earliest Traditions of Heroism and Victory.'

JOHN PAUL JONES' COTTAGE is now a museum dedicated to his memory, and the surrounding gardens of the Arbigland Estate, where Jones and his father worked, can be visited at certain times. In nearby Kirkbean church there is a baptismal font made of Portland stone, given by the American Navy in 1945, and dedicated to 'the first commander of the United States Navy'.

Kirkbean has another link with America. Born here in 1727 was James Craik, friend of George Washington and his physician during Washington's last illness. The first American President called Craik 'my compatriot in arms, my old and intimate friend'.

Threave Castle

Archibald the Grim

THREAVE CASTLE, one of the largest and strongest towers in Scotland, stands gaunt and still menacing on a small, grassy island in the middle of the River Dee, west of Castle Douglas. To reach it requires a ten-minute walk across fields and water-meadows until you come to a small jetty where hangs a bell. Toll the bell and the ferryman will row across from the island and take you to the castle harbour.

The castle rises 70 ft (21 m) high and has five floors, the topmost level being UNIQUE AMONGST SCOTTISH TOWERS. During a siege the defenders would retreat to this top floor, draw up the ladders and drop boulders or boiling oil on to the attackers from the parapet above.

Threave was built in the late 14th century by ARCHIBALD DOUGLAS, in order to secure his position as Lord of Galloway. He was known as Archibald the Grim because of his 'terrible countenance in warfare', and was the son of the Sir James Douglas entrusted with Robert the Bruce's heart. Archibald the Grim's own son married the eldest daughter of Robert III, Margaret Stewart, whose rich tomb can be found amongst the magnificent ruins of Lincluden Abbey near Dumfries.

Eventually, during the 15th century, the growing power of the Earls of Douglas began to alarm the King. In an act of open defiance, William, the 8th Earl, by all accounts 'one of the most horrible devils that ever appeared in Scotland', captured one of the King's friends, Patrick MacLellan of Kirkcudbright, and incarcerated him at Threave. Douglas had bribed one of MacLellan's servants to betray his master by promising him a ladleful of gold. The payment was settled by having the molten gold poured down the unfortunate man's throat. James II sent a letter to Douglas demanding the release of MacLellan, but Douglas refused to read it until after he had dined. While feasting, he had MacLellan hanged from the gallows knob which can still be seen protruding above the castle's main doorway, and which Douglas liked to boast 'never wanted its tassel'.

The King's Revenge

In 1452 James II finally murdered the 8th Earl, with his own hands, at Stirling Castle, and then set about demolishing all the Douglas strongholds. Threave Castle was the last to fall because the 8th Earl, aware of James's enthusiasm for artillery, had built a strong curtain wall around the outside of the tower to deflect cannon fire. After a two-month siege James called for his mightiest cannon, 'MONS MEG', to be brought into the fray, one of only two occasions on which the great gun was used. It had the desired effect.

Local tradition has it that Mons Meg was built by a blacksmith from nearby Castle Douglas called McKim, specially for the siege of Threave, although it is much more likely that the cannon came from Belgium, having been made at Mons, and was given to James II by his uncle, the Duke of Burgundy. Mons Meg is now on display outside Edinburgh Castle.

Tongland

A Flying Abbot, a Hot Blast and Cars for Women

Tiny TONGLAND on the River Dee, north of Kirkcudbright, has an extraordinary history for somewhere in the middle of nowhere. Once it was the site of a mighty abbey, founded in 1218 by Fergus, Lord of Galloway. All that remains now is a doorway incorporated into the 19th-century parish church. The last abbot of Tongland, an Italian alchemist called John Damian, 'the Frenzied Friar of Tongland', tried to fly from the walls of Stirling Castle for the benefit of James IV, but fell to earth in a dung heap and broke his leg (*see* Stirling).

Buried in the churchyard, in a granite mausoleum, is JAMES NEILSON (1792–1865), inventor of the hot blast technique for smelting iron. This system used pre-heated air rather than cold air for blasting coal, greatly reducing the amount of coal and coke needed to produce iron, and enabling iron makers to satisfy the ever-increasing demand for iron from the railway and shipbuilding industries.

Thomas Telford built the sturdy, battlemented TONGLAND BRIDGE across the deep Dee gorge in 1805, THE FIRST BRIDGE IN BRITAIN TO CARRY A ROAD ON INTERNAL SPINE WALLS RISING FROM THE ARCH RINGS. This was Telford's first bridge in Scotland.

For two heady years in 1921–22, Tongland was the proud manufacturer of fine motor cars. GALLOWAY CARS were constructed in a factory that had been used to build aero engines during the First World War. The firm was staffed almost exclusively by women, boasted THE ONLY FEMALE MANAGER OF A CAR PLANT IN BRITAIN, DOROTHY PULLANGER, and produced cars extremely popular with lady drivers.

Today, Tongland is mainly known for its art deco power station, opened in 1936 as part of the Galloway hydroelectric scheme.

Cardoness Castle

Impregnable

CARDONESS CASTLE lies about a mile to the south of Gatehouse of Fleet and is perched above the road atop a rocky knoll overlooking the Fleet Bay. It is reached by a steep climb, winding up through banks of lawn covered in waving flowers, past woods full of birdsong.

Cardoness was built by the McCulloch family in the mid-15th century. They came by the estate through marriage to the youngest daughter of the previous landowner – she was the sole survivor of a bizarre accident when her whole family fell through the ice on a frozen lake and drowned, ironically while celebrating the birth of an heir.

Cardoness was wellnigh impregnable. In medieval times the sea lapped at the base of the rock, the tower was out of reach of any artillery and the only approach was by scaling the cliff. The views from the top of the stairway across Fleet Bay and the surrounding countryside are unsurpassed. Cardoness is truly one of southwest Scotland's best-kept secrets. It is cared for by Historic Scotland.

Glen Trool

Bruce's First Stand

The scenery around GLEN TROOL, on Kirkcudbrightshire's wild northern border, is some of the most sublime in Scotland, with rugged mountains, waterfalls and pine forests.

On a crest at the eastern end of the glen, stands BRUCE'S STONE, a huge granite boulder that commemorates Robert the Bruce's victory over a superior English force in March 1307, while he was on the run after the murder of John Comyn at Dumfries. Across the blue ribbon of the loch are the steep crags of Muldonach, where Bruce and his small band of men hid in the dawn mist. Fifteen hundred of the Earl of Pembroke's troops advanced through the glen until they reached a point where the track squeezes into a narrow defile, and they were forced to dismount and continue on foot, single file, along its steeply sloping side. Bruce gave the signal, three short blasts on his bugle, and the Scots, perched high on the cliffs above, rained stones and boulders down on the men below, sweeping them off the mountainside and into the loch. Those who weren't crushed or broken took flight and the rout was complete. It was a turning-point in the War of Independence, THE FIRST VICTORY FOR THE SCOTS.

Well, I never knew this

ABOUT

KIRKCUDBRIGHTSHIRE

ORCHARDTON TOWER, sitting in a lovely green fold of hills above the Solway Firth, was built by the Cairns family in the 15th century and is THE ONLY ROUND TOWER HOUSE IN SCOTLAND.

Every year, on a summer Saturday, PALNAKIE, a little fishing town on the Urr Water estuary, hosts the World

Flounder Tramping Championships. Competitors shuffle along the mudflats using their bare feet to feel for the fish, and prizes are awarded both for the lightest and the heaviest catch.

Growing out of the rocky sands of SOUTHERNESS POINT is SCOTLAND'S SECOND OLDEST LIGHTHOUSE, solitary, rough-hewn and sturdy. It is now forgotten and neglected, but still loyally stands sentinel. Built in 1748, this is one of the most perfect structures in all Scotland.

THE MERRICK, in north Kirkcudbrightshire, is THE HIGHEST MAINLAND PEAK IN SOUTHERN SCOTLAND, at 2,764 ft (842 m).

East of the Merrick is Loch Enoch. On an island in the middle of this loch there is another small loch, forming A LOCH WITHIN A LOCH – the only such feature in Scotland.

In the shadow of lonely Criffell, before the high altar of the ruined abbey that looms massively over the little village of NEW ABBEY, lies THE FIRST SWEETHEART. The abbey here, called the New Abbey to distinguish it from Dundrennan, already a venerable 130 years old, was founded in 1273 by Devorgilla, Lady of Galloway. She was a great-great-grandaughter of David I and mother of John Balliol, Edward I's puppet king. Her husband, John Balliol, founded Balliol College at Oxford University. When he died in 1268, she had his 'sweet heart' embalmed in an ivory casket banded with silver, which she carried around with her until her own death in 1290. She was buried at New Abbey with the casket on her breast and the abbey became known as 'Dulce Cor', or 'Sweetheart Abbey', passing its name into the English language.

Also buried at Sweetheart Abbey is SIR WILLIAM PATERSON, founder of the Bank of England and the ill-fated Darien Scheme (*see* Lochmaben, Dumfriesshire).

Grand Prix racing driver DAVID COULTHARD was born in the busy village of TWYNHOLM, near Kirkcudbright, in 1971. The David Coulthard Museum and Pit Stop Diner, housed in a long whitewash building just off the High Street, claims to be 'the most complete collection of memorabilia for any Formula One driver, past or present, in the world'.

LANARKSHIRE

COUNTY TOWN: GLASGOW

Llanerch – forest glade (Welsh)

St Mungo's Cathedral, Scotland's most complete medieval cathedral

Glasgow

'The Beautifullest little city I have seen in Britain'

DANIEL DEFOE

GLASGOW IS SCOTLAND'S BIGGEST CITY. It was European City of Culture (1990) and UK City of Architecture and Design (1999). Once a byword for slums and industrial deprivation, the city's grand Victorian architecture is now vibrant with art galleries and museums, trendy pavement cafés and glitzy shopping malls. As it was possibly the world's first truly industrial city, now it is often referred to as the world's first post-industrial city.

The Cathedral

Glasgow's recorded origins go back even further than those of its near neighbour

Edinburgh, although the place where it all began is rather sidelined now. A mile or so to the northeast of busy George Square, on a small hill, is Glasgow's CATHEDRAL OF ST MUNGO. Here, in AD 590, St Mungo, also known as St Kentigern, Bishop of Strathclyde, established a small wooden church at 'Glas ghu' or 'beloved green place', where St Ninian had dedicated a Christian burial ground some 200 years before. David I consecrated the first stone church in 1136, and during the course of the 13th century this was replaced with the core of the present building. Today, St Mungo's is THE ONLY COMPLETE MEDIEVAL CATHEDRAL ON THE SCOTTISH MAINLAND and THE BIGGEST GOTHIC BUILDING IN SCOTLAND. The fact that it was the only Scottish cathedral to survive the Reformation undamaged is thanks to the courage of the ordinary folk of Glasgow who turned out in great numbers to defend their beloved church against the rampaging mob.

The cathedral is built on a sloping site, with the eastern end falling away to a burn, and so the east end of the cathedral has two storeys. St Mungo's tomb can be found amidst the waving forest of pillars and Gothic vaulting of the magnificent lower church, UNIQUE AMONGST BRITISH CATHEDRALS and St Mungo's glory.

The whole building is beautifully balanced, and the best place to appreciate the cathedral's noble proportions is from the melodramatic Necropolis, Scotland's first and most spectacular garden cemetery. It was established in 1833 by the Merchant's House of Glasgow and based on the Père Lachaise in Paris. Covering an entire hill, this city of the dead is a diverse collection of monuments, statues, tombs, sculptures and sarcophagi, designed in the architectural style of the city where the merchant had made his money. Almost every eminent Glaswegian of the day is buried here, or at least has a memorial here. One such memorial, put up by public subscription, is to William Miller (1810–72), the carpenter, poet and songwriter who gave us 'Wee Willie Winkie'. He died penniless and is actually buried at Tollcross cemetery, across the city.

In Cathedral Square is THE ONLY TRADITIONAL STATUE IN BRITAIN THAT MOVES. Made of lead, it shows William of Orange, dressed in the garb of a Roman Emperor, seated on a horse. When the statue was relocated from Glasgow Cross, the horse's tail broke off and was re-attached using a ball and socket. It now swings when the wind blows.

The University

Glasgow University was founded in 1451 and is SCOTLAND'S SECOND OLDEST UNIVERSITY, after ST ANDREWS. In 1870 the university moved into a vast, pinnacled, Gothic building on Gilmorehill, overlooking Kelvingrove Park in the city's west end. Designed by George Gilbert Scott, the massive edifice includes a tower over 200 ft (61 m) high, which dominates the area and provides a magnificent vantage-point over the city. THE HUNTERIAN MUSEUM, which forms part of the university, was bequeathed by Dr William Hunter and opened in 1807 as SCOTLAND'S FIRST PUBLIC MUSEUM.

Glasgow University

Trongate

Glasgow's early wealth in the 18th century was based on tobacco, with half of all the trade between Europe and the American colonies controlled from the city. The 'Tobacco Lords' became immensely rich and immensely grand. Their favoured gathering place was TRONGATE, near Glasgow Cross, where a special paved area known as the Plainstanes was reserved exclusively for them. Here they would strut in their red cloaks and tricorn hats, clearing the rabble out of the way with their silver-knobbed canes. Now a popular shopping street, the most notable structure in Trongate is the Tolbooth Steeple, 126 ft (38 m) high and ONE OF ONLY THREE CROWNED STEEPLES IN SCOTLAND. Sir John Moore (1761–1809), the hero of Corunna, was born at No. 90, Trongate. James Watt had a workshop where No. 32 now stands.

Glasgow Green

GLASGOW GREEN, to the east of the city centre, is Glasgow's oldest and biggest park and known as 'Glasgow's lung'. One quiet Sunday afternoon in May 1765 something happened on Glasgow Green that changed Glasgow, and the world, for ever. James Watt was strolling across the green, lost in thought and grappling with the problem of how to improve the Newcomen steam engine he was working on . . . *'I had not walked further than the golf-house when the whole thing was arranged in my mind.'* He had hit upon the idea of a separate condenser, and that one flash of inspiration was to put in motion the Industrial Revolution. The magic spot is now marked by a boulder. Forty years later BRITAIN'S FIRST MEMORIAL TO ADMIRAL NELSON was erected nearby.

Tolbooth Steeple

In 1873 Glasgow Rangers Football Club played their first match against Callander on Glasgow Green. GLASGOW RANGERS are one of Scotland's two premier football clubs, the other being Glasgow Celtic. The two teams are arch-rivals and their support is divided down religious lines, with Rangers fans almost exclusively Protestant and Celtic fans drawn from the Irish Catholic community. Collectively the two clubs are known as the 'Old Firm'. Today, Rangers play at IBROX STADIUM which, in 1939, hosted THE LARGEST CROWD EVER TO WATCH A LEAGUE MATCH IN BRITAIN, 118,567. In 1971, Ibrox was the scene of BRITAIN'S WORST SPORTING DISASTER, up to that time, when some spectators lost their footing while leaving the stadium via stairway 13, after an Old Firm match, and 66 people were asphyxiated or crushed under an avalanche of bodies.

CELTIC, formed in 1887, play at PARKHEAD STADIUM in the east end, and were THE FIRST-EVER BRITISH CLUB TO WIN THE EUROPEAN CUP, with a 2–1 victory over Inter Milan in the 1967 final.

Since 1903 international matches have been played at HAMPDEN PARK, THE WORLD'S OLDEST INTERNATIONAL FOOTBALL GROUND. Until 1950, when the Maracaña in Rio de Janeiro was completed, Hampden Park was THE LARGEST STADIUM IN THE WORLD. In 1937, the stadium hosted THE LARGEST CROWD EVER TO ATTEND A FOOTBALL MATCH IN EUROPE, 149,415 for a Scotland v. England match. Today Hampden Park is also home to SCOTLAND'S OLDEST FOOTBALL CLUB, QUEEN'S PARK, founded in 1867. THE WORLD'S FIRST INTERNATIONAL FOOTBALL MATCH was played in Glasgow between Scotland and England at the West of Scotland Cricket Club's ground at Hamilton Crescent in the Partick area of the city. The score was 0–0.

Modern Glasgow

At the centre of modern Glasgow is GEORGE SQUARE, home to more statues than any other square in Scotland, including SCOTLAND'S FIRST STATUE OF SIR WALTER SCOTT, erected in 1838.

In 1796 John Golborne began to dredge the shallow River Clyde so that large ships could sail right into the city. From that small beginning Glasgow grew into THE LARGEST SHIPBUILDING CENTRE IN THE WORLD. Today, the shipyards are gone but the riverside is being re-invigorated with exciting new architectural projects such as the futuristic SCOTTISH EXHIBITION AND CONFERENCE CENTRE known as the 'Armadillo', and the GLASGOW TOWER, THE ONLY TOWER IN THE WORLD ABLE TO REVOLVE THROUGH 360 DEGREES FROM THE GROUND UP and, at 412 ft (126 m) high, THE TALLEST FREE-STANDING BUILDING IN SCOTLAND.

Glasgow is also renowned for its libraries and museums. THE MITCHELL LIBRARY in North Street is THE BIGGEST PUBLIC REFERENCE LIBRARY IN EUROPE and holds THE WORLD'S LARGEST COLLECTION OF BOOKS ON ROBERT BURNS (3,500 volumes). THE BURRELL COLLECTION, housed in POLLOK HOUSE, is one of Scotland's most visited museums, and it was in Pollok House in 1931 that the National Trust for Scotland was conceived.

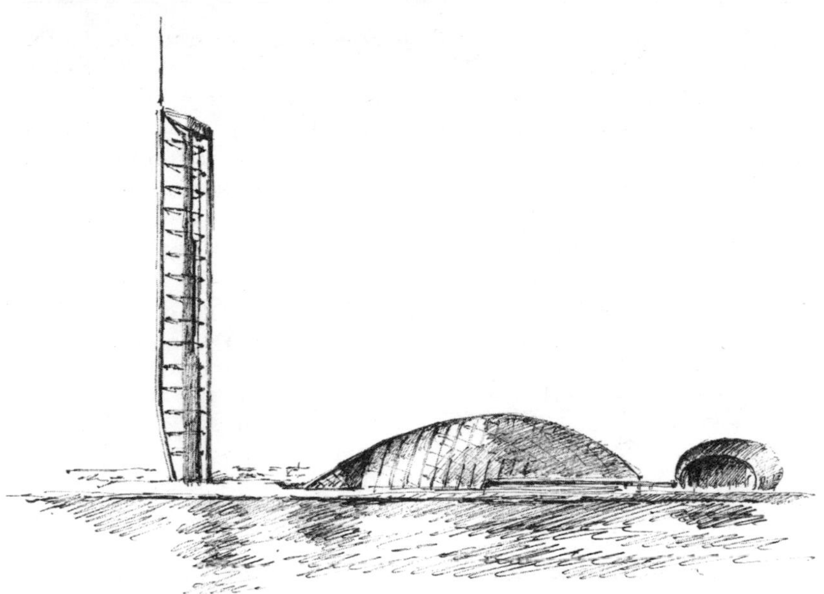

Scottish Exhibition and Conference Centre with Glasgow Tower

The *Glasgow Herald*, first published on 27 January 1783, is the longest continuously published daily newspaper in Britain.

BORN IN AND AROUND GLASGOW

CHARLES MACINTOSH (1766–1843), chemist. Invented the 'macintosh', THE WORLD'S FIRST WATERPROOF RAINCOAT.

ROBERT STEVENSON (1772–1850), engineer. Held the post of engineer to the Lighthouse Board for 47 years and was responsible for designing 18 Scottish lighthouses. He established a dynasty of 'Lighthouse Stevensons', and between 1790 and 1940 eight members of the Stevenson family built 97 lighthouses around the Scottish coast. He was the grandfather of the novelist Robert Louis Stevenson.

ALLAN PINKERTON (1819–84), the first 'private eye', born in the Gorbals. After emigrating to America in 1842 to avoid arrest for 'left wing' activities, he became CHICAGO'S FIRST FULL-TIME DETECTIVE and in 1850 started his own PINKERTON NATIONAL DETECTIVE AGENCY. The agency logo, an 'all-seeing eye', gave rise to the term 'private eye'. In 1861 Pinkerton foiled a plot to assassinate Abraham Lincoln on his way to his inauguration and was hired, by Lincoln, to organise a 'secret service' to gather military information in the Southern States during the Civil War. This was the forerunner of today's US Secret Service.

CHARLES RENNIE MACKINTOSH (1868–1928), architect. He developed the 'Glasgow Style', a fusing of art nouveau, Gothic and Scottish baronial. His masterpiece is the Glasgow School of Art, designed in 1896. Between 1897 and 1906 he designed and furnished a chain of tea rooms in Glasgow, commissioned by Kate Cranston as part of a campaign to discourage the drunkenness rife in the city. His best-known example is the Willow Tea Room, still operating in Sauchiehall Street ('Sauchiehall' meaning 'alley of willows').

JAMES MOLLISON (1905–59), aviator. In 1931 he flew from Australia to England in just under nine days, and in 1932 he married fellow aviator Amy Johnson. His list of firsts includes THE FIRST SOLO EAST-WEST CROSSING OF THE NORTH ATLANTIC in 1932, THE FIRST FLIGHT FROM ENGLAND TO SOUTH AMERICA in 1933, and THE FIRST FLIGHT TO INDIA in 1934.

BENNY LYNCH (1913–46), flyweight boxer, born in the Gorbals. In 1935 he became SCOTLAND'S FIRST-EVER WORLD BOXING CHAMPION.

ALASTAIR MACLEAN (1922–87) thriller writer, born at the manse in Shettleston, the son of a minister. A veteran of the Russian convoys in the Second World War, he used his experiences to write his first two thrillers, *HMS Ulysses* (1955) and *The Guns of Navarone* (1957). In 30 years from 1955 he wrote 30 books including *Ice Station Zebra* (1963) and *Where Eagles Dare* (1967) At one time was THE BEST SELLING NOVELIST IN THE WORLD. He is buried near his home at Celigny on Lake Geneva within feet of Richard Burton, star of the film version of *Where Eagles Dare*.

BILLY CONNOLLY, apprentice welder, actor and comedian, born in 1942. Known as the 'Big Yin', or 'Big One' due to his 6ft height.

Hamilton

Cheered to the Echo

HAMILTON was once the county town of Lanarkshire, and until 1920 was the site of Hamilton Palace, seat of the Dukes of Hamilton, Scotland's premier dukes. The grandest non-royal residence in Scotland was demolished when it started to fall into the coal-mines underneath. There used to be a grand avenue of trees, 2 miles (3.2 km) long, leading to Chatelherault, an elaborate hunting lodge now refurbished as a museum. The name is derived from the French dukedom bestowed upon the Hamilton's ancestor the 2nd Earl of Arran for his part in arranging the marriage of Mary, Queen of Scots to the Dauphin in 1558.

The most sensational leftover from the Hamilton Estate is the extraordinary, high-domed HAMILTON MAUSOLEUM, built in 1856 and modelled on the Castel St Angelo in Rome. It has a rare marble floor and a deep crypt, slowly becoming less deep as the heavy edifice sinks a little further each year.

The 10th Duke was married to a daughter of the eccentric and fantastically rich aesthete William Beckford of Fonthill Abbey, in Wiltshire, and

amongst the treasures he inherited was a rare and extremely valuable sarcophagus from Memphis in Egypt. The Duke wished to be buried in this, and the Mausoleum was designed to be a worthy resting-place for it. The sarcophagus was set on a black marble catafalque right at the centre of the mausoleum, while the rest of the Hamiltons were consigned to the vault below. Two stone lions guard the entrance, one alert, the other apparently sleeping, while Time, Death and Eternity are carved above the lintels of the three doors.

In 1921, because of the subsidence, the Duke's sarcophagus and all the other bodies were removed and reinterred in Bent Cemetery to the south of the town. The mausoleum is now open to the public and a visit is a memorable experience, for the structure possesses THE LONGEST AND DEEPEST ECHO OF ANY BUILDING IN BRITAIN. If the doors are slammed shut – they lock from the inside – or someone sings a few notes, the echo repeats and grows and deepens into an awesome harmony of sound. Several Americans, struck by the magic, have tried to buy the mausoleum with a view to taking it home, but to move it would be to risk losing the unique echo and so this remarkable place stays where it belongs – in Scotland.

Buried in BENT CEMETERY along with the Hamiltons – the Duke still in his sarcophagus – is SIR HARRY LAUDER (1870–1950), the comedian and music hall star who created the caricature, kilted image of a canny Scotsman. Born in Edinburgh's Portobello, he spent his teens as a pit boy in the coal-mines of Hamilton. Having won a singing competition in Arbroath as a lad, he launched his career at the Old Scotia Theatre in Glasgow and was soon THE HIGHEST-PAID ENTERTAINER IN SCOTLAND. His best-loved songs include 'I Love a Lassie', 'Roamin' in the Gloamin' and 'Keep Right On to the End of the Road'. He retired to the lovely old town of Strathaven, 6 miles (10 km) to the south of Hamilton, where he built himself a comfortable villa and named it Lauder Ha'.

Biggar

. . . and Better

BIGGAR is a busy, pleasant market town that sits astride the main route from the south-west of Scotland to Edinburgh. On either side of the wide, tree-lined main street there seem to be almost as many museums as shops, for Biggar has led an interesting existence. One of the museums resides in Gladstone Court, a reminder of the fact that the family of the Victorian Prime Minister, William Gladstone, hail from Biggar.

The attractive parish church dates from 1545, and was THE LAST CHURCH TO BE BUILT IN SCOTLAND BEFORE THE REFORMATION. It was built by the Fleming family, of Boghall, Mary Fleming being one of the 'four Marys'.

JAMES GILLRAY (1756–1815), THE FIRST BRITISH POLITICAL CARTOONIST, lived at Coulter, three miles south of Biggar. His superb and very funny portraits of figures such as King George III and Napoleon are extremely rare and valuable, as are the more risqué cartoons for which he became infamous.

GEORGE MEIKLE KEMP (1795–1844), the architect who designed one of the world's largest monuments to a writer, the Scott Monument in Edinburgh, was a native of Biggar. He drowned in the Union Canal before the monument was completed in 1846.

Albion Motors, at one time THE BIGGEST TRUCK MANUFACTURER IN THE WORLD, began life in THOMAS BLACKWOOD MURRAY's back yard in Biggar, where he built and tested the first Albion car. By 1899 Albion were established in Glasgow and in 1903 opened a purpose-built factory at Scotstoun. From 1910 Albion began to concentrate on trucks, and their famous motto 'Sure as the Sunrise' was recognised across the world. They merged with Leyland trucks in 1951; the firm then became British Leyland and eventually Leyland DAF, which went into administration in 1993. The name has been revived as Albion Automotives, a division of an American truck engineering company.

Leadhills

The Oldest Library and the Highest Railway

At 1,295 ft (395 m) above sea level LEADHILLS is THE SECOND HIGHEST VILLAGE IN SCOTLAND, after Wanlockhead, just across the border in Dumfriesshire. It possesses THE OLDEST SUBSCRIPTION LIBRARY IN BRITAIN, opened in 1741 by 23 lead miners who set up the Leadhills Reading Society. They named it the Allan Ramsay Library after the poet and bookseller, born here in 1686, who set up SCOTLAND'S FIRST CIRCULATING LIBRARY.

Also born in the village was WILLIAM SYMINGTON, inventor of the world's first steam boat (*see* Dumfriesshire).

In the cemetery is the grave of a lead miner called JOHN TAYLOR who died in 1770 at the age of 137.

Leadhills is the main station on the revitalised Leadhills and Wanlockhead railway, THE HIGHEST ADHESION RAILWAY IN BRITAIN. Built to service the lead-mines, the 2 ft narrow-gauge railway operated from 1901 to 1939 and was reopened by enthusiasts in 1996. Leadhills also boasts BRITAIN'S HIGHEST 9-HOLE GOLF COURSE.

New Lanark

From the Cradle to the Grave

NEW LANARK is an extraordinary surprise. To begin with you can't see it until you almost fall over the edge of the gorge in which it lies. Three huge sandstone mills, rows of houses and a chapel huddle together by the river in the narrowest of valleys, creating a harmonious picture that belies the hectic activity for which this place was once famous.

The valley was purchased in 1783 by a Glasgow banker called DAVID DALE, who went into partnership in 1785 with Richard Arkwright, founder of the world's first cotton factory at Cromford in Derbyshire. The plan was to exploit, on a grand scale, the fast-running Clyde to power the mill-wheels, as it tumbled through the gorge. Arkwright and Dale fell out over the trivial matter of where to site the belfry, but Dale carried on alone, and by 1795 the New Lanark Mills were THE BIGGEST IN BRITAIN and formed THE BIGGEST INDUSTRIAL SITE IN SCOTLAND.

In 1800, Dale handed New Lanark over to his son-in-law, Welshman ROBERT OWEN, who introduced a whole raft of innovative measures 'to commence the most important experiment for the happiness of the human race . . .' Purpose-built nurseries were put up to house the many child workers, and a village co-op store opened where workers and their families could buy good food at cost. THE INDUSTRIAL WORLD'S FIRST CRÈCHE ensured that working mothers could leave their children in safe hands, a school was established, and the minimum age for mill workers was raised from 6 to 12 so that the children could gain an education. Owen set up basic medical facilities and a sick fund, and also catered for leisure time with his Institution for the Formation of Character – the workers of New Lanark were literally looked after from the cradle to the grave.

Owen was a century ahead of his time, and New Lanark was able to operate without much change for some 200 years before the mills had to close in 1968. Today the whole site has been restored to create a thriving village with museums, rides and hands-on exhibitions. One of Scotland's top five attractions, New Lanark achieved World Heritage Status in 2001.

Well, I never knew this
ABOUT
LANARKSHIRE

Lanarkshire is SCOTLAND'S MOST DENSELY POPULATED COUNTY.

PATRICK HAMILTON, SCOTLAND'S FIRST PROTESTANT MARTYR, was born in Stonehouse in 1503. He was burned at the stake in St Andrews in 1528. The fire burned out too quickly and Hamilton was left badly burned but alive. In the end it took him six hours to die.

EAST KILBRIDE is THE LARGEST OF SCOTLAND'S NEW TOWNS and has THE LARGEST UNDERCOVER SHOPPING AREA IN SCOTLAND.

DUNGAVEL HOUSE, former hunting lodge of the Dukes of Hamilton, lies 6 miles (10 km) to the south of Strathaven on Dungavel Moor. After the demolition of Hamilton Palace in 1921, Dungavel became much more of a permanent residence. It was Dungavel House that Rudolf Hess was trying to reach when he parachuted into a field in Eaglesham on 10 May 1941 (*see* Renfrewshire). Dungavel House is now a refugee detention centre.

DAVID LIVINGSTONE (1813–73), the great explorer, was born, the son of a weaver, in a one-bedroom flat in Shuttle Row, a tenement block in Blantyre, 3 miles (5 km) north of Hamilton. He was THE FIRST EUROPEAN TO SEE THE VICTORIA FALLS, and died while looking for the source of the River Nile. Livingstone's expeditions were largely financed by James 'Paraffin' Young, from the profits of his West Lothian oil business. His birthplace is now a museum of his life.

CROOKSTON CASTLE, 5 miles (8 km) south of Glasgow city centre, was THE FIRST PROPERTY TO BE HANDED OVER TO THE NATIONAL TRUST FOR SCOTLAND, in 1931. Sir John Sterling Maxwell (1866–1956), the owner, was a founder member of the Trust. Crookston was the family home of Lord Darnley, second husband of Mary, Queen of Scots, and it is said that the couple were betrothed beneath a yew tree which stood near the castle. This yew was the only tree ever to appear on Scottish coins – the silver coins issued under Mary and Henry (Darnley) were known as Cruickston Dollars, and had a representation of the Crookston yew on the reverse.

ROBBIE COLTRANE, the actor, was born Robert MacMillan, in RUTHERGLEN, in 1950. He is best known for his role as 'Fitz', a criminal psychologist, in the *Cracker* television series. He has appeared in two James Bond films and plays Hagrid in the Harry Potter series.

The village of DOUGLAS stands on the banks of Douglas Water, the 'dubh ghlas', or black water, from which the powerful Douglas family get their name. In Old St Bride's Church, there is a clock given by Mary, Queen of Scots in 1565, THE OLDEST WORKING PUBLIC CLOCK IN SCOTLAND.

JAMES KEIR HARDIE (1856–1915) was born at HOLYTOWN near Motherwell. He lost his job as a miner, campaigning for better wages and conditions. In 1888 he founded the Scottish Labour Party, THE FIRST POLITICAL PARTY IN BRITAIN SET UP TO REPRESENT THE WORKING CLASSES, and, in 1892, he became THE FIRST-EVER LABOUR MP. In 1893, he founded the Independent Labour Party, forerunner of the modern Labour Party.

Midlothian

County Town: Edinburgh

Middle territory of *Loth*, grandfather of St Mungo

The Palace of Holyroodhouse, official residence of the British monarch in Scotland

Edinburgh

Athens of the North

EDINBURGH is Scotland's capital and without question one of the most dramatic and beautiful cities in the world. It is a city of contrasts, saluted as 'the Athens of the North' for its learning and handsome buildings, and as 'Auld Reekie' for the smoke that used to spew from its chimneys. No other city is divided so clearly between old and new. The Old Town is one of Europe's purest medieval towns, while the New Town is unsurpassed for the splendour of its Georgian landscape. Together they form a World Heritage Site (1999).

To the traveller emerging from Waverley station – THE ONLY STATION IN BRITAIN NAMED AFTER A BOOK – the dichotomy is immediately apparent. To the left, confusion, romance and intrigue; towering rock, dark walls, turrets and spires reaching into the sky, impossibly tall, like an early Manhattan. To the right, order and elegance, wide

streets and open squares. It is an intoxicating mix.

Dominating the city centre, from 270 ft (82 m) above, is the castle, SCOTLAND'S MOST VISITED TOURIST ATTRACTION. The volcanic plug on which it sits has been occupied for thousands of years, but the buildings there now date from the 12th century. At their heart is the minute ST MARGARET'S CHAPEL, SCOTLAND'S SMALLEST ROYAL CHURCH and THE OLDEST BUILDING IN EDINBURGH, whose simple stone interior is perfection. This replaced a wooden chapel built by Malcolm III's wife, the saintly Margaret. When she heard of her husband's death at Alnwick in 1093, her heart broke and she died right here.

In Queen Mary's Room in the 15th-century King's Lodging, Mary, Queen of Scots gave birth to her son Charles James, future James VI of Scotland and I of England. The birth was difficult and there are those who claim that Mary's baby was stillborn and another baby substituted in its place – from that time on a government minister was required to be present at every royal birth to see fair play, an awkward ritual performed for the last time at the birth of Princess Margaret at Glamis Castle in 1930.

Running down from the castle like a trickle of rain is the wondrous Royal Mile, 'the largest, longest and finest street . . . in the world', according to Daniel Defoe. The Royal Mile is made up of Castlehill, Lawnmarket, High Street and Canongate and is, in fact, one mile and 107 yards long. Every one of those yards is packed with history and legend. Still very much alive and bustling, the Royal Mile is lined with churches, shops and houses of every century from the 14th to the present day, a time capsule in stone. Mysterious, narrow passageways hurry off down steep stairways and through tunnels of stone, to hidden courtyards surrounded by tall, forbidding tenement blocks. In medieval times there was little space to expand, and so the tenements developed upwards and all the classes lived together, the rich aristocracy on the upper levels, professionals on the middle levels and manual workers and the poor occupying the lower levels.

Deacon Brodie

On the corner of Lawnmarket and Bank Street is Deacon Brodie's Tavern, just a few steps away from where Deacon Brodie, the original Jekyll and Hyde, was born in 1741. By day Brodie was a respectable cabinet-maker like his father, a burgh councillor, president of the craftsmen's guild, furniture-maker and carpenter to the gentry. He worked at all the best addresses in Edinburgh and was completely trusted. By night he was a gambler and a drunken womaniser with five illegitimate children and two mistresses. In order to fund this double life he began to rob the homes of his well-to-do friends, having made wax impressions of their house keys and copied them. The inevitable happened when one of Brodie's accomplices was caught and turned informer. Brodie fled, but was detained in Amsterdam, trying to find passage to America. He was brought back to Edinburgh and hanged at the Old Tolbooth near St Giles in 1788, one of the first victims of the new gallows that he himself, as the city carpenter, had designed and built. Robert Louis Stevenson, whose father owned furniture made by Brodie, used the story as the basis of The Strange Case of Dr Jekyll and Mr Hyde.

In the Outlook Tower just below the castle esplanade is the CAMERA OBSCURA, ONE OF ONLY THREE IN SCOTLAND, used by the civic planner Sir Patrick Geddes (1854–1932) as a slightly Orwellian 'sociological observatory' to study the masses in these teeming streets below.

GLADSTONE'S LAND, run by the National Trust for Scotland, is a finely preserved example of a typical 17th-century Old Town house, THE ONLY BUILDING IN EDINBURGH THAT STILL HAS ITS ARCADED FRONT.

ST GILES CATHEDRAL boasts THE FINEST OF SCOTLAND'S THREE CROWN STEEPLES, built in 1495, and sits on the site of Edinburgh's first church, founded here in the 9th century by the monks of Lindisfarne. As the senior church of Scottish Presbyterians, who do not countenance bishops, St Giles is not really a cathedral, although it did play that role for two short periods in the 17th century. John Knox was the minister of St Giles and is thought to have lived, and died, in John Knox House, a little further down. He is buried under parking space No. 44 in Parliament Square, once the burial ground of St Giles.

PARLIAMENT HOUSE is where the Act of Union was signed in 1707. The minutes of the final meeting of that Scottish Parliament stop in mid-sentence, at the point where the parliament dissolved itself. In 1999, Winnie Ewing MSP opened the new Scottish Parliament with the words 'The Scottish Parliament, adjourned on 25th March 1707, is hereby reconvened.'

A heart shape picked out in the cobblestones nearby depicts the 'Heart of Midlothian', a name coined by Sir Walter Scott for the OLD TOLBOOTH, the administrative centre of medieval

John Knox House

Edinburgh. In the 17th century this was a gaol, though not it seems a very secure one, for nearly everyone put there managed to escape. The first thing they would do on getting free was to spit on the gaol door with contempt. Today it is considered good luck, if not good manners, to spit on the middle of the heart. Hearts Football Club takes its name from here.

THE PALACE OF HOLYROODHOUSE, which sits at the eastern end of the Royal Mile, is now the official home of the monarch in Scotland.

Opposite Holyrood is the modernistic SCOTTISH PARLIAMENT BUILDING, designed by Catalan architect Enric Miralles, who did not live to see it opened in 2004. The original estimate for the building was around £50 million. It ultimately cost £431 million. From the outside the design is indefinable, but it nonetheless won the Stirling Prize for architecture in 2005. The Debating Chamber inside is breathtaking.

EDINBURGH'S FIRST RAILWAY, the horse-drawn Edinburgh to Dalkeith line, opened in 1831 and skirted Holyrood Park. It was known as 'the innocent railway' because, despite its carrying 400,000 passengers per year, there were no accidents. A fixed steam engine was needed to haul the wagons up through a steeply inclined tunnel, 1,050 ft (320 m) long, between Craigmillar and St Leonards. This section of line, on the southern perimeter of Holyrood Park, has been converted into a cycle route.

To the south of the Royal Mile is GREYFRIARS KIRK where, in 1638, the National Covenant was placed on a stone slab in the graveyard and signed, by rich and poor alike. The architect William Adam (1689–1748) is buried here, in a grand mausoleum built by his architect sons Robert, James and William. Somewhere in the kirkyard, unmarked and unlamented, lies the world's worst poet, William McGonagall (1825–1902). Keeping vigil outside the gates is GREYFRIARS BOBBY, the faithful Skye terrier who, for 14 years, watched over his master's grave. He was created a 'freeman of the city', given a special collar and asked after by Queen Victoria. When his own time came on 14 January 1872, he was laid next to his master beneath a red granite tomb donated by smitten Americans.

Behind Greyfriars kirkyard is the most satisfying building in Edinburgh, GEORGE HERIOT'S SCHOOL, opened in 1659. Heriot (1563–1624) was goldsmith to James VI and endowed the 'hospital' for the education of the 'fatherless bairnes of Edinburgh'. It was

THE FIRST BUILDING IN SCOTLAND TO BE BUILT TO A REGULAR DESIGN, having four sides, and four corner towers topped with four turrets, arranged around a courtyard.

EDINBURGH'S NEW TOWN was created in open fields to the north of the castle during the 1760s and 70s, to a grid plan by James Craig. It is THE MOST COMPLETE EXAMPLE OF AN UNSPOILED GEORGIAN TOWN IN BRITAIN.

PRINCES GARDENS was created by draining the shallow loch beneath the north side of the castle rock.

Scottish Enlightenment

City of Literature

In October 2004, Edinburgh became UNESCO'S FIRST CITY OF LITERATURE. It was a well-deserved accolade for a city that has succoured more than its fair share of genius. In the 18th century Edinburgh was home to a group of writers and thinkers who became known as the Scottish Enlightenment. They included the philosopher DAVID HUME (1711–76), who wrote a celebrated philosophical *History of England* at Riddle Court, 332 High Street; ADAM SMITH (1723–90), known as 'the Father of Economics' and author of *The Wealth of Nations*; and ADAM FERGUSON (1723–1816), known as 'the Father of Sociology' and best remembered for his *History of Civil Society*. Ferguson lived at Sciennes Hill House, about half a mile (1 km) south of the Royal Mile, and it was here that the 15-year-old Walter Scott met Robert Burns for the first and only time in his life.

RAMSAY GARDENS, off Castlehill, is named after the poet and bookseller ALLAN RAMSAY (1686–1758), who lived

George Heriot's School

there in a curious octagonal house he designed himself, which is still there. He established THE FIRST CIRCULATING LIBRARY IN BRITAIN, in 1725 (*see* Lanarkshire).

There is a plaque in Anchor Close, beside the City Chambers off Lawnmarket on the Royal Mile, on the site of WILLIAM SMELLIE's shop, where he edited and produced THE FIRST *ENCYCLOPAEDIA BRITANNICA*, in 1768. Smellie also published the Edinburgh edition of Robert Burns's poems, in 1787. JAMES BOSWELL, the biographer and friend of Dr Johnson, lived with his wife in Chessel Buildings, off Canongate, near where he was born in Blair's Land, Parliament Square, in 1740.

SIR WALTER SCOTT Bt (1771–1832) was born in a house on College Wynd, south of the Royal Mile, but the address most associated with him in later life was 39 Castle Street, in the New Town. KENNETH GRAHAME (1859–1932), author of *The Wind in the Willows*, was born nearby at No. 30.

ROBERT LOUIS STEVENSON (1850–94) was born at 8 Howard Place, near the Royal Botanic Gardens, and brought up at 17 Heriot Row, in the New Town. Stevenson spent the last years of his life in Samoa, taken there by his American wife Fanny, for the sake of his ailing health. The only belongings of his to be found in the city of his birth are in the Writer's Museum in Lady Stair House on the Royal Mile.

SIR ARTHUR CONAN DOYLE (1859–1930) was born at 11 Picardy Place, just below Calton Hill. In 1876 he studied medicine at Edinburgh University and attended the lectures of Dr Joseph Bell, whose remarkable powers of deduction inspired the creation of Sherlock Holmes. Dr Watson was based on Conan Doyle himself.

MURIEL SPARK (1918–2006) was born at 160 Bruntisfield Place, south of Edinburgh Castle, and set her novel *The Prime of Miss Jean Brodie* in one of Edinburgh's famous academies for girls.

IAN RANKIN, creator of INSPECTOR REBUS, lives in Edinburgh, where he sets many of his stories. Rebus's (and Rankin's) favourite pub is the Oxford Bar in Young Street.

HARRY POTTER was born at Nicolson's Café at 6a Nicolson Street, where J.K. ROWLING wrote most of her first Harry Potter story, while living in Leith.

In 1946, Edinburgh hosted BRITAIN'S FIRST FILM FESTIVAL, the International Festival of Documentary Films, at the Playhouse Cinema. The following year, 1947, saw the introduction of the first Edinburgh International Festival. Held in July/August, this now includes the 'Fringe' as well as film, television, jazz and literary festivals and THE WORLD'S BIGGEST MILITARY TATTOO on the castle Esplanade. It is THE LARGEST ARTS FESTIVAL IN THE WORLD.

BORN IN EDINBURGH

JOHN NAPIER (1550–1617), Laird of Merchiston Castle, where he was born. Napier discovered logarithms, a method for facilitating the calculation of complex figures, which helped to resolve navigational and astronomical puzzles, and enabled many subsequent scientific breakthroughs. He spent 20 years doing seven million calculations, and his log tables were published in Edinburgh in 1614. Napier University in Merchiston is named after him.

ALEXANDER GRAHAM BELL (1847–1922), inventor of the telephone.

ALASTAIR SIM (1900–76), actor, best remembered for his comic roles in such films as *The Happiest Days of Your Life* (1950) and *The Belles of St Trinians* (1954), and for his gloriously bewildered facial expressions in the 1960's BBC TV series, *Alastair Sim's Misleading Cases.*

SIR SEAN CONNERY, actor, born 1930. Found fame as the original James Bond in *Dr No* (1962) and a further six Bond films. Regarded by many as one of the greatest screen actors of his generation.

RORY BREMNER, comedian and impressionist, born the son of an army officer in Morningside, in 1961. Known best for his Channel Four television series BREMNER, BIRD and FORTUNE.

Inveresk

'The Finest Village and Most Healthy Place in Scotland'

Barely half a mile (1 km) inland from the bustle of Musselburgh lies, in the words of William Maitland, 'the beautiful Village of Inveresk, which from its Situation, Houses, and Salubrity of Air, is justly reckoned the finest Village and most healthy place in Scotland'. Today, 200 years later, those words still ring true for, thanks to the Inveresk Preservation Society and the National Trust for Scotland, Inveresk remains an almost flawless example of an 18th-century village, with wrought-iron gates, elaborate door knockers and lamp-posts, wide, shady pavements and handsome houses, mostly Georgian, but all of different styles, and all painted in traditional hues of orange and pink and russet. You half expect to see the residents in powdered wigs, or to hear a horse and carriage trotting along the street. But that would spoil the peace, which is absolute.

One of the colourful characters of Inveresk was the REVD ALEXANDER 'JUPITER' CARLYLE, minister from 1748 to 1805. It was he, in Moffat, along with John Home, who persuaded James Macpherson to publish his controversial Ossian Papers (*see* Dumfriesshire). A keen golfer, in 1758 he performed THE WORLD'S FIRST GOLFING TRICK SHOT, at his friend David Garrick's home by the Thames in London, when he chipped a golf ball through an archway into the river. And in 1775 he became the second winner of the Musselburgh Old Golf Club Cup.

Today another larger-than-life character lives in the village, TV chef Clarissa Dickson-Wright of The Two Fat Ladies.

Rosslyn

The Holy Grail?

There is nowhere else like it in Britain, possibly even the world. It is a sumptuous feast, almost too rich, a jungle of fruits and faces, leaves and animals that overwhelm the senses. There are stories in every nook and cranny, hidden meanings and signs accessible only to the chosen few. It is no wonder that ROSSLYN CHAPEL has for so long been the subject of mystery and intrigue, brought to a head by the publication in 2003 of Dan Brown's *The Da Vinci Code*.

Rosslyn Chapel was begun in 1447 by WILLIAM EARL ST CLAIR, last Prince of Orkney, and later 1st Earl of Caithness. Only the choir was completed, but the whole of the interior is luxuriantly decorated with carvings and sculptures of quite astounding brilliance. Biblical tales are depicted: Lucifer the Fallen Angel, the Seven Deadly Sins and the Seven Cardinal Values, the Dance of Death. There are pagan symbols, mythical beasts and dragons, and THE LARGEST NUMBER OF 'GREEN MEN' FOUND IN ANY MEDIEVAL BUILDING ANYWHERE. There are signs and mysterious emblems of Freemasonry and the Knights Templar. Plants that grow only in America such as aloe vera and maize are found here, carved in stone 50 years before Columbus sailed. There is also a winged heart, commemorating a previous St Clair, who accompanied James, Earl of Douglas and Robert the Bruce's heart on its abortive journey to the Holy Land.

The chapel was built over a former church, and no one seems to know what lies beneath. Do the Knights Templar lie there, dressed in armour, ready to defend their treasure, the Holy Grail? Or does the Ark of the Covenant? Or the Lost Scrolls of the Temple?

A visit to Rosslyn was George Meikle Kemp's inspiration for the Scott monument in Edinburgh.

Rosslyn raises many questions and gives up few answers, but the experience is unforgettable.

From the Chapel grounds there are fine views over the spectacular Rosslyn Glen, with glimpses of 14th-century Rosslyn Castle, perched on a lip of rock

The Prentice Pillar

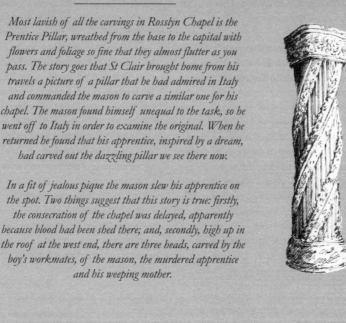

Most lavish of all the carvings in Rosslyn Chapel is the Prentice Pillar, wreathed from the base to the capital with flowers and foliage so fine that they almost flutter as you pass. The story goes that St Clair brought home from his travels a picture of a pillar that he had admired in Italy and commanded the mason to carve a similar one for his chapel. The mason found himself unequal to the task, so he went off to Italy in order to examine the original. When he returned he found that his apprentice, inspired by a dream, had carved out the dazzling pillar we see there now.

In a fit of jealous pique the mason slew his apprentice on the spot. Two things suggest that this story is true: firstly, the consecration of the chapel was delayed, apparently because blood had been shed there; and, secondly, high up in the roof at the west end, there are three heads, carved by the boy's workmates, of the mason, the murdered apprentice and his weeping mother.

above the river, where St Clair lived the life of matchless extravagance for which he gave thanks by building Rosslyn Chapel.

DOLLY THE SHEEP, THE WORLD'S FIRST LIVING CLONE, was manufactured just down the road at the Roslin Institute.

Well, I never knew this
ABOUT
MIDLOTHIAN

FETTES COLLEGE, in Edinburgh, is something of a breeding ground for politicians. Old boys include Selwyn Lloyd (1904–78), Foreign Secretary during the Suez crisis, Ian Macleod (1913–70), Edward Heath's Chancellor of the Exchequer for a few weeks before he died, and Labour Prime Minister, Tony Blair. James Bond attended Fettes after being expelled from Eton. His exploits at Fettes are described by Ian Fleming in *You Only Live Twice.*

Edinburgh's ROYAL BOTANIC GARDENS possess THE LARGEST COLLECTION OF RHODODENDRONS IN BRITAIN.

MUSSELBURGH claims to have THE OLDEST GOLF COURSE STILL IN USE IN THE WORLD, with documentary evidence showing that golf was played on the Musselburgh links in 1672.

MURRAYFIELD STADIUM hosted THE WORLD'S FIRST INTERNATIONAL RUGBY MATCH, in 1925, in which Scotland beat England 14–11. The stadium also holds the world record for attendance at a rugby match, set when 104,000 saw Scotland play Wales in 1975.

Scotland's principal port until the mid 19th century, LEITH was the departure point for the ill-fated Darien Expedition in 1698 and the site of SCOTLAND'S FIRST DRY DOCK in 1720.

Some 13 miles (21 km) south of Edinburgh is BORTHWICK CASTLE, THE BIGGEST AND HIGHEST PEEL TOWER IN SCOTLAND. It is 110 ft (34 m) high.

In 1958, THE WORLD'S FIRST TRAFFIC CONES were manufactured at Castle Mills in Edinburgh by Uniroyal Ltd.

JENNER'S STORE, in Edinburgh's Princes Street, was established in 1838. Until taken over by the House of Fraser in 2005, it was THE OLDEST INDEPENDENT DEPARTMENT STORE IN THE WORLD.

MORAYSHIRE

COUNTY TOWN: ELGIN

Thought to be from the Gaelic for 'land of the seagoing people'

Elgin Cathedral – The Lantern of the North

Elgin

'A very agreeable place to live in'
DANIEL DEFOE

ELGIN, the ancient capital of Moray and long-time seat of the Bishops of Moray, lies on the banks of the River Lossie, amidst the lush barley fields and meadows of the Laich of Moray. Like most Scottish towns it has often been crushed to earth, only to rise again more grand than before. Elgin was the northern limit of Edward I's march through Scotland in 1296. The castle where he stayed has long since vanished, the site marked by a tall column in honour of the Duke of Gordon. The long climb to the top of the column is rewarded by fine views stretching as far as the Cairngorms and the Caithness Mountains. In 1390, Elgin was razed to the ground by the Wolf of Badenoch (*see* Perth).

In the High Street is Braco's Bankhouse, where William Duff accu-

Elgin Cathedral

Consecrated in 1224, Elgin Cathedral, known as 'the Lantern of the North', was once the most noble of all Scotland's churches and THE SECOND LARGEST CATHEDRAL IN THE COUNTRY *after St Andrews. 'The Ornament of the Realm, the Glory of the Kingdom' was how the sorrowful Bishop of Moray described his cathedral, after the Wolf of Badenoch had done his worst.* IT IS THE ONLY ANCIENT BRITISH CATHEDRAL WITH DOUBLE AISLES TO THE NAVE, *and even the ruins are awesome, as is its picturesque setting beside the river. Rebuilt in the 15th century, the cathedral fell into neglect after the Reformation and was dealt a fatal blow when the central tower collapsed in 1711, taking what was left of the 298 ft (91 m)-long nave with it. Now the twin 90 ft (27 m) western towers, which can be climbed, gaze with dignity down a grass-carpeted, roofless nave to the empty rose window in the east. The well-preserved, 15th-century, octagonal Chapter House next to it has a glorious vaulted ceiling, supported from a central column,* UNIQUE IN SCOTLAND, *save for that at Incholm Abbey in Fife. It is thought that the body of Duncan was buried here at Elgin, after his murder by Macbeth in 1040, before being removed and reinterred on Iona.*

mulated the fortune that built Duff House, and ultimately earned his descendants a Dukedom.

Curiously the name of Elgin is probably best known to the world because of a controversy that has no direct connection to the city at all. The ELGIN MARBLES, which were named after the Earl and not the city, were brought to England from Athens in 1805 by Thomas Bruce, 7th Earl of Elgin, in a genuine effort to save them from destruction. The expense bankrupted the Earl, who sold them to the British Museum in 1816, where they can be seen to this day. Removing the marbles from Greece was controversial at the time and the arguments still rage to this day, with the Greek government constantly demanding their return.

Birnie

A Country Cathedral

Elgin was not Moray's first cathedral. That honour goes to the sturdy little church at BIRNIE, a few miles to the south, THE OLDEST PARISH

CHURCH IN CONTINUOUS USE IN SCOTLAND. Built in 1140 on the site of a Celtic church dedicated to St Brendan the Navigator, Birnie sits in the middle of a circular mound down a tiny country lane to nowhere. It has one of the few remaining Norman chancel arches in Scotland, and one of the loveliest – slightly crooked but ageless, and beautiful in its simplicity.

Simon de Tonci, 4th Bishop of Moray, who died in 1184, is buried in the churchyard, and the tiny church possesses a number of special treasures, including a square bell called the Coronach Bell, over 1,000 years old, inherited from the former church and reportedly blessed by the Pope. Birnie is also inordinately proud of its Hairy Bible, dated 1773 and bound in unshaven calfskin. Birnie is a very remarkable place, lost in deep country, quiet and modest but more important than many a grand palace or castle. Just to sit for a while in the churchyard at Birnie is to experience Scottish history in the raw.

After Birnie, the cathedral moved to Spynie, just north of Elgin, in 1207. Here the Bishops of Moray made themselves a fine palace to live in, which remained as their residence for over 500 years. David's Tower at Spynie, named after Bishop David Stewart, was built in 1600 with five floors and a vaulted basement, ONE OF THE LARGEST TOWER HOUSES IN SCOTLAND.

Lossiemouth

Jets, Dunes and Socialism

LOSSIEMOUTH is a smart stone town, laid out on a grid pattern, with a good harbour that serves as the port of Elgin. There are some sandy beaches, great sea views and the regular scream of jet engines overhead, from the Tornados of nearby RAF Lossiemouth, established here in 1939.

At the mouth of the River Lossie, a pedestrian bridge gives access to the wide, golden East Beach and, sheltering in the lee of the sand dunes, are a collection of single-storey, stone fishermen's cottages, grouped around a grassy square. At No. 1, Gregory Place, there is a stone plaque marking the birthplace of the socialist politician JAMES RAMSAY MACDONALD (1866–1937).

MacDonald had an inauspicious start to life as the illegitimate son of a maidservant, Mary Ramsay, and a farm worker from the Black Isle. He was attracted to socialism while studying in Bristol and in 1894 joined the Independent Labour Party, set up the previous year by Keir Hardie (see Lanarkshire).

In 1897 he married Margaret Gladstone, a great-niece of Lord Kelvin and daughter of Dr John Gladstone, founder of the YMCA. Although she died tragically young in 1911, Margaret gave MacDonald three sons and three daughters, and her private income enabled MacDonald to pursue his political career free from financial worries. Tall, handsome, a powerful orator and noted intellectual thinker with great organisational skills, he was elected leader of the Labour Party in 1911 and became recognised as LABOUR'S FIRST GREAT PARLIAMENTARIAN. He resigned as leader, however, in 1914, refusing to support Britain's involvement in the First World War.

By 1922, his pacifist views had become fashionable and he once again became party leader, in 1923–24 becoming THE FIRST-EVER LABOUR PRIME MINISTER as the head of a minority administration. He won another election in 1929 and appointed the FIRST-EVER FEMALE CABINET MINISTER, Margaret Bondfield. In 1931, MacDonald was expelled from the Labour party for what they saw as his betrayal in forming a coalition government to tackle the great economic depression of the time. He nonetheless won the 1931 General Election as leader of a National Government. In 1935, he lost his seat to the Labour candidate Emanuel Shinwell and died on a cruise to South America in 1937. He is buried in the churchyard at Spynie, 3 miles (5 km) south of Lossiemouth.

'We hear war called murder. It is not: it is suicide.'

James Ramsay MacDonald

'We know that he has, more than any other man, the gift of compressing the largest amount of words into the smallest amount of thought.'

Winston Churchill on
James Ramsay MacDonald

Fochabers

Soup

FOCHABERS is a pleasant, spacious place, laid out at the end of the 18th century by John Baxter to replace an older village that stood in the way of the extension of Gordon Castle, seat of the 4th Duke of Gordon. The castle is now much diminished, and not open to the public, but was once described as 'the most magnificent edifice north of the Forth'.

An employee of the Duke of Gordon who made good was George Baxter, one of 50 gardeners at the castle. In 1868 he opened a small grocery shop in Fochabers, marketing the abundant local produce from the fertile Laich of Moray, known as 'the Granary of the North'. George's wife Margaret began to make jams and conserves in the back of the shop, which became very popular with the Duke and his friends, and the Baxters' reputation started to spread. In 1928 their son William set up a production line for canning beetroot which has grown into THE BEST SELLING BRAND IN BRITAIN. The following year William's wife Ethel, taking advantage of the plentiful supply of venison from the castle estate, came up with a

recipe for what became known as Royal Game Soup, the first in a long line of famous BAXTER'S SOUPS, such as Cock-a-Leekie and Scotch Broth, which have made the Baxter name famous across the world. Today, the Baxter's factory on the River Spey west of Fochabers has become a tourist attraction in its own right.

Forres

Of Witches and Watch Towers

FORRES is a very ancient burgh and was once a very important place. King Duncan held his court at Forres, and Macbeth was on his way here when he met three of the witches for which Forres was then notorious (*see* Nairnshire).

On the south side of the road to Kinloss, east of Forres, is the Witches Stone, which marks the spot where they used to burn the Forres witches.

Also on the eastern outskirts of Forres, now encased in a glass cabinet, is the 9th-century SUENO'S STONE, 23 ft (7 m) high and THE TALLEST PICTISH STONE IN SCOTLAND. The intricate carvings are of Runic knots, and animals and warriors in battle. When the stone was rediscovered in 1726 it was thought, mistakenly, to commemorate Swein Forkbeard, King of Norway.

High up above Forres, on a wooded hill, is the 70 ft (21 m) NELSON'S TOWER, put up in 1806 as THE FIRST MONUMENT IN BRITAIN TO COMMEMORATE NELSON'S VICTORY AT THE BATTLE OF TRAFALGAR. The tower also acted as a beacon, an observatory and a lookout post. The steep climb to the top of the hill, and then up the tower stairs is rewarded by fantastic views over the Moray Firth to the Caithness mountains – and the good people of Forres even provide a pair of binoculars with which to appreciate the spectacle.

Well, I never knew this
ABOUT
MORAYSHIRE

MORAYSHIRE is also known as Elginshire.

THE MORAY FIRTH is SCOTLAND'S LARGEST BAY.

At the mouth of the Spey are THE LARGEST SHINGLE BANKS IN SCOTLAND. They are constantly shifting, and in size they are second only to Chesil Beach in Dorset.

GARMOUTH, a pretty village on the west bank of the Spey north of Fochabers, is where Charles II landed in 1650 after his exile on the Continent, and it was here that he was forced to sign the Solemn League of Covenant, intended to enforce the Presbyterian religion in Scotland.

GORDONSTOUN SCHOOL occupies a house built in 1616 by the Marquess of Huntly near the village of Duffus. In 1934 the property was purchased and a fee-paying school established under the stern headmastership of Dr Kurt Hahn, who had escaped to Britain after being imprisoned by the Nazis. The school is noted for its character-building principles, winter runs in the Scottish hills and the wide variety of tough, practical training the pupils receive. The Duke of Edinburgh attended Gordonstoun, as did the Prince of Wales, Princes Andrew and Edward, and Lara Croft. Prince Charles was deeply unhappy there.

Carved out of the rock at Burghead, is the ancient and mysterious BURGHEAD WELL, a round chamber, 15 ft by 15 ft (4.6 x 4.6 m) and 12 ft (3.6 m) high, with a deep pool at its centre, surrounded by a narrow walkway. A Celtic head found carved in the wall suggests that this could have been a place of worship in Pictish times, when a common means of sacrifice and execution was by drowning. The pool was later sanctified for use as a Christian baptistry. A key can be obtained from a nearby house.

DALLAS, the great Texan city that spawned a soap opera of the same name, has its origins in Morayshire. In 1279, William de Ripley obtained the lands and tiny village of DALLAS, on the River Lossie, 6 miles (9.6 km) southeast of Forres. On being knighted, he changed his name to Sir William of Dallas. His descendants emigrated to America and, in 1844, one of them, George Mifflin Dallas, became Vice-President of the United States. Dallas in

Texas was named after him. Dallas means 'watery valley'.

The first settlement at FINDHORN was buried by sand in 1694, and the second lies at the bottom of the sea after another storm in 1701. Today's Findhorn is famous for the FINDHORN FOUNDATION, founded in a caravan park in 1962 by Dorothy Maclean and Peter and Eileen Caddy. The Foundation is a centre for exploring spiritual and alternative ways of life and has expanded hugely to include arts and crafts businesses, an education centre and an eco village. During the 1970s, Findhorn enjoyed a reputation for apparently nurturing fruit and vegetables that grew to several times the size of normal produce.

NAIRNSHIRE

COUNTY TOWN: NAIRN

Uisage n Earn – 'river of the alder trees' (Gaelic)

Cawdor Castle, which possesses the only surviving drawbridge at a private castle in Scotland

Nairn

All ye tourists who want to be away
From the crowded city for a brief holiday
The town of Nairn is worth a visit,
I do confess,
And it's only about fifteen mile
from Inverness

WILLIAM MCGONAGALL

NAIRN makes a not unreasonable claim to be the sunniest and driest place in Scotland and, with two sandy beaches and a couple of top golf courses, it is not surprising that this old fishing town is a popular resort, sometimes called 'the Brighton of the North'.

Nairn is the county town and, indeed, the only town of the little county of Nairnshire. It is one of the oldest royal burghs in the north-east, but has been much rebuilt and there are few buildings of note, although narrow streets and quaint cottages give the FISHERTOWN area down by the harbour an attractive, old-world feel.

Dr Johnson, on a visit here in 1773, said, 'At Nairn, we may fix the verge of the Highlands,' and, indeed, the town has often been described as being on the dividing line between Highland and Lowland. At one time there were two distinct communities in Nairn, the fishermen and the crofters, who lived at different ends of the High Street. The fishermen spoke only Gaelic and the crofters English, prompting James VI to boast, 'There is a town in my kingdom so vast that the people who live at one end of the street cannot understand the people who live at the other end!'

On 15 April 1746, the Duke of Cumberland celebrated his 25th birthday at Nairn on the eve of the Battle of Culloden.

The 1st VISCOUNT WHITELAW (1918–99), Margaret Thatcher's ferociously loyal Deputy Prime Minister, and one of the most decent and respected men in British politics, was born in Nairn. As Margaret Thatcher commented, 'Every Prime Minister needs a Willie.' Nairn is evocatively depicted in David Thomson's prize-winning memoir, *Nairn in Darkness and Light.*

Cawdor Castle

Tree House

Unspoiled CAWDOR CASTLE is magnificent and moody, with its deep dry moat, brooding square tower, portcullis, iron-studded doors, winding stairways, gloomy secret passages and THE ONLY SURVIVING DRAWBRIDGE AT A PRIVATE CASTLE IN SCOTLAND. Macbeth may not have actually murdered Duncan here, but it feels like the sort of place where he might have done, although certainly in an earlier building if so, for the keep, the oldest part of what we see today, dates only from about 1400.

The original name of the land and castle was Calder, and the family were CALDERS OF THAT ILK. This was pronounced Cawdor by the locals, and Cawdor is the name Shakespeare picked up when he came, as some believe, to visit Scotland to research his play.

When, in the 14th century, the Thane decided to treat himself to a new fortress, he was guided by a dream to load up a donkey with a chest of gold, let it go free, and build his castle where the donkey lay down to rest. If he did this, he was told, his family would prosper. The honest creature wandered around for a bit, chomping on a thistle here and a bit of grass there, and finally settled in under a holly tree. The obedient Thane erected the keep around the tree, and now the ancient holly, long since dead, but still standing, can be seen growing out of the floor of the dungeon and up through a hole in the ceiling. For years, it was assumed to be a hawthorn tree and, indeed, the room where the tree resides is known to this day as the Thorn Tree Room. Modern scientific examination has proved the tree to be, in fact, a holly, dating from 1372.

Although the family has certainly prospered, their history has been chequered. In 1499, the Campbells of Argyll picked up the Cawdor title by kidnapping, after her father died, the young, red-haired heiress, Muriel

Calder, and forcibly marrying her off to a Campbell. The death of the 6th Earl and 25th Thane of Cawdor, in 1993, triggered a frightful fuss because he broke the tradition of centuries and left the castle to his second wife, rather than his son, the 7th Earl. The ramifications rumble on, but somehow this just adds to the atmosphere that is Cawdor.

Well, I never knew this ABOUT NAIRNSHIRE

Nairnshire, though small in size, is not the smallest county in Scotland. It does, however, have THE SMALLEST POPULATION.

CULBIN FOREST, which stretches between Nairn and Findhorn, and is shared with Morayshire, was once an area of sand dunes known as 'THE SCOTTISH SAHARA'. The removal of grasses for thatch had denuded the existing dunes which, in 1694, were swept up by a westerly gale, engulfing the whole community of Culbin, dwellings, a church, the great house of Kinnaird and a mass of livestock. Today the land has been stabilised by the planting of trees and hardy grasses, but occasionally the sand shifts to reveal bits of the lost buildings underneath.

CULBIN FOREST is home to many different species of wildlife such as deer, badgers and foxes, but perhaps the most exotic inhabitant is the rare capercaillie, THE LARGEST GAME BIRD IN BRITAIN. It looks like a small turkey, is very noisy and can be quite aggressive. The capercaillie became extinct in Britain in 1783 but was re-introduced from Sweden in 1837.

The BLASTED HEATH where Macbeth encountered the three witches, while on his way to meet Duncan at Forres, lies about 6 miles (10 km) east of Nairn, on the border with Morayshire, just before Brodie Castle. The land is wooded and farmed now but, about 400 yards (366 m) to the north of the main road down a little lane, there is a bare hillock that looks as though it might be a suitable spot for sorcery.

The 17th-century BOATH DOOCOT, at AULDEARN, stands sentinel above the marshy fields where Charles I's Scottish commander, the Marquis of Montrose, defeated a far stronger army of Covenanters at the Battle of Auldearn in 1645.

The doocot, ONE OF THE OLDEST IN SCOTLAND, stands at the top of a high

motte, all that survives of the Castle of Eren, constructed by William the Lion (William I) in 1180. Boath House, nearby, was built in 1825 for the Dunbar family and has been described as the 'most beautiful Regency house in Scotland'. It is now a hotel.

The detached and fortified bell tower at ARDCLACH, a few miles south of Nairn, was built in 1655 and is UNIQUE IN SCOTLAND. It stands above the village on the top of a hill, so that the church bell can be heard from afar, and also to act as a watch-tower.

ORKNEY

COUNTY TOWN: KIRKWALL

Ork Ay – 'Whale Island' (Norse)

Kirkwall Cathedral, Britain's most northerly cathedral

Kirkwall

A Norse Cathedral

KIRKWALL has been the capital of Orkney since Norse days, and was important long before that, owing to its strategic position at the centre of Mainland, the largest of the Orkney islands, beside a sheltered and well-protected bay. Orkney was ceded to Scotland, along with Shetland, in 1468, as part of the dowry of Princess Margrethe of Denmark, betrothed to the future James III; the Norwegians, however, have never formally recognised the islands as a part of Scotland. Kirkwall certainly feels much more Norse than Scottish. It is a lovely town

of narrow, twisting streets and steep, crow-stepped and gabled stone houses, clustered proudly round the magnificent red and yellow sandstone ST MAGNUS CATHEDRAL, a church that would grace any city in the kingdom. St Magnus is ONE OF ONLY TWO COMPLETE PRE-REFORMATION CATHEDRALS IN SCOTLAND, the other being St Mungo's in Glasgow, and St Magnus is UNIQUE IN BEING OWNED, NOT BY THE CHURCH, BUT BY THE PEOPLE OF KIRKWALL.

As the Normans built mighty churches throughout England, so their Norsemen cousins in Orkney built St Magnus, which was founded in 1137 by Earl Rognvald of Orkney, in memory of his uncle and predecessor, Magnus. Earl Magnus, a scholarly and peace-loving man, was lured on to the island of Egilsay in 1116, by his rival cousin Earl Haakon, who stove Magnus's head in with an axe and buried him in the church at Birsay. Miracles were attributed to the grave site and Magnus was made a saint in 1135. His nephew Rognvald swore that if he attained the Earldom of Orkney, he would build a grand church in his uncle's honour, and he did just that. The story of Magnus's death was thought apocryphal until 1919 when, during restoration work, a casket containing bones and a skull with a great gash in it, as from an axe blow, was discovered embedded in one of the great pillars of the cathedral.

St Magnus took over 300 years to complete and has been added to and restored over the years. Its beauty and power lies, as with Orkney itself, in its rugged simplicity. It is, in fact, one of the smaller cathedrals in Britain, but gives the impression of being much larger, and effortlessly dominates the bustling and self-sufficient town. When you enter by the west door, the ruddy-hued vista of sturdy Romanesque pillars, marching away to a glorious east window, takes the breath away.

Beside the cathedral are the remains of the BISHOP'S PALACE, where King Haakon IV of Norway came after being defeated at the Battle of Largs in 1263. He fell ill and died here, and was buried in St Magnus over the winter, after which his body was taken to its final resting-place in Bergen Cathedral.

Next to it is the palace of the hated Earl of Orkney, Patrick Stewart, grandson of James V. Begun in 1607, it was never finished after the Earl was hanged for treason in 1615. Earl Patrick, it seems, had no intention of stinting himself: even roofless, the palace is regarded as one of the most accomplished examples of Renaissance architecture in Scotland.

Orkney's Prehistoric Treasures

Oldest Known Village and Largest Chambered Cairn

The Orkney Islands POSSESS A HIGHER CONCENTRATION OF PREHISTORIC MONUMENTS THAN ANYWHERE ELSE IN NORTHERN EUROPE and Mainland's 5,500-year-old Neolithic collection was granted World Heritage status by UNESCO in 1999.

Skara Brae

In 1850 one of Orkney's legendary storms whipped off the covering of sand to reveal SKARA BRAE, 5,000 years old, THE OLDEST KNOWN PREHISTORIC VILLAGE IN EUROPE. Built before the Pyramids were even thought of and situated beside a glorious curve of bay on the west coast of Mainland, 7 miles (11 km) north of Stromness, Skara Brae was engulfed by a mighty sandstorm and lay hidden and undisturbed for 4,500 years. Dug deep into the soil are a number of ingeniously constructed stone houses: comfortable, sheltered from the wind and equipped with stone beds, tables, cupboards and fireplaces. Everything looks so new and so complete, as if the inhabitants have just popped out to the shops, that it is remarkably easy to connect with the lives of these people from so long ago.

Maes Howe

MAES HOWE, 3 miles (4.8 km) north-east of Stromness, is the finest burial chamber in Europe, THE LARGEST CHAMBERED CAIRN IN BRITAIN. Built around 2800 BC, the grass-covered mound is 36 ft (11 m) high and 300 ft (91 m) in circumference. Inside, a long narrow passageway leads to a central chamber with a number of smaller chambers off it, all lined and roofed with massive stone slabs. Maes Howe is superior to and far more sophisticated than its older cousin Newgrange in Ireland, but is similarly aligned as a calendar – at sunset on midwinter day the sun shines along the entrance passage and illuminates the central chamber. Abandoned in 2000 BC, Maes Howe slept untouched for 3,000 years until discovered by the Vikings in the middle of the 12th century. They broke in and looted the tombs, leaving behind a fascinating display of runic graffiti, THE LARGEST SINGLE COLLECTION IN EUROPE, which, when translated, say things like 'Haermund Hardaxe carved these runes' and 'Ingigerth is the most beautiful of women'.

The roof later fell in and Maes Howe was left alone again until 1861, when it was rediscovered by a Victorian landowner, excavated and restored to the immaculate condition we see it in today. Maes Howe is cared for by Historic Scotland.

The Ring of Brodgar

Situated between two lochs north of Maes Howe, the RING OF BRODGAR is a wide stone circle of almost perfect shape, probably built not long after Maes Howe to track the movement of the sun. There were originally 60 stones in the circle, of which 36 remain, some upright, some as broken stumps. Comedian Billy Connolly started something of a trend when he danced naked round the Ring of Brodgar for his *World Tour* television series.

Scapa Flow

A Watery Grave

With an expanse of 56 square miles (14,500 ha), encircled and protected by the Orkney Islands, SCAPA FLOW is one of the largest natural harbours in the world, and has been used by sailors and fishermen since the islands were first inhabited. In the 17th century, Stromness, standing at the mouth of Hoy Sound, the western entrance, became the main European trading post of the Hudson's Bay Company – 90 per cent of the original employees of that company were Orcadians.

Scapa Flow really proved its worth as a naval anchorage during the two world wars. In 1914, a German submarine was discovered prowling in the harbour, and so the Royal Navy sank a number of old ships to form barriers at the harbour entrances. In May 1916, the British Grand Fleet sailed from here to the Battle of Jutland, THE LAST EVER SET PIECE BATTLE AT SEA.

In June that year, FIELD MARSHAL THE 1ST EARL KITCHENER OF KHARTOUM, the British Commander-in-Chief, war hero and the face on the 'Your Country Needs You!' recruitment posters, dropped in on Scapa Flow while on his way to St Petersburg to hold talks with the Tsar. After dining on board the flagship he transferred to HMS *Hampshire* and put to sea. Just off Birsay, having passed through Hoy Sound, the *Hampshire* struck a mine, exploded and sank immediately, with few survivors.

In 1919, after the Armistice, the neutralised German High Seas Fleet were held at Scapa Flow, while negotiations were in progress to end the war. The German commander, ADMIRAL VON REUTER, was mistakenly led to believe that war was about to resume and, to save his ships from falling into enemy hands, he ordered the entire fleet of 74 vessels to be scuttled. At 10.30 on the morning of 21 June the pre-arranged signal 'Paragraph Eleven – Confirm' was hoisted and, in front of an astonished group of schoolchildren on a boat trip around Scapa Flow, the most powerful fleet in the world sank slowly beneath the water, THE GREATEST LOSS OF SHIPPING TONNAGE IN A SINGLE DAY IN HISTORY. Remarkably, no one was drowned but, in the confusion, as the British struggled to beach as many of the sinking ships as possible, nine German sailors were shot dead, THE LAST CASUALTIES OF THE FIRST WORLD WAR. During the 1920s and 30s many of the ships were salvaged in THE LARGEST OPERATION OF ITS KIND EVER TO BE ATTEMPTED, but there are still eight ships at the bottom of Scapa Flow and divers come from around the world to explore the wrecks.

In October 1939, during the Phoney War at the beginning of the Second World War, a German U-boat found its way through the narrow Holm Sound from the east and torpedoed HMS *Royal Oak*, which went to the bottom with 800 men on board. Many of them are still entombed in the wreck, now a war grave and marked by a buoy. Winston Churchill heeded the warning that Scapa Flow was not impregnable, and sent 13,000 Italian prisoners of war to Orkney to construct a series of concrete barriers across the eastern side of Scapa Flow. Known as THE CHURCHILL BARRIERS, these remarkable feats of engineering not only made Scapa Flow secure but also provided a series of useful permanent causeways linking the chain of islands between South Ronaldsay and Mainland.

The 550 Italian prisoners who were housed at Camp 60 on the little island of Lamb Holm left another legacy, which has now become one of Orkney's most popular attractions, the wonderfully ornate ITALIAN CHAPEL. This extraordinary creation, standing improbably on a bare hill above the sweeping grey wastes of Scapa Flow, was fashioned out of two Nissen huts joined end to end, using only concrete and imaginative paintwork. In the 1960s some of the Italians were invited back to Orkney to help restore the chapel.

On 16 March 1940, during an abortive air raid on Scapa Flow, a bomb was dropped on a number of small

stone cottages at Bridge of Waithe, 4 miles (6.4 km) to the east of Stromness. Six people were injured and one young man, 27-year-old farm labourer James Isbister, was killed, becoming THE FIRST CIVILIAN TO BE KILLED ON BRITISH SOIL IN THE SECOND WORLD WAR. Willie Farquhar, who was injured in the same attack, repaired his cottage and opened it as a watering-hole for the servicemen stationed in Orkney. It became known as the Golden Slipper and proved hugely popular as nearby Stromness was 'dry' at the time. The cottage can still be seen, and many older Orcadians have happy and colourful memories to share of the legendary Golden Slipper.

STROMNESS is no longer dry, but a thriving port, consisting mainly of one delightful long, narrow street, that winds its way up to a headland, past shops and handsome stone houses, backing on to the sea with their own jetties. Stromness was Sir John Franklin's last landfall before his doomed expedition in 1845. And it was Orcadian JOHN RAE, buried in St Magnus Cathedral, who later discovered the fate of Franklin and his men.

Just outside Stromness is the ORKNEY FUDGE FACTORY.

Hoy

Old Man

During the two world wars Lyness, on the south-east of HOY, acted as the main centre of operations for Scapa Flow. Huge oil tanks were excavated out of the hills behind the town to store fuel for the fleet, and one of the old pumping stations on the harbour front has been turned into the Scapa Flow Visitor Centre. In the nearby Naval Cemetery are buried the victims of the Battle of Jutland and the bodies that were recovered from the *Hampshire* and the *Royal Oak*. Across the water on FLOTTA, the 200 ft (61 m) high gas flare from the vast oil terminal which began operation in 1976 can be seen day and night. About 10 per cent of Britain's North Sea oil output has come ashore at Flotta since then.

Hoy is the second largest of the Orkney Islands and, scenically, the most spectacular. Ward Hill, at 1,570 ft (479 m), is the highest point in Orkney, and the cliffs of St John's Head on the west side of the island rise sheer for 1,140 ft (347 m), THE HIGHEST VERTICAL SEA CLIFFS IN BRITAIN. The distinctive 'OLD MAN OF HOY', which can be seen across the Pentland Firth from the Caithness coast, is BRITAIN'S TALLEST SEA STACK, 450 ft (137 m) high. It was thought to be unclimbable until 1966, when Chris Bonington got to the top, along with Rusty Baillie and Tom Patey. They repeated their feat in front of the television cameras for a pioneering outside broadcast in 1967.

Sheltered from the Atlantic wind in a deep valley near the middle of Hoy is BERRIEDALE WOOD, THE MOST NORTHERLY NATURAL WOOD IN BRITAIN and home to THE ONLY HAZEL TREES ON ORKNEY. Nearby is the mysterious DWARFIE STONE, a huge free-standing block of red sandstone, hollowed out as a burial chamber or dwelling place some 5,000 years ago, THE ONLY KNOWN ROCK-CUT TOMB IN BRITAIN. In 1850

Major William Mouncey took up residence in the stone for a while and decorated the walls with Persian graffiti, in memory of his time as a spy in the Middle East. The initials of Hugh Miller, Cromarty's famous geologist, are also inscribed on the stone.

On Tuesday, 17 October 1939, ground artillery hit a Junkers Ju 88, which crashed and exploded on Hoy, to become THE FIRST ENEMY AIRCRAFT TO BE BROUGHT DOWN OVER BRITAIN IN THE SECOND WORLD WAR.

Well, I never knew this ABOUT ORKNEY

Orkney is an archipelago of more than 70 islands, 17 of them inhabited. It covers an area of 377 square miles (976 sq km), of which more than half is taken up by Mainland, the largest island. There are some 20,000 people in Orkney, most of whom live in the main towns of Kirkwall and Stromness. Orcadians see themselves as 'farmers with boats', as opposed to neighbouring Shetlanders, who see themselves as 'fishermen with crofts'.

Thanks to the Gulf Stream, the weather is not too harsh although the winds can be savage – it is said that when the wind drops in Orkney everyone falls over.

Growing in a private garden near the road between Kirkwall and Stromness are THE MOST NORTHERLY PALM TREES IN THE WORLD – probably.

THE BIGGEST BROWN TROUT EVER CAUGHT IN THE BRITISH ISLES was taken from Stenness Loch. It weighed 29 lbs (13 kg).

The HIGHLAND PARK DISTILLERY, above Kirkwall, is BRITAIN'S NORTHERNMOST DISTILLERY.

SCOTLAND'S ONLY MEDIEVAL ROUND CHURCH can be found at ORPHIR, 9 miles (14 km) west of Kirkwall. It was built in 1123 by Earl Haakon, the murderer of Magnus, perhaps as a penance. He had made a pilgrimage to the Holy Land, and the Church of St Nicholas is modelled on the Church of the Holy Sepulchre in Jerusalem. Only the apse remains standing.

PEEBLESSHIRE

COUNTY TOWN: PEEBLES

Pebyll – 'tent' (Celtic)

Traquair House, the oldest inhabited house in Scotland

Peebles

Peebles for Pleasure

PEEBLES is a pleasant market and county town on the River Tweed, famous for its salmon fishing. Its name comes from the Celtic 'pebyll', or tent, and the area was probably a camping site for early nomadic tribesmen, just as it is now for walkers and explorers of the Border hills.

THE CHAMBERS INSTITUTION in the High Street is a reminder that Peebles was the birthplace of William Chambers (1800–83) and his brother Robert (1802–71), who founded the publishing house that gives us *Chambers Encyclopaedia* and *Chambers Dictionary*. They were inspired by reading an old encyclopaedia that Robert found in the attic when he was a boy. Their family house, in a narrow street called Biggiesknowe, is marked by a plaque.

The turreted 16th-century building now occupied by the Chambers Institution was previously called Queensberry Lodging and was the birthplace of William Douglas, 4th Duke of

Queensberry (1724–1810), known as 'Old Q'. A member of the Hellfire Club, he was a notorious gambler and philanderer who bathed in milk 'to maintain his potency'. His summer retreat was the formidable 13th-century peel tower of Neidpath, with walls 12 ft (4 m) thick, which stands on a high rock above a loop in the River Tweed, to the west of Peebles.

To the north of the town, and now forming the centrepiece of a large caravan park, is a fine Georgian house called ROSETTA, built in 1814, for his retirement, by DR THOMAS YOUNG (1773–1829), a physicist and surgeon who went on the expedition to the Nile delta which brought back the ROSETTA STONE. The stone was discovered in 1799 near the Egyptian town of el Rashid (Rosetta) by soldiers of Napoleon's army, who were digging the foundations of a new fort. When the English defeated the French in Egypt, at the Battle of Alexandria in 1801, they took possession of the stone and, in 1802, it was put on show in the British Museum, where it can be seen today. The Rosetta Stone is inscribed in three languages, Egyptian, Greek and hieroglyphics, and Thomas Young was THE FIRST MAN TO DECIPHER THE HIEROGLYPHS, by matching them up with the other two languages. Young's work enabled scholars to finally read the language of the Pharaohs, and this in turn led to the discovery of many of their tombs and artefacts. Inside the house is a plaster-cast replica of the Rosetta Stone which can be examined on request.

Traquair

Unopened Gates

TRAQUAIR HOUSE, near Innerleithen, is THE OLDEST INHABITED HOUSE IN SCOTLAND. It was built as a royal hunting lodge around AD 950 and over the centuries has been visited by 27 kings and queens, including Alexander I, Edwards I and II and Mary, Queen of Scots. Traquair was given by James III to his favourite, William Rodgers, who was later forced to give it up to the King's uncle, the Earl of Buchan. He passed it on to his illegitimate son, James Stuart, who was killed at Flodden and whose descendants, the Maxwell Stuarts, live there to this day. The original 12th-century stone peel tower has been incorporated into the northeast corner of the later house largely built in the 17th century by John Stuart, the 1st Earl of Traquair. This is perhaps the most unpretentious and 'Scottish' of all Scotland's big houses, not grand or elaborate, but old and grey and mellowed, with corbelled turrets, rows of dormer windows and a lived-in feel that is very appealing.

The Stuarts are, and always have been, staunch Catholics, and the homely, unspoilt house is full of the features and personal effects of a family who have had to live under constant threat. The Priest's Room has a secret stairway, and there are hidden doors and passageways, priest holes and vestments that can be disguised as counterpanes. It was in the King's Room, in the peel tower, that Queen Mary stayed with her husband Lord Darnley, shortly before he was murdered in Edinburgh, and she left behind a quilt that she embroidered herself. Darnley was chastised by the 4th Laird for his coarse manners and for referring to the Queen as a 'mare'.

In 1900 a mural painting dating from 1530 was discovered beneath the wallpaper in the Museum Room and is thought to be THE EARLIEST MURAL OF ITS KIND IN SCOTLAND. A special treasure is a rare Jacobean Amen glass engraved with a toast to the 'true born Prince of Wales'.

The 'true born Prince of Wales', Bonnie Prince Charlie, visited Traquair in 1745. When he departed, the Bear Gates (a.k.a. the 'Steekit Yetts', or Stuck Gates) at the end of the long drive were closed and locked behind him, and the 7th Earl declared that they would not be opened again until a Stuart sat upon the British throne once more. They have never been opened since.

Laid out on the site of the 18th-century parterre at the rear of the house is SCOTLAND'S LARGEST HEDGED MAZE, planted in 1981, first with cypress trees and later with beech. It covers half an acre (0.2 ha) and the walk to the centre is over a quarter of a mile (0.4 km).

Beneath the private chapel is a brewhouse, renovated and reopened in 1965, which produces a range of powerful home-made ales, similar to those once enjoyed by Bonnie Prince Charlie himself.

Broughton

John Buchan's Inspiration

The Green, a pleasant, white-painted house in Broughton's main street, was the home of John Buchan's maternal grandparents. The writer spent many happy holidays here as a boy and set his first novel, *John Burnet of Barns*, at nearby Barns Manor. Buchan's parents met and married in the FREE CHURCH IN BROUGHTON, and this has now been turned into THE JOHN BUCHAN CENTRE, dedicated to his extraordinary career as a barrister, soldier, statesman and author of some 50 books. The church has a memorial window to a local man called Hannay, from which Buchan took the name for his hero, Richard Hannay.

JOHN BUCHAN, 1st LORD TWEEDSMUIR, was born in Perth in 1875. He is best known for his spy novel *The Thirty-Nine Steps*, published in 1915, and made into a film three times so far. He was also a war correspondent for *The Times*, Director of Reuters, worked for British Intelligence during the First World War, and was a hugely popular Governor-General of Canada. He died in office, after a stroke, in 1940, and is buried at Elsfield in Oxfordshire, where he lived in the Manor House.

Buchan's sister Anna lived at Bank House, beside the parish church in Peebles. She was also a popular novelist who wrote as 'O. Douglas'.

Well, I never knew this ABOUT PEEBLESSHIRE

LYNE CHURCH, perched on a hill beside the road some 4 miles (6 km) west of Peebles, was built in 1645 and IS THE SMALLEST CHURCH IN SCOTLAND.

ST RONAN'S WELL, at Innerleithen, was made famous by Sir Walter Scott's novel of that name, published in 1823. The writer came here as a boy, hoping the sulphurous waters would cure his polio. Robert Burns also visited what he called the 'famous spa' in 1787.

The round-arched Norman doorway in the porch of STOBO CHURCH is one of the oldest surviving examples of ecclesiastical architecture in Scotland.

The castellated STOBO CASTLE, built in 1811, is home to one of Britain's most exclusive health clubs.

THE DAWYCK ARBORETUM, part of the National Botanic Gardens, is the finest in Scotland and possesses A UNIQUE COLLECTION OF TREES planted over the last 300 years by the local Veitch, Naesmyth and Balfour lairds. As well as a number of record-breaking Douglas firs planted from seeds brought back from North America by David Douglas (*see* Scone, Perthshire), Dawyck is home of THE UNIQUE DAWYCK BEECH, first discovered growing here in 1860 and the progenitor of this variety of beech tree all over the world. In 1650, SCOTLAND'S FIRST HORSE CHESTNUT TREE was planted here, and in 1725, SCOTLAND'S FIRST LARCH.

JOHN BUCHAN took his title of Lord Tweedsmuir from the tiny village of TWEEDSMUIR, on the old coach road that runs along the narrow Tweed valley, 15 miles (24 km) southwest of Peebles. Seven miles (11 km) further south, close to where the counties of Dumfriesshire, Lanarkshire and Peeblesshire meet, and marked by a road-side sculpture, is TWEEDS WELL, source of the River Tweed.

PERTHSHIRE

COUNTY TOWN: PERTH

Perth – thicket (Celtic)

Dunblane Cathedral – 'I know not anything so perfect in its simplicity . . .' John Ruskin

Perth

Fair City

The 'Fair City' of PERTH is a former royal burgh and county town of Perthshire. It stands at the head of the Tay estuary between two meadows called North and South Inch, lending itself to a trick trivia question – 'What is the smallest town in Scotland? Answer: Perth, which is between one and two inches . . .'

From the 12th to the 15th centuries, largely due to its proximity to Scone and the Stone of Destiny, Perth vied with Dunfermline to be the capital of Scotland. It might have become the permanent capital but for a dastardly deed that took place here in 1437. King James I, who had made Perth the centre of his court, was brutally murdered at his favourite residence, the former Blackfriars monastery, by a group of disaffected nobles led by the Earl of Atholl. As the assassins battered at the door, James tried to escape through a sewer, while one of the Queen's ladies-in-waiting, Catherine Douglas, barred the door with her arm, in place of the bar which had been removed beforehand. However, the sewer tunnel had been sealed off at the end with a grill, on James's orders, to prevent him losing tennis balls down there. The King was trapped and most foully done to death. The Queen fled to Edinburgh for safety, and the coronation of her six-year-old son, James II, took place there rather than at Scone. From that time on Edinburgh was the capital.

The rise of the Protestant faith in Scotland, or Reformation, originated at Perth in May 1559, when the fiery preacher John Knox gave his famous sermon in St John's Church, denouncing the idolatry of the Catholic Church. The inflamed congregation rampaged through the city destroying religious treasures and defacing the churches.

There has been a church on the site of St John's for over 1,000 years, but the present ST JOHN'S CHURCH, dating from the 15th century, is the oldest surviving building in Perth, and gives the town its older name of St Johns Town, now borne by the local football team, St Johnstone.

The Salutation Hotel in South Street has a good claim to be THE OLDEST HOTEL IN SCOTLAND and there is a stone in the courtyard bearing the date 1619. Bonnie Prince Charlie is known to have stayed here, in room 20, and The Beatles took tea in the hotel lounge.

Scone

Destiny and Freedom

SCONE is the heart of the kingdom, site of the old Pictish capital to where Kenneth MacAlpin, King of the Scots, came in AD 843 to unite two peoples under one crown and create the fledgling nation. MacAlpin brought the Stone of Destiny with him, on which the Kings of Dalriada, Argyll were enthroned. From that time on, all Kings of Scotland, including Macbeth in 1040, were crowned on the Moot Hill at Scone, seated upon the Stone of Destiny.

John Balliol, in 1292, was THE LAST SCOTTISH KING TO BE CROWNED ON THE STONE AT SCONE. Four years later, King Edward I of England seized the Stone and took it to London, where it remained underneath the Confessor's Coronation Chair in Westminster Abbey for the next 700 years – if, that is, the Scots handed over the real thing. Some think that the genuine

Stone was hidden away on Dunsinane Hill, and a substitute given up in its place.

Although the Stone was no longer there, Scone remained the coronation site of the Scottish kings for another 350 years. Robert the Bruce was crowned here in 1306, and the Stuart dynasty was given legitimacy when the first Stuart king, Robert II, was crowned at Scone in 1371. The last coronation at Scone was that of Charles II on New Year's Day in 1651, just before he went off to the Battle of Worcester.

Eventually the old palace of Scone was granted to Sir David Murray, a friend and strong supporter of James VI. The most celebrated of Murray's descendants was WILLIAM MURRAY, 1st EARL OF MANSFIELD, THE FIRST SCOT TO BECOME LORD CHANCELLOR and, arguably, the greatest lawyer of all time.

In 1771, Lord Mansfield presided over the contentious case of James Somerset, a black slave brought over from America by a Scotsman called Charles Stewart. When they arrived in London, Somerset escaped and sued for his freedom. At the end of a tense and intimidating court case, and despite powerful arguments put up by vested interests, who warned that giving slaves their freedom would bring down the British Empire, Lord Mansfield found in favour of Somerset. 'Fiat justicia, ruat coelum,' he declared – 'Let justice be done, though the heavens fall.'

It was the most immense, courageous, far-reaching and dramatic ruling ever handed down in a court of law. It meant liberty that day for some 15,000 slaves in Britain and led ultimately to freedom for slaves across the world.

Today, a long driveway winds through manicured parkland to SCONE PALACE, the present building being a

A Picture Paints a Thousand Words

Hanging on a wall in Scone Palace is an enchanting portrait by Johann Zoffany of two young women, smiling annd holding hands. One is black, the other white; both are richly attired and aristocratic. They are Dido Elizabeth Belle and her cousin Lady Elizabeth Murray, great-nieces and adopted daughters of Lord Mansfield. Dido was the daughter of a black slave girl and Mansfield's nephew Sir John Lindsay; Elizabeth the daughter of another nephew, the 7th Viscount Stormont. The childless Earl had brought them both up at Kenwood House, his London home, as his own daughters. It was a great scandal at the time but could Lord Mansfield's well known admiration for his beautiful adopted daughter Dido have influenced his decision to free James Somerset?

Georgian Gothick refurbishment of the former abbot's palace commissioned by the 3rd Earl of Mansfield and completed in 1802. Highlight of the interior is the Royal Long Gallery, built in 1618, THE LONGEST ROOM IN SCOTLAND at 142 ft (43 m). Charles II walked along the Gallery to his coronation in 1651.

A little to the north of the palace is the MOOT HILL, complete with a replica of the Stone of Scone.

Not far from the Moot Hill, towering above the other trees in the Pinetum, is a mighty Douglas fir, grown from a seed sent home from North America in 1826 by DAVID DOUGLAS. A much respected botanist, after whom the Douglas fir is named, Douglas began life as an under-gardener at Scone, before setting off to explore the trees and plants of the North American continent. He discovered some 200 new species before being gored to death by a wild bison, after falling into a hidden pit dug by the natives designed to catch bison rather than botanists.

Comrie

The First Seismologists

The little EARTHQUAKE HOUSE AT COMRIE, set high up on a knoll above the village, with a solitary Scots pine for company, was put up in 1874. It is EUROPE'S SMALLEST LISTED BUILDING. Comrie, which sits right above the Highland Boundary fault line, is known as 'the earthquake capital of Scotland'.

In the 18th and 19th centuries Comrie suffered a number of earthquakes, and some of the local people began to take an interest and record them. The Revd R. Taylor and the Revd S. Gilfillan were two early enthusiasts, later joined by the village postmaster,

Peter Macfarlane, and the cobbler, James Drummond. They became known as the 'Comrie Pioneers', and their observations resulted in the setting up in 1839 of a Committee for the Investigation of Scottish and Irish earthquakes.

Mr Milne, a member of this committee, devised the term 'seismometer' and its associated words, thereby making the Comrie Pioneers THE FIRST 'SEISMOLOGISTS'. Professor J.D. Forbes of the Committee designed THE FIRST SEISMOMETER. The Committee also discovered that the epicentre of an earthquake could be determined by the intersection of two or more lines of direction.

Blair Atholl

The Last Private Army

BLAIR CASTLE, seat of the Dukes of Atholl and the Clan Murray, is SCOTLAND'S MOST VISITED HISTORIC HOUSE. The Duke of Atholl is THE ONLY PERSON IN BRITAIN ALLOWED TO RETAIN HIS OWN ARMY, the Atholl Highlanders. THE SOLE REMAINING PRIVATE ARMY IN EUROPE, they date back to the times when Atholl functioned as a small kingdom of its own within Scotland. The Atholl Highlanders fought bravely at Culloden on Prince Charles's side and, in that same year, 1746, Blair Castle achieved the distinction of becoming THE LAST PLACE IN BRITAIN TO BE BESIEGED. The Atholl Highlanders first appeared as a ceremonial bodyguard in 1839 when they escorted the Duke's heir, Lord Glenlyon, to the Eglinton Tournament at Irvine (*see* Ayrshire).

Inside the Atholl Country Collection in the village of Blair Atholl is the Caledonian Challenge Shield, BRITAIN'S LARGEST TROPHY. Carved from oak it is over 9 ft (2.7 m) high and 6 ft (1.8 m) across, and was designed in 1861 by J. Clark Stanton as a shooting trophy. It is still competed for today.

Dunkeld

An Early Ecclesiastical Capital

DUNKELD is one of the loveliest surprises in all Scotland, an unspoiled, 18th-century cathedral city, hidden away in trees on the banks of the River Tay. Dunkeld gives the impression of being undiscovered, which is its charm, but in its day this little town was one of the most important places in Scotland.

When Kenneth MacAlpin, first King of Scotland, established his capital at nearby Scone in AD 843, he brought with him from Iona the relics of St Columba, and placed them in the Celtic monastery in Dunkeld for safe-keeping. Dunkeld became the ecclesiastical capital of the kingdom and seat of Scotland's senior bishop, until St Andrews took over in the middle of the 10th century.

DUNKELD CATHEDRAL, reached by a short walk from the market square, down a lane of whitewashed stone cottages, sits in glorious leafy gardens down by the river. It is extraordinarily impressive, with a very long, roofless nave and a choir that is now used as the parish church. Although there has been a church of some sort here since the 6th century, most of the remains we see today date from the 14th and 15th centuries. In 1560 the cathedral was wrecked by a Reformation mob from Perth.

ST COLUMBA's relics are thought to be buried under the chancel steps. Behind the carved oak chancel screen there are some interesting medieval monuments, including the headless effigy of Bishop Sinclair, chaplain to William Wallace and Robert the Bruce, and to the notorious Wolf of Badenoch, Alexander Stewart, Earl of Buchan and youngest son of King Robert II. Censured by the Bishop of Moray for being unfaithful to his wife, the Wolf of Badenoch took his revenge by sacking the town of Forres and burning down the cathedral at Elgin in 1390. He was eventually forced by his brother, Robert III, to wear sackcloth and ashes in the Blackfriars monastery at Perth, in penance for his crimes.

In the ruined nave is the grave of Count Rohenstart, or Rouenstuart, grandson of Bonnie Prince Charlie by the Prince's illegitimate daughter Charlotte and the Archbishop of Rouen. The Count died in a carriage accident while visiting Scotland in 1854. Nearby lies William Cleland, leader of the defending Government forces in the Battle of Dunkeld, when the town was attacked by Jacobites after the Battle of Killiecrankie in 1689.

The battle more or less destroyed Dunkeld, and most of the buildings in the town centre date from after that time. The result is extremely handsome, with picturesque streets lined with 17th-century houses and a wide square dominated by the Atholl Memorial

Fountain, dedicated in 1866 to the 6th Duke of Atholl, who brought piped water to the town.

Many of the houses have been restored and some are looked after by the National Trust for Scotland, whose bookshop is located in THE ELL HOUSE in the square. Its name derives from the 'ell' measure fixed to its outside wall – an ell being an old Scottish measure, equivalent to about 37 inches (91.5 cm), used by weavers.

Birnam

Peter Rabbit and Macbeth's Doom

On the opposite bank of the River Tay, across Telford's elegant bridge of 1809, is the village of BIRNAM. The doddery Birnam Oak is practically all that is left of Shakespeare's 'great Birnam Wood which came to Dunsinane' and spelt the end for Macbeth. The Birnam Oak stands beside BRITAIN'S LARGEST SYCAMORE TREE.

Beatrix Potter used to holiday in Birnam as a child, and it was while staying here that she wrote the letter that was to become *The Tale of Peter Rabbit.* She is commemorated by the BEATRIX POTTER GARDENS.

Dunsinane Hill is about 12 miles (19 km) away from here and can be seen from the top of Birnam Hill. It is a conspicuous summit in the Sidlaw Hills, 1,012 ft (308 m) high with a flat top, and is supposed to have been the site of Macbeth's castle. According to legend, the genuine Stone of Destiny was hidden on Dunsinane Hill by the monks of Scone, who sent King Edward I home with a fake – dug from a quarry near Oban.

BORN IN PERTHSHIRE

ROB ROY MACGREGOR (1671–1734), the outlaw, was born at GLENGYLE, on the north shore of Loch Katrine. Named 'roy' for his red hair, MacGregor suffered from the proscription of the MacGregor name after the Glenfruin massacre (*see* Dunbartonshire) and made a living as a cattle dealer, providing safe passage through the lowlands in return for protection money. He was dispossessed of his lands in BALQUHIDDER by the Duke of Montrose after his drover, a Macdonald, absconded with his money, leaving MacGregor to renege on a debt. He spent the next years cattle rustling and blackmailing and took part in the Jacobite uprisings of 1708 and 1715, before receiving the King's Pardon in 1725. His exploits became legendary, with tales of amazing escapes and heroic sword fights against great odds, and his life was much romanticised in Sir Walter Scott's novel of 1818, *Rob Roy.* He is buried in the churchyard at BALQUHIDDER, with his wife and two of his sons.

ROBERT STIRLING, the inventor of the hot air engine, was born in CLOAG in 1790. In 1816, while a parish minister at Galston, in Ayrshire, Stirling invented the external combustion engine, an idea that has recently been rediscovered and taken up. Put simply, fuel, which can be of any type, is sealed within a cylinder containing a piston. At one end of the cylinder the fuel is heated so that it expands and is moved by the piston to the opposite end of the cylinder, where it is cooled and re-compressed, moving the piston back again to restart the cycle. Since the fuel never leaves the cylinder and is used over and again, and there is no explosive combustion, it is very fuel efficient, quiet to operate and there are no polluting exhaust fumes. For all these reasons the Stirling engine is being enthusiastically redeveloped for any number of modern applications from submarine engines to central heating boilers.

Well, I never knew this ABOUT PERTHSHIRE

Perth boasts THE OLDEST REPERTORY THEATRE IN SCOTLAND.

The deeply satisfying ROUND TOWER AT ABERNETHY is one of only two Irish Celtic-style round towers in Scotland. The other is at Brechin. Abernethy is 75 ft (23 m) high with Romanesque windows in the belfry which suggest it was built in the late 11th century. A Pictish stone at the foot of the tower reflects the fact that Abernethy was an important Pictish stronghold. In 1072, Malcolm III (Canmore) bowed the knee to William the Conqueror at Abernethy. Two miles (3.2 km) outside the village of Dunning, beside the road, there is a monument to MAGGIE WELLS, with an inscription that reads 'burnt here – as a witch – 1657'. It is THE ONLY MEMORIAL TO A WITCH IN SCOTLAND and has a cross at the top, perhaps indicating the remorse of those responsible.

In the Parish Church of St Bean at FOWLIS WESTER you can see a piece of McBean tartan that has been to the moon. It was transported there, in 1969, by the astronaut ALAN BEAN, lunar module pilot on *Apollo 12*, and the fourth man to walk on the moon.

The GLENTURRET DISTILLERY near Crieff, established in 1775, is the home of The Famous Grouse and THE OLDEST DISTILLERY IN SCOTLAND. The Famous Grouse is THE BEST-SELLING WHISKY IN BRITAIN.

The first shot of the American War of Independence, fired by Scottish American EBENEZER MUNRO of the Lexington Minutemen, was quite likely fired from a pistol made at DOUNE near Dunblane. During the 17th and 18th centuries the village was famous for making the best pistols in the world. Thomas Cadell, considered to be the master of his craft, set up the business in 1646, and his descendants continued to produce accurate, good-quality pistols at Doune for many generations.

DOUNE CASTLE was used as a location for the 1975 comedy film *Monty Python and the Holy Grail.*

The 19th-century MODEL VILLAGE OF FORTINGALL sits at the head of GLEN LYON, at 25 miles (40 km) THE LONGEST GLEN IN SCOTLAND. Nearby is the site of a Roman camp where Pontius Pilate is said to have been born. He was the son of a Roman officer sent by Augustus Caesar to command a unit against the Picts, and a local woman. The rather mothy FORTINGALL YEW in the churchyard, now supported by stakes, is thought to be anything up to 3,000 years old, THE OLDEST LIVING THING IN EUROPE. In 1769 it had a girth measured at 56 ft 6 ins (17 m).

Lonely LOCH TAY, overlooked by Ben Lawers, Perthshire's highest mountain at 3,984 ft (1,214 m), is the source of the RIVER TAY, SCOTLAND'S LONGEST RIVER. The Tay is 120 miles (193 km) long and has THE LARGEST VOLUME OF WATER OF ANY RIVER IN BRITAIN.

Rannoch Station, standing between Loch Rannoch and the desolate Rannoch Moor, is BRITAIN'S LONELIEST RAILWAY STATION.

PITLOCHRY stands at the geographical centre of Scotland and is THE FURTHEST SCOTTISH TOWN FROM THE SEA. The town has its very own dam, thrown across the River Tummel to create Loch Faskally. The building of the dam required the creation of a 'fish ladder', a series of pools one above the other, to allow spawning salmon to make their way upstream. The ladder has a number of glass walls so that visitors may watch the leaping salmon.

THE EDRADOUR DISTILLERY, in the hills above Pitlochry, is THE SMALLEST DISTILLERY IN SCOTLAND. Edradour has for a long time been popular in America, and when the SS *Politician* was wrecked off Eriskay, in 1941, a large percentage of the quarter of a million whisky bottles on board were Edradour.

KEATHBANK MILL, a 19th-century former jute mill on the banks of the River Ericht at Rattray, houses THE LARGEST WATER-WHEEL IN SCOTLAND.

The Blairgowrie/Rattray region is sometimes called THE RASPBERRY CAPITAL OF THE WORLD.

The CAIRNWELL PASS on the A93 between Blairgowrie in Perthshire and Braemar in Aberdeenshire reaches a height of 2,199 ft (670 m), making it THE HIGHEST MAIN ROAD IN BRITAIN.

Running alongside the A93, as it bypasses the village of MEIKLEOUR, is THE TALLEST HEDGE IN THE WORLD, the Meikleour Beech Hedge. It is 580 yards (530 m) long and averages 100 feet (30 m) in height, attaining 120 ft (37 m) at the northern end. It was planted in 1745, as a boundary hedge, by Jean Mercer and her husband Robert. Not long afterwards Robert was killed at Culloden and Jean went to live in Edinburgh, leaving the hedge to grow at will. It is now cared for by the Meikleour Trust, and cut and re-measured every ten years in an operation that takes four men six weeks to complete.

Buried on INCHMAHOME ISLAND on the Lake of Menteith is ROBERT BONTINE CUNNINGHAME GRAHAM (1852–1936), FIRST PRESIDENT OF THE SCOTTISH LABOUR PARTY, which he co-founded with Keir Hardie in 1888. In 1934, at the age of 82, he became president of the newly formed Scottish National Party. He was THE FIRST MP ever to be suspended from the HOUSE OF COMMONS FOR SWEARING. The offending word? 'Damn!'

JAMES CRICHTON (1560–82) was born at CLUNIE CASTLE. A brilliant student, he was learned in philosophy and the sciences and fluent in Greek, Latin, Arabic, French, Hebrew, Italian, Spanish and English. He was also an excellent horseman, swordsman and musician. His attributes brought him to the attention of the Duke of Mantua in Italy, who appointed him to his Council. The Duke's son, jealous and fearful for his own position, waylaid Crichton one dark night and stabbed him to death. James Crichton was the model for the capable butler in James Barrie's play *The Admirable Crichton.*

Britain's current top tennis player, ANDY MURRAY, was born in DUNBLANE on 15 May 1987.

The popular resort town of CALLANDER, at the foot of the Trossachs, featured as Tannochbrae in the television series *Dr Finlay's Casebook*, based on the books of A.J. Cronin.

RENFREWSHIRE

COUNTY TOWN: RENFREW

Rhen frwd – 'flowing river'

Paisley Abbey – Cradle of the Royal House of Stuart

Renfrew

First in the Air

The old county town of RENFREW is the oldest burgh, and the sole royal burgh, in Renfrewshire. In 1157 Malcolm IV gave the lands of Renfrew to WALTER FITZALAN, FIRST HIGH STEWARD OF SCOTLAND. FitzAlan led Malcolm's army to victory over Somerled, Lord of the Isles, at the Battle of Renfrew in 1164, finally bringing the Western Isles under the control of the monarchy. His Steward was given the Isle of Bute in recognition of his victory (*see* Mount Stuart, Buteshire).

In 1315, Walter, the sixth High Steward, married Marjorie, daughter of Robert the Bruce (Robert I). The next year, heavily pregnant, Princess Marjorie was thrown from her horse, while riding through Renfrew at a place called the Knock. She was taken to Paisley Abbey, where she

died, but her child was somehow saved and grew up to ascend the throne as Robert II. A memorial called Queen Bleary's Cross used to mark the spot.

In 1404 Malcolm III made his son James (later James I) Lord Renfrew, a title now held by the heir to the Scottish throne, currently Prince Charles.

In the 19th century, Renfrew grew into a major industrial centre attracting many engineering and shipbuilding firms. In 1895, Babcock and Wilcox built THE BIGGEST BOILER-MAKING WORKS IN THE WORLD IN RENFREW.

Renfrew has been at the heart of Scotland's aviation history since the early 20th century. It was the home of GLASGOW'S FIRST AIRPORT and was THE FIRST MUNICIPAL AIRPORT IN SCOTLAND. Flying from Renfrew, then known as Moorpark Aerodrome, began in 1912. The first regular passenger air service from Glasgow flew from Renfrew Airport on 27 April 1933 bound for Campbeltown. A London service followed shortly afterwards.

Renfrew's Air Ambulance Service was initiated on 14 May 1933, when a pilot with Midland and Scottish Air Ferries, JIMMY ORWELL, flew from Renfrew to Islay to help a fisherman with acute peritonitis. It is THE OLDEST AIR AMBULANCE SERVICE IN THE WORLD.

The famous 602 'City of Glasgow' air squadron was based at Renfrew until 1933 and then moved down the road to Abbotsinch. In 1933 the squadron's COs David McIntyre and the Duke of Hamilton became THE FIRST MEN TO FLY OVER MOUNT EVEREST (*see* Prestwick, Ayrshire). 602 Squadron was THE FIRST AUXILIARY SQUADRON TO BE ISSUED WITH SPITFIRES, and two pilots from 602 Squadron were THE FIRST SPITFIRE PILOTS TO SHOOT DOWN A GERMAN AIRCRAFT, when they brought down a Junkers 88 over the Firth of Forth on 16 October 1939.

In August 1965 Renfrew Airport was at the centre of a media frenzy when MUHAMMAD ALI, OR CASSIUS CLAY as he was then, landed there on his way to an exhibition fight in Paisley.

The airport closed in 1966. Glasgow's airport is now located at ABBOTSINCH, nearby in Renfrewshire.

Paisley

Cradle of the Royal House of Stuart

PAISLEY has a surprisingly spacious and elegant town centre with fine classical buildings and attractive gardens surrounding one of Scotland's least known, but most impressive churches, Paisley Abbey.

PAISLEY ABBEY stands on the site of a Celtic monastery dedicated to St Mirren, who brought Christianity to this part of Scotland in the 6th century. In 1163 Walter FitzAlan, the first High Steward of Scotland, founded a priory here for 13 monks from Much Wenlock in Shropshire, where the FitzAlan family had originally come from. The priory was largely destroyed by the English in 1307, as a reprisal for supporting William Wallace, the son of a Renfrewshire knight, who had been educated by the monks from Paisley. What we see today are the restored remains of the 14th-century building.

From the outside the Abbey is handsome but not special, except for the deeply recessed west door, a remnant of the original Norman foundation. Inside, the soaring Gothic architecture is complemented by some of the most glorious 19th- and 20th-century stained glass of any church in Britain, with work by Burne-Jones and Kempe, and a beautiful Great East Window by the renowned stained-glass artist Dr Douglas Strachan (1875–1950).

In the south wall of the chancel is Paisley's greatest surprise, one of the most sublime modern stained-glass

windows in Britain, a tapestry of light and colours, simple and yet dazzling. It is the work of Glasgow-based artist John Clark, and was dedicated in 1988 in memory of James Shaw of the Society of Friends.

In St Mirren's chapel there is a UNIQUE SCULPTURED STONE FRIEZE, depicting episodes from the life of the saint. The name St Mirren lives on in the name of Paisley's football team.

The burial place of Marjorie Bruce, daughter of Robert the Bruce, wife of the 6th High Steward and mother of King Robert II (*see* Renfrew), is marked by an impressive tomb and effigy on the north side of the chancel. Also buried in Paisley Abbey are six High Stewards and the wives of Robert II and Robert III.

Thread Capital

Paisley owes its pre-eminence as a thread-manufacturing centre to a remarkable woman called CHRISTIAN SHAW, born in 1685, the daughter of the Laird of Balgarran, an estate 5 miles (8 km) north of Paisley. At the age of 11, she began having fits, which she blamed on a coven of local witches. She named 21 people, seven of whom were sentenced to death and burned at the stake.

When Christian was 32, her husband, a clergyman named Miller, died leaving her some money, and she decided to go on a tour of northern Europe to study how the Dutch made the best thread in Europe. By careful observation, and by using a touch of industrial espionage, Christian Shaw brought back the secrets of the Dutch trade to Balgarran, where she set up in business, selling high-quality products to her aristocratic friends, who would show them off on their travels to London.

In this way Paisley's fame spread, and by the time mass production of thread came along with new machinery in the 18th century, Paisley was already regarded as THE THREAD-MAKING CAPITAL OF BRITAIN.

The name of Paisley is known across the world for THE PAISLEY SHAWL, a colourful garment woven from wool or silk, once worn by new brides on their first outing after getting married. The famous Paisley pattern was copied from the Hindu and Arabic designs on shawls brought back from Kashmir by Scottish soldiers in the service of the East India Company.

In 1826 James Coats began building a series of huge thread mills by the River Cart. The Clark family followed, and by the time Coats and Clark merged Paisley had become THE BIGGEST COTTON THREAD PRODUCER IN THE WORLD. Around the same time, Paisley was THE FIRST TOWN IN BRITAIN TO ADOPT THE JACQUARD LOOM from France, which enabled intricate patterns to be woven at the same high speed as plain fabrics.

Some of the thread factories are still there, although thread manufacturing ceased in Paisley in 1984. J. & P. Coats has become Coats plc, with headquarters in Middlesex. A wonderful collection of Paisley shawls can be seen in the Paisley Museum, SCOTLAND'S FIRST MUNICIPAL MUSEUM, opened in 1870, the gift of Sir Peter Coats.

Golden Shred

In 1859 JAMES ROBERTSON, a former thread mill worker, opened his own grocery shop in Causeyside Street. One of his first business decisions was to take pity on a travelling salesman from whom he bought a barrel of bitter oranges which then wouldn't sell. Robertson's wife Marion was reluctant to waste the oranges and decided to make them into marmalade.

Marmalade was already being made in Scotland by Keiller's of Dundee (*see* Angus), but Marion Robertson hit upon a recipe that removed some of the bitterness while maintaining the essential flavour of the oranges. She coined the name 'Golden Shred', and the product, initially produced from the back of the grocery shop, was an instant success, with the Robertson's Company being formed in 1864. Today Robertson's Golden Shred is one of the fastest-selling preserves in Britain, and Robertson's one of the biggest preserve makers in the world.

BORN IN PAISLEY

ALEXANDER WILSON (1766–1813), ornithologist, who wrote the first authoritative book on American birds. In 1810 he met and inspired the celebrated author of bird books, Audubon.

KENNETH MCKELLAR, tenor, born in 1927.

FULTON MACKAY (1922–87), actor, best known for his role as the prison warder Mr Mackay in the BBC TV comedy series *Porridge* with Ronnie Barker.

JOHN BYRNE, artist and writer of TV series *Tutti Frutti*, born in 1940.

TOM CONTI, actor, born in 1941.

GERRY RAFFERTY, singer and composer, best known for the hit song 'Baker Street', which featured a haunting saxophone riff and reached No. 3 in the UK charts in 1978. He was born in 1947.

ANDREW NEIL, outspoken newspaper editor and TV political commentator, born in 1949.

DAVID TENNANT, actor, best known as Doctor Who, born in 1971.

DAVID SNEDDON, winner of the inaugural *Fame Academy* in 2002, born in 1978.

The late US President Ronald Reagan's mother's family emigrated to America from Paisley. In 1991, Reagan and his wife Nancy attended a service at the church in Paisley where his Wilson ancestors are buried.

Eaglesham

Sprechen Sie Deutsch?

EAGLESHAM, one of Renfrewshire's most attractive villages, was planned in the 18th century by the Earl of Eglinton. One long V-shaped street leads up the hillside towards the high moors. Wide at the bottom, it narrows towards the top, with meadows, trees and a small stream tumbling down the middle. There are some fine buildings from the period, including the church which sports an eagle atop the spire. Quiet, stolid, the sort of place where nothing much happens. You might think.

Late on the night of 10 May 1941, local ploughman David McClean was minding his own business at home on the farm near Eaglesham, when his ruminations were disturbed by the sound of an aeroplane stuttering overhead. It coughed and died, there was a moment of chilling silence, then a crump. McClean rushed outside to investigate. He heard a fluttering sound from above and a shadowy figure floated out of the night sky, landing in a heap on the other side of the field.

McClean didn't hesitate. He took up his pitchfork and ran across to where the intruder was trying to extricate himself from the folds of his parachute. Wincing with pain, the man stood up, dusted himself down, and announced in a guttural German accent, 'I have an important message for the Duke of Hamilton.'

Well, McClean wasn't having any nonsense like that. Pitchfork at the ready, he escorted the fellow back to his cottage and called the Home Guard. While awaiting their arrival, with true Scottish hospitality, he brewed them both a cup of tea.

When the home guard arrived, McClean learned to his astonishment that sitting in his kitchen drinking tea was none other than Adolf Hitler's deputy, RUDOLF HESS.

Quite why Hess had flown 800 miles across the North Sea from Hanover, in a Messerschmitt 110, to crash land in the middle of the night in a bleak Scottish field, no one really knows. It is thought that he was attempting to reach Dungarvel, the Duke of Hamilton's home, a few miles away in Lanarkshire. Hess had met the Duke, then the Marquess of Clydesdale and a fellow flying enthusiast at the 1936 Olympics, and apparently he wanted to broker a peace treaty with the British, prior to Hitler's invasion of Russia, so that Germany would not have to fight on two fronts.

Hitler disowned Hess and claimed he had gone mad, that the mission was a desperate attempt by Hess to ingratiate himself with either the British or his Führer.

Whatever the truth, the events of 10 May 1941 certainly brought the sleepy village of Eaglesham to the attention of the world.

In 1960 Eaglesham became THE FIRST VILLAGE IN SCOTLAND TO BE LISTED AS A PLACE OF SPECIAL ARCHITECTURAL AND HISTORICAL INTEREST.

BORN IN RENFREWSHIRE

WILLIAM WALLACE (1270–1305) was born in ELDERSLIE, a large village to the west of Paisley. There is a huge Wallace Monument at the village centre where the Wallace Day Gathering takes place every year. Nearby is a very old yew, badly damaged by a storm in 2005, under which Wallace is said to have played. A cutting from this legendary tree has been planted outside the new Scottish Parliament building in Edinburgh.

WILLIAM KIDD was born in GREENOCK around 1645, the son of a minister. He emigrated to New York where, as a sea captain, he defended American and English trade routes against the French. In 1695 he received a royal commission to act as a 'privateer', running down pirates in the Indian Ocean.

While he was away, times changed and the authorities began to frown upon the privateers, branding them pirates. When Captain Kidd captured the *Quedah Merchant* and its valuable cargo, he was arrested on his return to Boston and sent for trial in England. He was tried and hanged in 1701, his body left swinging on the gibbet over the Thames as an example to others.

The cargo of the *Quedah Merchant* has never been found. It is thought that Captain Kidd buried it on a lonely Caribbean island, while en route to Boston, possibly Gardiner's Island or Block Island – treasure hunters are still searching for it to this day.

Captain Kidd's story has been embellished and glamorised over the years in tales such as Robert Louis Stevenson's *Treasure Island.* His legend has grown until he has become the epitome of the swashbuckling, sword-fighting buccaneer so beloved of children and Hollywood. Captain Kidd and his crew are indeed the original 'Pirates of the Caribbean'.

JAMES WATT (1736–1819) was born in GREENOCK. Watt's father repaired nautical instruments and constructed the first crane in Greenock, so the young James grew up with a ready interest in complex machinery and gadgetry and 'making things work'. When he was given an early Newcomen steam engine to repair he spotted the inefficiencies of the design and started to think about how he could improve it. The answer, he suddenly realised one day while walking across Glasgow Green (*see* Lanarkshire), was a separate condenser.

After nine years of frustration and financial difficulties Watt went into partnership with the Birmingham businessman Matthew Boulton, and together they were able to build steam engines that powered the Industrial Revolution and changed the world for ever.

Watt's inventions made him a very rich man and he gave back to his birthplace in the form of money to found a scientific library, as an addition to the famous Greenock Library, founded in 1783, THE SECOND OLDEST SUBSCRIPTION LIBRARY IN SCOTLAND, after Kelso.

In 1882 the British Association decided to give his name to the basic unit of electrical power, the watt, and thus his name is commemorated on every light bulb in the world.

Watt is buried alongside Matthew Boulton in Handsworth Church in Birmingham. In Greenock he is remembered with the James Watt College and a cairn in Greenock Cemetery.

WILLIAM COLLINS (1789–1853), publisher, was born in EASTWOOD, on the outskirts of Glasgow. He became a teacher and set up a bookselling and publishing business to produce religious books for his students. HarperCollins, still connected with Glasgow, is now part of Rupert Murdoch's News Corporation media empire.

SIR WILLIAM ARROL (1839–1913), engineer, was born in HOUSTON, near Paisley, the son of a spinner. As an engineer he was responsible for constructing the replacement Tay Railway Bridge, the

Forth Railway Bridge and Tower Bridge in London, as well as Bankside power station, now the Tate Modern. He also built Arrol-Johnston cars (*see* Dumfries).

RICHARD WILSON, actor, was born in Greenock in 1936. He is best known for his role as grumpy pensioner Victor 'I don't believe it!' Meldrew in BBC TV's *One Foot in the Grave.* He was Rector of Glasgow University from 1996 to 1998.

Well, I never knew this ABOUT RENFREWSHIRE

In 1688, in a shed at the end of the pier in GOUROCK, Glasgow merchant and Provost Walter Gibson discovered the fish-curing technique that gave the 'red herring', or kipper, to the world. The expression 'red herring', meaning a diversion from the basic issue, comes from the practice of drawing a strong-smelling smoked or 'red' herring across the path of a hunted animal to confuse the scent for the pursuing dogs.

JAMES 'PARAFFIN' YOUNG (1811–83), the chemist who founded the world's oil industry (*see* West Lothian), is buried at INVERKIP.

Early 19th-century ARDGOWAN HOUSE near Inverkip, home of the Shaw-Stewart family, is known as the 'finest country house in Renfrewshire'. It served as a military hospital during both world wars and in 1941 became THE FIRST HOSPITAL IN SCOTLAND TO BE DAMAGED BY GERMAN BOMBS.

The *R34* airship, the first aircraft to fly the Atlantic both ways, in 1919, was built by Beardmores at INCHINNAN, just outside Renfrew.

In the early 1960s the nearby LINWOOD CAR PLANT was THE FIRST CAR FACTORY TO BE OPENED IN SCOTLAND SINCE THE SECOND WORLD WAR. It produced Hillman Imps until 1976, then various Chrysler models until 1979, when Peugeot Citroën bought the plant. SCOTLAND'S LAST CAR PLANT, it closed in 1981. Before 1914 there were over 40 car manufacturers in Scotland.

Ross and Cromarty

County Town: Dingwall

Ros and *crom bahd* – 'moor' and 'bay with crooked coastline' (Celtic)

The Tolbooth in Tain, Scotland's Oldest Royal Burgh

Dingwall

Macbeth's Birthplace

DINGWALL, in Norse, means 'meeting place' or 'place of the parliament' and Dingwall was indeed, for many years, on the frontier of Norse-held northern Scotland and the Scottish south. Macbeth was born in Dingwall Castle in 1010. At the beginning of the 13th century, Scottish kings finally gained permanent control of Dingwall and it was made a royal burgh in 1226 by Alexander II.

In the 13th century, Dingwall Castle became the main stronghold of the Earls of Ross. In 1475, in retaliation for the Earl making a secret treaty with Edward IV of England, James III confiscated the Earldom and conferred the title on to the second son of the monarch.

In 1843 Dingwall was recognised as the county town of Ross and Cromarty.

In the churchyard of St Clement in Dingwall there is an obelisk erected by George Mackenzie, 1st Earl of Cromartie, who died in 1714. He is actually buried somewhere to the south of the monument in order to frustrate his wife, who had been much looking forward to 'dancing on his grave'.

The DINGWALL CANAL, designed in 1817 by Thomas Telford, is BRITAIN'S NORTHERNMOST CANAL. It fell into disuse with the arrival of the railway but is slowly being restored for leisure use.

High above Dingwall, on a hill to the south, is THE NATIONAL MEMORIAL, a 100 ft (30 m) high tower erected in 1907 to the memory of local hero Major-General Sir Hector Macdonald (1853–1903), known as 'Fighting Mac'. He was born the son of a crofter at Muir of Allangrange on the Black Isle and joined the Gordon Highlanders at the age of 17. Macdonald was one of the few ordinary soldiers of his era to rise from the rank of private to commanding officer of a Highland Brigade, at a time when commissions were the prerogative of wealth or connections. He served with honour in India, Afghanistan, the Sudan, South Africa and Ceylon and in 1901 was knighted by Edward VII. In 1903, some high-ranking officers, embittered at having been passed over for command by a man from such humble beginnings, raised false allegations of homosexuality against Macdonald and leaked them to the newspapers. Macdonald, fearful of bringing disgrace down on his family, took his own life in a Paris hotel. Embarrassed by the scandal, his family tried to have Macdonald buried in secret at Edinburgh's Dean Cemetery, but in Scotland 'Fighting Mac' was a hero and some 30,000 people turned out to pay their respects.

It is Major-General Sir Hector Macdonald who appears on the Camp Coffee label. Camp Coffee is made at Paisley in Renfrewshire, and was created in 1885 for Gordon Highlanders serving in India, who wanted a drink that they could brew quickly and easily on their campfires.

Cromarty

'The jewel in the crown of Scotland's vernacular architecture'

CROMARTY sits at the tip of the Black Isle and is an almost perfect small 18th-century burgh. A walk along Church Street is like walking through a film set, one sublime house after another until you come to Cromarty's *pièce de résistance*, the East Church, 'one of the finest post-Reformation churches in Scotland' and the subject in 2006 of a BBC Television *Restoration* programme. The church is 17th century but the interior was remodelled on a T plan in 1739 with wooden lofts or galleries and a central pulpit. It is exquisite.

Inside the church there is a commemorative plaque to Sir Thomas Urquhart of Cromarty (1611–60), a renowned eccentric who composed an extraordinary book on mathematics. He also penned the story of his ancestry back to Adam and Eve, and a work entitled *Logopandecteision*, in which he proposed the introduction of a universal language. In 1652 he wrote THE FIRST SCOTTISH NOVEL, called *Ekskybalauron, or The Discoverie of a most Exquisite Jewel*, based on the life of James 'the Admirable' Crichton (*see* Perthshire). He was best known for his bawdy translations of the comic works of the 16th-century French novelist François Rabelais. He died in 1660, laughing uncontrollably at the news of Charles II's restoration to the throne.

In 1760 George Ross acquired Cromarty and set about rebuilding it in the style of the period, creating the town we see today. He was responsible for the harbour, the brewery, the splendid Court House and handsome Cromarty House as well as a rope works opened in the 1760s, one of the first factories in Scotland.

Cromarty's most famous son was HUGH MILLER (1802–56), who began his working life as a stonemason and taught himself all about geology. He gathered and studied fossils from all over Scotland and wrote eloquently about the history of the earth. His collection of over 6,000 fossils formed the core of the Royal Scottish Museum's display. Miller was a staunch evangelical Christian and edited *The Witness*, the newspaper of the Free Church of Scotland, THE SECOND BIGGEST NEWSPAPER IN THE COUNTRY. He was a heated opponent of the emerging theories of evolution, and his struggle to reconcile his religious beliefs with his scientific discoveries caused bouts of depression. During one of these bouts he took his own life.

Hugh Miller's birthplace in Church Street, now in the care of the National Trust for Scotland, is THE ONLY THATCHED HOUSE IN CROMARTY. It was built with Spanish gold, in 1711, by one John Fiddes, who went off to be a buccaneer on the Spanish Main, after being rejected by a local girl, Jean Gallie. When he returned, dripping with doubloons, Jean had been widowed and so they married and lived happily ever after in the long, low cottage that John constructed for them. Hugh Miller later complained that Fiddes, dressed in his buccaneering blue greatcoat, still haunted the place fifty years after his death.

Like so much of Scotland's east coast, Cromarty Firth has benefited from North Sea oil. In 1972, a construction and repair yard for drilling platforms opened at Nigg, across the mouth of the Firth from Cromarty, with, at the time, THE LARGEST DRY DOCK IN THE WORLD.

Today SCOTLAND'S SMALLEST CAR FERRY carries just two vehicles at a time between Cromarty and Nigg across the mouth of the Firth. The ferry uses a rare turntable system which can come as a surprise to those who have not experienced it before. The startled look on the faces of unsuspecting drivers, when their horizon suddenly spins around and they find themselves staring back at where they have just come from, provides hours of innocent amusement for the ferryman.

Chanonry Point

Dolphin Watch

CHANONRY POINT on the Black Isle is THE BEST PLACE IN BRITAIN TO SEE DOLPHINS. It is situated at the end of a spit of land that extends for over a mile out into the Moray Firth, home for over one hundred years to THE MOST NORTHERLY DOLPHIN POPULATION IN THE WORLD. The mouth of the Firth is so narrow here that the dolphins have to swim close to the shore and it is possible at high tide to see them fishing and playing at remarkably close quarters. To watch these graceful, intelligent creatures performing and joyously showing off, somersaulting and leaping about in the waves, is one of Scotland's most magical and unforgettable treats.

Scotland's Nostradamus

A stone memorial at Chanonry Point marks the spot where the BRAHAN SEER was put to death by his patron, the Countess of Seaforth, in the 17th century. Kevin Mackenzie, the Brahan Seer, was a labourer on the Earl of Seaforth's Brahan estate and amongst other things he foretold was the Battle of Culloden: *'Oh! Drumossie, thy bleak moor shall, ere many generations have passed away, be stained with the best blood of the Highlands. Glad am I that I will not see the day.'*

He also predicted North Sea oil – '*black rain that will bring riches to Aberdeen*' – and the fact that Scotland would have its own Parliament again when *'men could walk dry shod from England to France'*. Well, the Channel Tunnel has made possible the latter, and the first Scottish Parliament since 1707 opened for business in 1999.

There was one thing that he did not foresee. Questioned by the Countess of Seaforth about why her husband had not come home from Paris, the Brahan Seer at first feigned ignorance, but when she insisted, he confessed that the Earl was in fact gambolling there with a woman far more beautiful than she. Well, no woman wishes to hear something like that, so quite naturally the Countess had the wretched man tossed into a burning barrel of tar, but not before he had predicted the extinction of the Seaforth line, when the last Earl would see all his sons die before him. Sure enough, that is what happened. In 1815, the last Lord Seaforth died having outlived his four sons and the title became extinct. The estates passed to his sister, widow of the great Admiral Sir Samuel Hood. Brahan Castle is today a ruin.

Eilean Donan

A Symbol of Scotland

When people throughout the world think of the Scottish Highlands they picture romantic EILEAN DONAN, perched on a small island at the mouth of Loch Duich near Kyle of Lochalsh. It is the most photographed castle in Scotland, everything an ancient Highland fortress should be. Yet less than one hundred years ago it was a pile of rubble, having been blown to smithereens by Royal Navy warships during the Jacobite uprising of 1719, when it housed a Spanish garrison supporting the Old Pretender.

Home of the MacRaes, Eilean Donan was restored at vast cost by

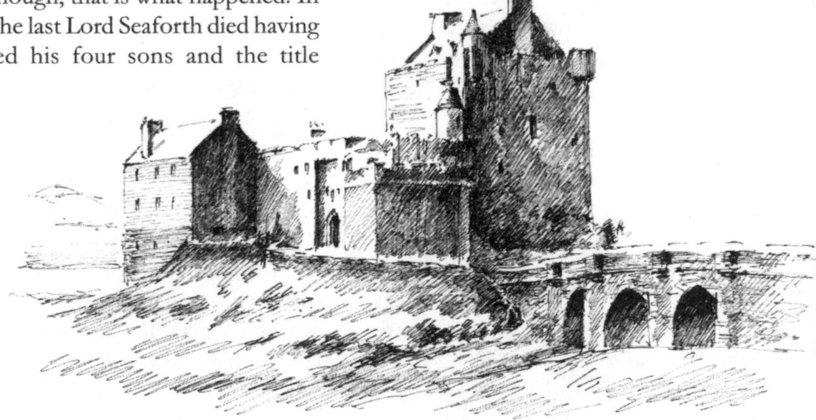

Lieutenant-Colonel John MacRae Gilstrap between 1920 and 1932. Since then it has appeared many times on the silver screen, most notably in the 1986 film *Highlander* and as MI6 northern headquarters in the 1999 James Bond adventure *The World is Not Enough*.

Well, I never knew this ABOUT ROSS AND CROMARTY

The airfield at RAF Evanton closed in 1947 but during the 1960s it was used as THE MOST NORTHERLY MOTOR RACING CIRCUIT IN BRITAIN.

PETER FRASER (1884–1950), New Zealand's longest-serving Labour Prime Minister (1940–49), was born in FEARNS, near Tain.

TAIN is SCOTLAND'S OLDEST ROYAL BURGH, with a charter dating from 1066. The Glenmorangie Distillery can be found northwest of the town.

At 135 ft (41 m) high, the lighthouse at TARBAT NESS is THE THIRD HIGHEST LIGHTHOUSE IN SCOTLAND, after Ronaldsay and Skerryvore. It was built by Robert Stevenson in 1830.

THE BLACK ISLE is so called because it is so rarely whitened by snow.

BALNAGOWAN CASTLE, on the shores of Cromarty Firth near Alness, is an ancient seat of the Ross family. Parts of the castle date from the 14th century, but most of what we see today is 18th and 19th century. In 1972 Balnagowan was bought for £60,000 by MOHAMED AL FAYED, the owner of Harrods.

The FALLS OF GLOMACH, or 'Gloomy Falls', at 375 ft (114 m) are twice as high as Niagara Falls and THE SECOND HIGHEST FALLS IN BRITAIN. The Allt a' Ghlomaich or 'Chasm' river is fed by three small lochs and falls some 500 ft (152 m) into the River Elchaig through a deep gorge. The drop is broken by a buttress half way down, but the water is airborne for 220 ft (67 m) at the main falls, THE GREATEST SINGLE DROP OF ANY WATERFALL IN BRITAIN. The spectacle is breathtaking and the noise, as the water tumbles down through such a narrow, confined space, is awesome. The falls are reached by a five- or six-hour round walk through wild and lonely terrain, from the car park at Dorusduain off the A87 near Shiel Bridge.

Washed by the Gulf Stream and tucked away beside an inlet of Loch Carron, PLOCKTON has an idyllic Mediterranean feel, with palm trees and gaily painted houses set behind lush gardens. Between 1995 and 1997 Plockton became the fictional Highland village of Loch Dubh, the new beat of laid-back policeman Hamish Macbeth, transferred here from the mean streets of Glasgow, in the BBC television series of that name starring Robert Carlyle.

In 1942 scientists from the Ministry of Defence laboratory at Porton Down detonated six 'anthrax' bombs on a small deserted island in beautiful GRUINARD BAY to see what happened to the unfortunate flock of sheep they had been placed there. The sheep all died within days and the island was quarantined until 1987, when a new team of scientists went in to clean the island up. Gruinard has now been pronounced free of contamination.

The BEALACH NA BA, or 'Pass of the Cattle', over the Applecross Mountains attains a height of 2,053 ft (626 m), and is THE THIRD HIGHEST ROAD IN BRITAIN. The single-track road has 5 miles (8 km) of zigzag corners, dizzying drops and 1 in 4 gradients, and is the only road in Scotland to have a warning sign at the bottom to deter learner drivers. The views from the summit, particularly towards the Cullins of Skye, are matchless.

BEINN EIGHE NATIONAL NATURE RESERVE, covering 10,500 acres (4,250 ha) of Wester Ross, was established in 1951 as BRITAIN'S FIRST NATURE RESERVE.

STRATHPEFFER is BRITAIN'S MOST NORTHERLY SPA.

ROXBURGHSHIRE

COUNTY TOWN: JEDBURGH

Hroc's burgh – Hroc's castle (Old English)

Melrose Abbey, the first Cistercian house in Scotland and the loveliest of the Border abbeys

Jedburgh

'Would That I Had Died in Jedburgh . . .'

JEDBURGH, pronounced 'Jeddart', is the county town of Roxburghshire and stands plumb in the middle of the county. In medieval times the Borders Justiciary Court sat here and dispensed a rather summary kind of justice known as 'Jeddart Justice', which involved hanging the miscreant first and trying him later. In defence of their town the people of Jedburgh would wield the fearsome 'Jeddart staff', a long pole tipped with a metal hook or axe head, and then play with the severed English heads in a type of ball game known as 'Jeddart hand-ba''. The game is still played on Shrove Tuesday, but because of a shortage of severed heads they now play with footballs.

The long rows of socketless windows and arches that make up JEDBURGH

ABBEY loom above the town like some sort of mighty guard dog. The abbey was founded in 1138 by David I, sacked at least nine times by the English, and each time was painstakingly restored by the monks, at least until the last occasion. Although roofless, the abbey is the most complete of the Border churches and remains an impressive structure, the finest example of the Romanesque in this part of Scotland.

In 1409, Jedburgh Castle held out as the last English stronghold in Scotland and was eventually demolished on the orders of the Scottish Parliament.

The pretty, turreted MARY, QUEEN OF SCOTS HOUSE is where the tragic Queen stayed for five weeks in 1566. While she was here she learned that her lover, the 4th Earl of Bothwell, had been injured in a skirmish and she rode over to Hermitage Castle to see him, returning on the same day, a total distance of some 40 miles (64 km) across wild and dangerous country. In doing so she fell from her horse, caught a fever and nearly died. In later life, when a prisoner of Elizabeth I in England, she reflected ruefully, 'Would that I had died in Jedburgh . . .'

SIR DAVID BREWSTER (1781–1868), INVENTOR OF THE KALEIDOSCOPE, was born in Jedburgh, as was Conservative MP MICHAEL ANCRAM, in 1945.

Kelso

'The most romantic, if not the most beautiful place in Scotland'

SIR WALTER SCOTT

Founded in 1128, KELSO ABBEY was the first, the biggest and the wealthiest of all David I's Border abbeys and, for many years, the Abbots of Kelso held the honour of precedence in the Scottish hierarchy. Now in the care of Historic Scotland, the abbey ruins stand not far from Kelso's elegant, cobbled centre, THE LARGEST MARKET SQUARE IN SCOTLAND.

Built in 1803, Kelso's handsome bridge across the River Tweed was John Rennie's first major bridge, and the prototype for his Waterloo Bridge in London. It is here that the Teviot and the Tweed rivers converge and form a deep pool known as the JUNCTION POOL, which provides some of the best salmon fishing in Scotland.

In 1770 SCOTLAND'S FIRST PUBLIC DISPENSARY opened in Kelso, and in the 19th century a fishmonger's shop in

Kelso became THE FIRST BUILDING IN SCOTLAND TO BE LIT WITH GAS.

Just outside Kelso, to the west, a few grassy mounds indicate the site of the royal burgh of Roxburgh, once the fourth most important burgh in Scotland. In the 12th century, Roxburgh Castle was the chosen seat of King David I, and if Roxburgh had not had the misfortune to lie on the front line in the various Border wars with England, it could well have become the Scottish capital. Alexander III was born there in 1241, and thereafter the castle changed hands numerous times. In 1460, after the castle had been occupied by the English for 100 years, James II made a determined effort to win it back. The Scottish king did win the castle back, but at the expense of his own life, when a cannon exploded and blew off his leg, causing him to bleed to death. The spot where he fell is now marked by a holly tree. The Scots then completely dismantled the castle, and the community that had grown up around it slowly withered away, until not a trace remained. The small village of 'New' Roxburgh, some 3 miles (5 km) to the south, begun as an overflow for 'Old' Roxburgh, has retained the name.

The paltry remains of Roxburgh lie in the spreading grounds of FLOORS CASTLE, seat of the Duke of Roxburgh and THE LARGEST INHABITED CASTLE IN SCOTLAND.

The castle consists of a 17th-century tower house that was enlarged in 1721 by William Adam and then added to by William Playfair from 1838 to 1849. Floors Castle stood in for Greystoke Castle in the 1984 film *Greystoke, the Legend of Tarzan Lord of the Apes*, directed by Hugh Hudson and starring Christopher Lambert as Tarzan and Sir Ralph Richardson as Lord Greystoke. The real Greystoke Castle is in Cumberland but was not deemed suitable for filming.

Abbotsford

A Scottish Treasure House

ABBOTSFORD HOUSE, 2 miles (3.2 km) west of Melrose, is a very personal expression of SIR WALTER SCOTT's life, the 'greatest historical novel he has left for posterity', and a veritable treasure-house of Scottish heritage and artefacts. Incorporated into the house are a door from Edinburgh's Tolbooth and carved oak panels from Dunfermline's Old Kirk, while the main entrance is modelled on a porch from Linlithglow Palace and the entrance hall is floored with black and white marble from the Hebrides. For his armoury, Scott assembled Rob Roy's broadsword, a pocket book made by Flora Macdonald, a crucifix belonging to Mary, Queen of Scots, the keys to Loch Leven Castle, a glass engraved by Robert Burns and that essential possession of every self-respecting house in Scotland, a lock of Bonnie Prince Charlie's hair.

Perhaps the most intriguing room is the library, where Scott's unsurpassed collection of 20,000 Scottish books is housed beneath a carved cedar-wood roof copied from that of Rosslyn Chapel. This last has brought fans of *The Da Vinci Code* flocking to Abbotsford, convinced that Scott must have somehow uncovered the secret of the Holy Grail, in much the same way that he tracked down the Honours of Scotland (*see* Kincardineshire).

Abbotsford has been open for the public to explore since about 1840, one of Scotland's first tourist attractions. It remains almost unchanged since Scott lived there, and the highlight of any visit is the cosy, intimate and wonderfully evocative study where he wrote the *Waverley* novels.

Scott bought the ramshackle farm of Clartyhole, or 'dirty hollow', on the banks of the Tweed, in 1811, and the first thing he did was to change the name to Abbotsford, after the nearby river crossing used by the abbots of Melrose, centuries before. For the next 12 years he proceeded to buy up as much of the surrounding land as he could afford, extending the 100 acre (40 ha) estate tenfold, and transforming the farmhouse into his grand baronial 'conundrum castle', all paid for out of the royalties from his hugely successful books. Two years after he had completed the house, his publishers Archibald Constable & Co. and his printers James Ballantyne & Co. went bust, and as Scott was part-owner of each he nobly dedicated the rest of his life to writing ceaselessly to pay off the debts. The effort exhausted him and he died in the dining-room at Abbotsford, overlooking his beloved Tweed, one autumn day in 1832.

Walter Scott was born in Edinburgh in 1771. He suffered from polio as a boy and spent much of his youth recuperating at his grandfather's home near Kelso. It was during this time that he explored and came to love the countryside and legends of the Borders. He is best remembered as a champion of Scotland, who promoted Scotland's history and created the romantic image of a wild and beautiful land filled with heroic clans and ancient kingdoms. His orchestration of the visit of George IV in 1822 helped to reintroduce much of the Highland culture that had been stamped out after the Jacobite uprisings of 1715 and 1745, and established tartan as the national dress. His greatest novels were written before he fell into debt and included such titles as *Waverley* (1814), *Rob Roy* (1818), *The Heart of Midlothian* (1818) and *Ivanhoe* (1819). He was married in 1797 to Charlotte Charpentier, a French *émigrée*, and they had four children. He was created a Baronet in 1820 and died in 1832.

Melrose

'If thou wouldst view fair Melrose aright,
Go visit it by the pale moonlight'

SIR WALTER SCOTT,
'THE LAY OF THE MINSTREL'

MELROSE sits in the shadow of the Eildon Hills whose three distinctive peaks made such an impression on Sir Walter Scott. Legend tells us that King Arthur sleeps beneath the tallest hill and will ride forth with his knights when Britain is threatened.

Warm, pink Melrose Abbey, THE FIRST CISTERCIAN HOUSE IN SCOTLAND, was founded by David I in 1136. It is considered to be the loveliest of the Border abbeys with rich carvings on the southern walls and two magnificent windows, the great east window and the window in the north transept with its magnificent crown of thorns. The tracery is beautiful beyond description, delicate and light yet strong enough to survive the years. In the chapter house are the remains of a tiled floor, one of only two in Scotland, the other being at Glenluce in Wigtownshire.

Most thrilling of all, beneath the floor at Melrose, a lead casket was found containing the heart of Robert the Bruce, returned here after its abortive journey to the Holy Land. Melrose was Bruce's favourite abbey, and in 1322 he granted it £2,000 to help with the rebuilding after it had been destroyed by Edward II. The sum exceeded the entire Scottish Treasury at the time. The casket was uncovered during restoration work and has been reburied with a plaque marking the spot. Alexander II is buried here also.

Well, I never knew this
ABOUT
ROXBURGHSHIRE

A little to the east of Melrose is NEWSTEAD, SCOTLAND'S OLDEST INHABITED VILLAGE, on the site of the Roman fort of Trimontium, set up by Agricola in AD 80. At the end of St John's Wynd, a plaque identifies the location of THE FIRST MASONIC LODGE IN SCOTLAND, established by the masons constructing Melrose Abbey. The Lodge moved into Melrose in 1742.

Buried in the churchyard at LINTON is THOMAS ELLIOT of Clifton Park, who is credited as THE FIRST MAN IN SCOTLAND TO OWN A PRIVATE MOTOR CAR, a Panhard imported from France in 1895.

George Johnston, who designed and made the early Arrol-Johnston cars (*see* Dumfriesshire), also lays claim to this accolade.

There seems to be something in the air of EDNAM, a little village near Kelso. Two musicians of great note were born here, JAMES THOMSON (1700–48), who wrote the words to 'Rule Britannia', and HENRY FRANCIS LYTE (1793–1847) who penned the hymns 'Praise My Soul, the King of Heaven' and 'Abide with Me'. The latter has provided succour and comfort to people everywhere in moments of great hardship – soldiers sang the words in the trenches during the First World War, and Nurse Edith Cavell recited them as she faced execution by the Germans as a spy in 1915.

In the town centre of HAWICK is a statue to JIMMY GUTHRIE, world champion TT rider in the 1930s, born in Hawick in 1897. He was killed while competing in the German Grand Prix in 1937. The life-size bronze statue nearby is of STEVE HISLOP, winner of 11 Isle of Man TT titles and twice British Superbike champion. Born in Hawick in 1962, he died in a helicopter crash in the Teviot valley in 2003.

SIR CHAY BLYTH, who in 1970 became the first person to sail single-handed around the world the wrong way, or against the trade winds, was born in Hawick in 1940.

SELKIRKSHIRE

COUNTY TOWN: SELKIRK

Sele's Kirk – Sele's church (Old English)

Sheriff Courthouse: Selkirk's seat of power

Selkirk

A Story of Three Statues

SELKIRK was the site of the first abbey in the Borders, founded by David I in 1113. However, in 1128, the monks were moved to Kelso 'on account of the inconvenient accommodation . . .' The old county town rises on a series of terraces to over 600 ft (183 m) above the River Ettrick, and from a distance, creates an attractive vista of turrets and spires. Selkirk was once famed for shoe-making and the people of the town are still known as 'souters' or shoe-makers. Down in the valley, along the river-banks, are numerous 19th-century tweed mills, some of which are still active.

The story of Selkirk is told in statues. In Market Square there is a statue of a man called FLETCHER, the sole survivor of the 80 Selkirk 'souters' who marched proudly off to Flodden with James IV in 1513. Fletcher returned alone, waving above his head a blood-stained English banner he had captured in the midst of the slaughter. He flung it down despairingly in the market-place, and the flag now hangs in the small museum in Haliwell's House, THE OLDEST BUILDING IN SELKIRK. Every year, in June, the scene is re-created during the Selkirk Common Riding, when the Selkirk dead of all wars are commemorated by the casting down of embroidered banners in the square while the town band plays the Selkirk lament, 'Flowers of the Forest'.

At the other end of the High Street there is a statue to the African explorer MUNGO PARK (1771–1806), who was born 4 miles (6.4 km) away on his father's farm near the village of Foulshiels. Trained to be a surgeon, he sailed as a doctor with the East India Company to Sumatra, where he caught the exploring bug. In 1795 he was sent by the African Association to map the course of the River Niger. When he returned to Scotland he set up a medical practice in Peebles, but was soon yearning for the big skies of Africa and went back to the Niger in 1895 to search for the source of the river. His statue is holding a scroll inscribed 'Die on the Niger', words from the final letter he sent just before setting off into the unknown: '... though I were myself half dead, I would still persevere; and if I could not succeed in the object of my journey, I would at least die on the Niger.' He did die on the Niger, trapped in the Bussa Rapids in Nigeria, and killed by natives.

Back in Market Square stands a third statue, this one to Sir Walter Scott, who was Sheriff of Selkirkshire from 1799 until his death in 1832. In 1818 Scott unearthed THE SELKIRK SILVER ARROW, which had been placed in a chest for safekeeping in the 17th century, and then forgotten. It was fashioned in 1660 from silver taken off a gypsy and competed for annually by local Borders archers until 1674. When the first stirrings of possible Jacobite troubles were felt, the arrow was hidden away. The winners had attached their medallions to it, and when the arrow was rediscovered by Sir Walter Scott, nine original medallions were found with it.

Scott invited the Royal Company of Archers, the monarch's official bodyguard in Scotland, to come and compete for the arrow against the local archers. It was duly won by a Royal Archer called Charles Nairn, and taken back to the Archers Hall in Edinburgh, where it resides to this day. The silver arrow is still competed for amongst the Royal Company of Archers, but all attempts by Selkirk to have the Selkirk Silver Arrow returned to the town of its origin have so far been rebuffed.

Yarrow

Shepherds, Wizards and Explorers

The brief beauty of the lonely Yarrow Valley, 14 short miles (23 km) from lovely St Mary's Loch to Ettrick Water, has inspired writers and poets for generations. Sir Walter Scott, as ever, sang its praises. At a deep pool near Foulshiels he came across Mungo Park, tossing pebbles into the water and watching the bubbles rise. 'This is how I measure the depth of an African River,' the explorer told him when Scott expressed surprise at this seemingly vacuous exercise.

William Wordsworth came and wrote 'Yarrow Unvisited', 'Yarrow Visited' and 'Yarrow Revisited', but it was Wordsworth's guide, Yarrow's own son JAMES HOGG, 'THE ETTRICK SHEPHERD', who captured its flavour to perfection.

James Hogg was born at Ettrick Hall in 1770 and farmed in the Ettrick Hills for most of his life. He taught himself to read and write and went round collecting the songs and ballads of the Borders, which he played on his fiddle. He also wrote books and poems about the Borders that found great acclaim in Edinburgh and London. His most celebrated work was *The Private Memoirs and Confessions of a Justified Sinner*, published in 1824. Sir Walter Scott was introduced to James Hogg as someone who could furnish him with local material, and the two became great friends. Hogg acted as the local guide and provided Scott with tales and folklore, while Scott helped and encouraged the Ettrick Shepherd to have more of his own work published. In 1832, Hogg was offered a knighthood by George IV but declined. He died in 1835 and is buried in Ettrick churchyard, a few hundred yards from the site of the cottage where he was born. A statue to him stands beside St Mary's Loch.

There is an exhibition on James Hogg in an outhouse at Bowhill and another one at AIKWOOD TOWER, a 16th-century peel tower near Ettrickbridge, once owned by the Scott family, now lived in by Sir David Steel, the former leader of the Liberal Party. Aikwood was at one time thought to have been the home of the 'wizard' MICHAEL SCOTT, who is possibly, according to Sir Walter Scott, buried in Melrose Abbey. Michael Scott was a 13th-century intellectual, lawyer, mathematician and student of theology, whose study of arcane books and manuscripts had him labelled as a wizard. Revered for his learning throughout Europe, his advice was sought by the Holy Roman Emperor Frederick II and the Pope. He was said to possess the gift of prophecy and foresaw his own death: that he would be felled by a pebble falling on his head. Just in case, he made himself a metal helmet for protection, but removed it while attending mass, and sure enough a pebble did indeed drop from the church ceiling and struck him on the head. He died shortly afterwards.

James Hogg and Sir Walter Scott would frequent TIBBIE SHIELS INN, which sits on a narrow spit of land between St Mary's Loch and the smaller Loch of the Lowes, at the head of the Yarrow valley. Tibbie Shiels was a widow called Isabella Shiels who supported herself and her six children by taking in paying lodgers. The inn became something of a cultural and

intellectual haunt visited by, amongst others, Thomas Carlyle, Robert Louis Stevenson and William Gladstone. The inn is still in existence and a popular watering-hole for travellers on the Upland Way which runs nearby.

Bowhill

'When summer smiled on Sweet Bowhill, and July's eve with balmy breath, waved the bluebells on Newark Heath . . .'
SIR WALTER SCOTT

The early 19th-century pile of BOWHILL on the River Yarrow, 3 miles (5 km) west of Selkirk, is the principal Border home of the great Scott dynasty of Buccleuch, distant cousins of Sir Walter Scott, who was a frequent visitor. The old Victorian Game Larder has been converted into the intimate 72-seat BOWHILL LITTLE THEATRE, which puts on a full programme of drama and music throughout the year.

Two miles (3.2. km) up river on the Bowhill estate, set on the crest of a low hill, is the ruined NEWARK CASTLE, once a hunting lodge. From the 12th century, the Scotts acted as rangers in the surrounding Ettrick Forest, and would accompany the various Scottish monarchs who came here to take advantagc of the fine hunting grounds. On one such occasion, a young ranger Scott grappled with a cornered stag that was threatening the King's life, seizing it by the antlers and tossing it over his shoulder. From this act of courage came the name 'Buck-Cleuch' or Buccleuch.

Galashiels

Sour Plums

GALASHIELS is an ancient industrial town famed for its tweed and woollen mills, the earliest of which was founded as far back as 1588. By 1890 there were 21 mills in the town, of which only a handful are still in operation. The word 'tweed' is not derived from the River Tweed but from a clerical error by an English clerk, who misspelt the Scots word 'tweels', meaning woollen fabrics.

Galashiels is the largest of the two Selkirkshire towns. The town motto, 'Soor Plums', dates back to 1337 when the townsfolk surprised a party of English soldiers searching for wild plums in the local woods, and killed the lot of them.

In 1503, in front of the old Mercat Cross, Henry VII's daughter Margaret Tudor of England was betrothed to James IV of Scotland, a marriage which led to the Union of Crowns in 1603.

The town's War Memorial, described by H.V. Morton as 'the most perfect town memorial in the British Isles', commemorates the 635 men from Galashiels killed in the First World War, out of a population of 14,500.

Well, I never knew this ABOUT SELKIRKSHIRE

As Sheriff of Selkirkshire, Walter Scott was required to spend at least four months each year in the area, and from 1804 he lived at his cousin's home ASHIESTIEL, 'a decent farm house overhanging the Tweed' some 7 miles (11 km) north of Selkirk. This was his first home in his beloved Borders, and he spent eight happy years here, writing *The Lay of the Last Minstrel*, *Marmion* and *The Lady of the Lake*, as well as the abortive first draft of *Waverley*. When his lease ran out in 1811, Scott and his family moved to a small farm near Melrose which became Abbotsford (*see* Roxburghshire).

Off the market-place in Selkirk is the shop where ROBBIE DOUGLAS, a baker in Victorian days, invented SELKIRK BANNOCK, a round fruit loaf made from local butter and sultanas imported specially from Turkey. Douglas would only bake when exactly the right ingredients were available, a policy that paid off in 1867 when Queen Victoria was visiting the town and selected his Selkirk bannock from amongst all the proffered delicacies.

Until 2006, Waverley Mill in Galashiels was home to Lochcarron of Scotland, THE LARGEST PRODUCER OF TARTAN IN THE WORLD. Lochcarron, who are the exclusive manufacturers of the Diana, Princess of Wales Memorial Tartan, have now moved to new premises in Selkirk.

At 2,756 ft (840 m), BROAD LAW is THE HIGHEST MOUNTAIN IN THE BORDERS and THE SECOND HIGHEST MOUNTAIN IN SOUTHERN SCOTLAND, after the Merrick in Kirkcudbrightshire.

SHETLAND

COUNTY TOWN: LERWICK

Hjaltland – 'High land' (Norse)

Shetland Pony

Lerwick

Britain's Northernmost Capital

LERWICK, the capital of Shetland, is THE MOST NORTHERLY TOWN IN BRITAIN and sits in the middle of Shetland's largest island, Mainland. The only town on Shetland, it has a population of 7,500. Lerwick was first developed by the Dutch to service their fishing fleet in the 17th century. The town has boomed since the discovery of North Sea oil in the 1970s and there are many new houses, but the picturesque old fishing town by the harbour is unspoiled and packed with restaurants and shops, while the sea front throngs with a colourful mixture of pleasure craft and fishing boats.

Held every year on the last Tuesday in

January, Lerwick's main festival is 'Up Helly Aa', based on a pagan Norse ritual marking the end of the dark days of winter. A Viking longboat is paraded through the streets escorted by men in Viking costume carrying torches. The boat is then ceremoniously burned, before everyone retires to the pubs and bars to celebrate.

A little to the north of Lerwick is Bod of Gremista, an 18th-century fishing booth that was the birthplace in 1792 of Arthur Anderson, the co-founder of P&O ferries. In 1844, P&O inaugurated THE WORLD'S FIRST PLEASURE CRUISE, giving a free passage to the writer William Makepeace Thackeray, in return for favourable publicity.

Scalloway

Former Capital

While they are only 7 miles (11 km) apart, Scalloway and Lerwick sit on different seas, Lerwick on the North Sea and Scalloway on the Atlantic Ocean. A few miles to the north, at Mavis Grind, an isthmus just 150 ft (46 m) wide separates the two seas.

Until 1708 Scalloway was the capital of Shetland. It is still dominated by SCALLOWAY CASTLE, built in 1600 by the despotic Earl Patrick Stewart, using forced labour and mortar mixed with blood. Earl Patrick, whose father was an illegitimate son of James V, is still reviled in Shetland memory for his brutality in imposing Scottish feudal law on the islands. He was hanged in 1615 for trying to expand his power in the islands at the expense of the King – his execution had to be delayed while he was taught the Lord's Prayer.

When Lerwick became the capital, Scalloway Castle was allowed to fall into disrepair. Although partially restored over the last century, the castle is now marooned amongst modern harbour developments and storage towers and appears rather melancholy, but there is plenty to explore and there are fine views from the upper levels. The castle key can be obtained from the nearby Shetland Woollen Company shop.

In Norse days, the 'Ting', or annual parliament, of Shetland was held on the Lawting Holm, a small promontory jutting out into Loch Tingwall, 2 miles (3.2 km) to the north of Scalloway. Nearby is TINGWALL KIRK, the 'Mother Church' of Shetland, built in 1790 on the site of the Church of St Magnus; it is the seat of the Archdeacon of Tingwall, Shetland's senior church official. The

prehistoric standing stone off the road between Tingwall and Scalloway is known as THE MURDER STONE – murderers were made to run to it from Lawting Holm, pursued by relatives of the person they had murdered. If the murderer reached the stone alive, he was allowed to live.

During the Second World War, Scalloway was the main base for 'THE SHETLAND BUS', a fleet of small boats operated by Norwegian Resistance and Britain's Special Operations Executive to ferry agents and supplies secretly to and from Nazi-occupied Norway. The operation was run from an isolated farmhouse called Flemington, further north on Mainland. The full story of this heroic outfit is told in the Scalloway Museum in Main Street.

Up t' North – Unst

Northern Highlights

UNST IS THE NORTHERNMOST ISLAND OF THE BRITISH ISLES. There is no more land between Unst and the North Pole.

OUTER STACK on Muckle Flugga is THE MOST NORTHERLY POINT IN THE WHOLE OF BRITAIN. It lies 170 miles (274 km) north of John o' Groats and only 400 miles (644 km) from the Arctic Circle. The lighthouse here is BRITAIN'S MOST NORTHERLY LIGHTHOUSE and was built in 1858 by Thomas Stevenson, father of the writer Robert Louis Stevenson, whose novel *Treasure Island* was inspired by a visit to Unst in 1869. The map of Treasure Island is remarkably similar to the map of Unst.

HERMA NESS on Unst is THE MOST NORTHERLY POINT OF BRITAIN THAT CAN BE REACHED ON FOOT.

The Methodist church at HAROLDSWICK, completed in 1993, is THE MOST NORTHERLY CHURCH IN BRITAIN. From here a track leads to the dunes of Norwick beach and then on to BRITAIN'S MOST NORTHERLY HOUSE, at Skaw.

BURRAFIRTH has BRITAIN'S MOST NORTHERLY GOLF COURSE – as opposed to THE MOST NORTHERLY GOLF CLUB, which is on Whalsay.

BRITAIN'S MOST NORTHERLY POST OFFICE is in the Unst village of BALTASOUND.

MUNESS CASTLE, a fortified tower house dating from 1598 on the southeast tip of Unst, is THE MOST NORTHERLY CASTLE IN BRITAIN.

Whalsay

Georgian Finery

WHALSAY is home to the finest Georgian house in Shetland, Symbister House, which sits on a hill overlooking the harbour. It was built of granite blocks in 1823 by the 6th Robert Bruce of Symbister and boasted courtyards, stables, a mill, a doocot, a farmhouse and, most impressive of all, a high-rise, three-seat outside lavatory. All this cost Bruce £30,000 and eventually bankrupted him. The last laird died in 1944, and since then Symbister House has been used as a school.

Throughout the 1930s 'Hugh MacDiarmid', the firebrand communist poet Christopher Grieve, lived on Whalsay, in a croft house called Sodom (from the Norse 'sud-heim', or 'southern house'). From here he kept up a lively correspondence with writers, thinkers and columnists of the day until called up to fight in 1942.

Fair Isle

FAIR ISLE, 33 miles (53 km) from the southern tip of Shetland, and 27 miles (43 km) from the northern tip of Orkney, is THE MOST ISOLATED SETTLEMENT IN BRITAIN.

On 20 August 1588, *El Gran Grifon*, the flagship of the Duke of Medina, Admiral of the Spanish Armada, was shipwrecked on the rocks of a cove on the east coast of Fair Isle. The Duke and 200 of his men had to spend a miserable two months on the island as unwelcome guests, although there is some suggestion that the intricate patterns for which Fair Isle knitted garments are known were introduced by the Spanish sailors.

Fair Isle is famous for its hand-knit sweaters made from fine yarns, stranded into a double layer, which produce a warm, durable but lightweight garment. Fair Isle sweaters have been much imitated around the world, but the only source of the genuine article is Fair Isle itself, where a small co-operative called Fair Isle Crafts makes the traditional sweater using hand-frame machines, labelled with Fair Isle's own trademark. In 2004 Fair Isle was granted the status of a Fairtrade island.

In 1954 Fair Isle was bought by the National Trust for Scotland from George Waterson, former Scottish Director of the Royal Society for the Protection of Birds, who had purchased the island after the Second World War and founded a bird observatory there.

Mousa

'Brochs' are Iron Age stone towers of a type found only in Scotland. There are 500 or so scattered across the country, and the wonderful broch on MOUSA, an uninhabited island off the east coast of Mainland at Sandwick, is the best preserved broch in Scotland. It is thought that brochs were used, rather like medieval church towers, as places of refuge, as lookout towers and as places for safe storage. The Mousa broch was built around 1 BC, and the remains are 40 ft (12m) high, with walls 12 ft (3.6m) thick. Alcoves are cut into the walls, probably for storage, and a stone staircase winds up between the walls to a parapet at the top of the broch, from where you can look down into the interior or out across the island. You can get to Mousa by ferry from Sandwick.

Jarlshof

Right on the southern tip of Shetland near Sumburgh is one of the most exciting and informative archaeological sites in Europe. JARLSHOF was discovered in the late 19th century when a storm washed away part of the cliff and revealed the layers of ancient structures that had been hidden away underneath. What is so remarkable about Jarlshof is that there are fine examples of every type of dwelling over a period of 4,000 years, from the Stone Age until the end of the 17th century. There are walls and hearths from the Stone Age and the Bronze Age, underground chambers and a broch from the Iron Age, four Pictish wheel houses from AD 400 to 500, a Norse village from the 12th century, a medieval farmhouse and, finally, the Old House of Sumburgh built by the ruling Stewart family in 1604 and abandoned at the end of the 1600s.

Well, I never knew this ABOUT SHETLAND

Shetland lies 110 miles (177 km) northeast of mainland Scotland. The capital, Lerwick, is further north than Moscow and on the same latitude as St Petersburg, Cape Farewell in Greenland, and Anchorage in Alaska. It lies closer to Bergen in Norway than to Edinburgh. and is as far from London as is Milan.

Shetland was Norse until 1468, when the islands were mortgaged to Scotland as part of the dowry of Princess Margrethe of Denmark, betrothed to the future James III. When Margrethe's father, Christian I, could not pay the balance, the lands were annexed to the Scottish crown.

There are over 100 islands in Shetland, but only 15 that are inhabited. Shetland has a population of 22,000 – half of whom live within 10 miles (16 km) of Lerwick.

The area of Shetland is 553 square miles (1,433 sq km), but the total length of the archipelago is 70 miles (113 km), the same distance as from Edinburgh to Aberdeen. Shetland has 900 miles (1,450 km) of coastline and nowhere is further than 3 miles (5 km) from the sea.

Shetland's highest point is RONAS HILL, near the northern tip of Mainland, which is 1,475 ft (450 m) high. A rare combination of Arctic and Alpine plants grow near the top and there is a prehistoric chambered burial cairn at the summit.

Shetland used to be, and sometime still is, called ZETLAND, which is the old Norse version of the name. There is still a Marquess of Zetland.

In November 1939, THE FIRST BOMBS DROPPED ON GREAT BRITAIN IN THE SECOND WORLD WAR fell on SULLOM. There were no casualties and little damage.

SULLOM VOE oil terminal, where great quantities of North Sea oil are pumped ashore, is THE LARGEST OIL AND LIQUEFIED GAS TERMINAL IN EUROPE.

Until 1975, FETLAR was home to BRITAIN'S ONLY PAIR OF BREEDING SNOWY OWLS.

The tiny but inhabited OUT SKERRIES are the nearest part of Shetland to Norway.

KAME CLIFFS on the west coast of Foula, 30 miles (48 km) west of Lerwick, are 1,200 ft (366 m) high, THE SECOND HIGHEST SEA CLIFFS IN BRITAIN, after those on St Kilda. In 1938, Michael Powell's *The Edge of the World*, about the removal of the last inhabitants from St Kilda, was filmed here.

THE SHETLAND PONY is only 42 inches (107 cm) high at the shoulder when full grown. Bred as a tough little workhorse for pulling ploughshares and other farm equipment on the islands, they were found to be useful for hauling trucks down the coal-mines after child labour was banned. Today they are popular as pets all over the world.

STIRLINGSHIRE

COUNTY TOWN: STIRLING

Srevelyn – Velyn's dwelling (Gaelic)

Wallace Monument, sited where William Wallace watched the English army cross Stirling Bridge before the battle in 1297

Stirling

The Key to Scotland

STIRLING is a beautiful and historic town which, in March 2002, became Scotland's sixth and newest city, an honour granted by the Queen Elizabeth II in celebration of her Golden Jubilee. With its cobbled streets, lined with lovely old buildings, leading up to a royal castle on the crown of a volcanic rock, it feels like a mini Edinburgh, and for many years during the Stewart reign it was the virtual capital of Scotland.

Stirling stands at what historically was the lowest bridging point on the Forth River, and at Scotland's narrowest point, right on the cusp of the Highlands and the Lowlands. Stirling is the gateway, with Stirling castle the key. The magnificent, panoramic view from the castle battlements takes in Scotland's rich central plains, the industrial reaches of the Forth, the stark Highland line to the north and three defining battlefields.

There must have been some sort of fortification on such a strategic position for a long time, but the first proper records of life on the rock come from the 12th century, when Alexander I dedicated a chapel in 1110. He died there in 1124, as did William the Lion in 1214. During the War of Independence in the 14th century Stirling was THE LAST CASTLE IN LOWLAND SCOTLAND TO SURRENDER TO EDWARD I. Having long barred his way to the north, it eventually succumbed in 1304. Ten years later, after Edward I's death, the English garrison was besieged by Robert the Bruce's brother Edward, and it was agreed that, if the castle wasn't relieved by 24 June 1314, the English would surrender. It was while on his way to relieve the garrison at Stirling that Edward II was defeated at Bannockburn.

In 1425, James I took up residence at Stirling after his exile in England, and one of his first acts was to execute his cousin the Duke of Albany – the Duke's father had usurped James's weak father Robert III, and run Scotland as Governor for 18 years while James was held captive. Albany was beheaded, along with his two sons and the Earl of Lennox, at a place just north of the castle where you can still see the gruesome Beheading Stone.

In 1437, the six-year-old James II was brought to Stirling for safety after James I was murdered by disgruntled nobles at Perth. When he was 21, James II ran the disagreeable Earl of Douglas through with his dagger and threw the body out of the window, where it was buried without ceremony. The remains were uncovered in 1797 when a new garden, since named the Douglas Garden, was being laid out beneath the castle walls.

James III was born at Stirling in 1451 and then murdered nearby in 1488, by an unknown assassin, after fleeing wounded from the Battle of Sauchieburn, fought over much the same ground as Bannockburn.

James IV then started on a major building programme at Stirling which included the Chapel Royal and Great Hall, the grandest medieval hall in Scotland.

James V set about turning

Stirling Castle into a palace, creating the finest Renaissance building in Scotland. In 1543, aged nine months, Mary was crowned Queen of Scots in the Chapel Royal, and in 1566 her son James was baptised there. He came back in 1594 as James VI of Scotland and I of England, to have his own son Prince Henry baptised in the new Chapel Royal, which had been refurbished on his orders.

After this, royal attention switched to London, and Stirling castle went through a number of incarnations and rebuilding programmes. One of Scotland's three Royal Castles, along with Edinburgh and Dumbarton, today Stirling is run by Historic Scotland and houses the Museum of the Argyll and Sutherland Highlanders.

Just down the hill from the castle is the 16th-century Church of the Holy Rood, THE ONLY CHURCH WHERE A SCOTTISH MONARCH WAS CROWNED THAT IS STILL IN USE TODAY. The Coronation of the infant James VI as King of Scotland was held here in 1567, accompanied by a sermon from John Knox. The original oak roof is the best in Scotland.

AROUND STIRLING

Brigs and Battlefields

The first of the great battles fought near Stirling was the BATTLE OF STIRLING BRIDGE on 11 September 1297, when William Wallace defeated the superior forces of Edward I. Some remains of the original wooden bridge where the fighting took place have been found about half a mile to the north of the castle at KILDEAN, the location today of EUROPE'S LARGEST LIVESTOCK MARKET.

THE AULD BRIG, seen from the castle, dates from the early 1400s. It was one of the most vital bridges in Scotland, as the only throughway to the north, until 1833, when Robert Stevenson built a new bridge just downstream. Pedestrians can still use the Auld Brig, crossed by every Scottish king from James I to Charles I, and it is fitting that there should be a fine view from here of the great Wallace Monument, one of Scotland's best-loved landmarks, perched on the tip of Abbey Craig, 2 miles (3.2 km) to the east.

THE WALLACE MONUMENT, completed in 1869, is 220 ft (67 m) high and has 246 steps to the top. Hanging from an inside wall is Wallace's heroic two-handed broadsword – experts say this sort of sword did not exist for another 200 years, so it must have given him quite an advantage on the battlefield.

The site of the most famous victory in Scottish history lies to the south of Stirling at BANNOCKBURN, where the battlefield of 1314 is overlooked by a huge statue of Robert the Bruce on his horse and a rotunda protecting the Borestone where Bruce raised his standard. The story of the battle is told in the Bannockburn Heritage Centre run by the National Trust for Scotland.

invented the hot blast furnace and installed one at Carron, greatly improving productivity.

The Carron Ironworks also moved into domestic products, many of them designed by the celebrated Adams brothers. Manhole covers, grates, postboxes and red telephone boxes, seen not just in Britain but around the world, were made by Carron.

The Carron Ironworks closed in the 1980s and the buildings were demolished except for the entrance clock tower, which has been kept as a museum.

In 1886 the Grahamston Iron Company of Falkirk forged THE LARGEST IRON GATES EVER MADE, for showing at the Edinburgh Exhibition. Standing over 26 ft (8 m) high and weighing 20 tons, they were brought back to Falkirk after the exhibition and erected outside the Grahamston Ironworks in Gowan Avenue.

Well, I never knew this ABOUT STIRLINGSHIRE

The Smith Art Gallery and Museum in Stirling is the proud owner of THE WORLD'S OLDEST FOOTBALL, which dates from around 1540, and was discovered behind the oak panelling in the bedchamber of Mary, Queen of Scots in Stirling Castle. The Museum is also home to the Stirling Stone, THE WORLD'S OLDEST CURLING STONE, inscribed 1511 and found at the bottom of a pond in Dunblane. Curling was originally played on frozen rivers and ponds.

HENRY CAMPBELL-BANNERMAN (1836–1908), Prime Minister from 1905 to 1908, was Liberal MP for Stirling for 40 years from 1868 until his death. He added 'Bannerman' to his name in order to inherit a fortune from a maternal uncle.

STIRLING CASTLE was the setting for the 1960 film *Tunes of Glory*, starring Alec Guinness and John Mills. The story is about a disturbing conflict within the Officers' Mess, and the Army refused to allow filming inside the castle, so interiors had to be constructed at Shepperton Studios.

The Coal for the Carron foundry came from the Kinnaird estate owned by James Bruce (1730–94), the African explorer. Bruce travelled throughout East Africa in 1769 to 71 and was THE FIRST MAN TO VERIFY THE SOURCE OF THE NILE. On his return, London society, goaded on by Dr Johnson, was dismissive of his exotic adventures and he retired to Kinnaird to write his memoirs, which were published in 1790 to great public acclaim. He did not live long to enjoy his vindication, but died after falling down the front steps of Kinnaird House while helping a lady into her carriage. He is buried in the churchyard at nearby Larbert. Kinnaird House is now a guesthouse.

Scotland's most unusual architectural folly is the PINEAPPLE at Dunmore House near AIRTH, a summer-house retreat built in 1791, crowned with a wonderful 45 ft (14 m)-high cupola in the form of a stone pineapple. Run by the National Trust for Scotland, it can be rented from the Landmark Trust.

IRN BRU was first brewed as 'Iron Brew' in Falkirk in 1875, by Robert Barr.

Sutherland

County Town: Dornoch

Sudrland – southernland (Norse)

Dornoch Cathedral, the most northerly cathedral on the British mainland

Dornoch

Most Northerly Cathedral and Championship Golf

Built of the mellow pink local sandstone, DORNOCH, former royal burgh, county town of Sutherland and seat of the Bishops of Caithness, is actually more like a Cotswold village than a frontier highland town. Gilbert of Moravia began the handsome little cathedral in 1222, and the first service was held here in 1239. Gilbert died in 1245 and was THE LAST SCOTSMAN TO BECOME A SAINT BEFORE THE REFORMATION. Over the years the cathedral became somewhat neglected and in 1835 William Burn, sponsored by the

Duchess of Sutherland, began to restore the fabric. The work was completed thanks to the generosity of Andrew Carnegie, who is commemorated by three windows in the north wall of the chancel. Sixteen Sutherlands are buried in the cathedral.

Dornoch cathedral is THE MOST NORTHERLY CATHEDRAL ON THE BRITISH MAINLAND and THE FIRST SCOTTISH CATHEDRAL TO HAVE A WOMAN MINISTER. In December 2000, the paparazzi descended on Dornoch to witness the christening of pop singer Madonna's son Rocco in the cathedral.

Opposite the cathedral is 16th-century Dornoch Castle, built as a palace for the Bishops of Caithness and now a hotel.

The name of Dornoch is celebrated far and wide in golfing circles. The course at the Royal Dornoch Golf Club is rated at No. 15 in the world, and is THE MOST NORTHERLY CHAMPIONSHIP GOLF COURSE IN THE WORLD. Dornoch also lays claim to being THE THIRD OLDEST GOLF CLUB IN THE WORLD. The game was brought here in the 16th century by monks from St Andrews, who came to work at the cathedral and found at Dornoch a similar 'links' landscape to that which they had left behind at St Andrews.

Skibo Castle

'If there is a heaven on earth, it is here'
ANDREW CARNEGIE

SKIBO CASTLE, hidden away down a long private drive west of Dornoch, is home to the exclusive Carnegie Club, the biggest private employer in Sutherland. There has been some sort of a castle at Skibo since the 13th century, but the present baronial pile was built between 1899 and 1903 for ANDREW CARNEGIE, the Dunfermline-born steel magnate and philanthropist, as a holiday home for himself and his wife. Carnegie filled the house with all the latest facilities and gadgetry, including an Olympic-size indoor swimming pool and an electric lift installed personally by Mr Otis whose family had invented the safety lift. While enjoying his summer retreat Carnegie would often invite

influential friends to stay for informal discussions and on the issues of the day. Edward VII, Gladstone, Lloyd George, Rudyard Kipling and the Rockefellers all enjoyed visits to Skibo.

After Andrew Carnegie died in 1918, his family continued to use Skibo, but the property became somewhat neglected, until bought in 1990 and restored to its former glory by businessman Peter de Savary. He transformed Skibo into an exclusive luxury country club and hotel and the setting for celebrity weddings. Those who have been married at Skibo include the actor Robert Carlyle of *Hamish Macbeth* fame, Ewan MacGregor from *Star Wars*, Ryder Cup golfer Sam Torrance, and the American actress Ashley Judd, who was married there to West Lothian-born Indy car racing driver Dario Franchitti. Perhaps most famously, pop star Madonna wed film producer Guy Ritchie at Skibo in December 2000. Amongst those on the guest list were Sting, Pavarotti, Gwyneth Paltrow, Donatella Versace and Michael Douglas.

Skibo no longer hosts celebrity weddings. Only members of 'the most exclusive club in the world', the Carnegie Club (membership fee £20,000), can marry there now. Non-members are allowed to stay at the hotel once, and once only.

Dunrobin

Bavaria Comes to the Highlands

DUNROBIN is one of the most extraordinary sights in Scotland, a vast, flamboyant, fairytale castle of pinnacles and turrets set high on a cliff above the cold North Sea – Bavaria come to the Highlands. Hidden within all this extravagance is an ancient 13th-century seat, one of the oldest continuously inhabited houses in Britain. The Earldom of Sutherland dates back to 1235, when the Scottish Kings took these northern lands back from the Norse and scattered titles and territories to their friends and supporters. The original keep was built in about 1275, and this was added to over the years, mainly during the reign of Charles II and in the 18th century. This older house now forms the west

wing, while the joyously unrestrained ocean façade that greets the world today was shaped in the mid-19th century by Sir Charles Barry, architect of the Houses of Parliament. Barry also laid out the formal gardens, which were inspired by those at Versailles and remain virtually unchanged since they were created.

Dunrobin has 189 rooms, is THE MOST NORTHERLY OF SCOTLAND'S GREAT HOUSES and the largest residence in the northern Highlands. The upper floors are said to be haunted by the daughter of the 14th Earl, who fell to her death climbing from an attic window while attempting to elope.

The Clearances

Making Way for Sheep

The name of Sutherland will always be associated with the notorious Highland Clearances of the early 19th century, carried out by the 1st Duke of Sutherland. The Battle of Culloden in 1746 saw the destruction of the clan system whereby tenants paid off their chieftains by military service. Instead, landowners began to demand financial rents which the impoverished Highland labourers and farmers were unable to pay. In 1792, known as 'the year of the sheep', the hardy Cheviot sheep was introduced to Scotland. Its ability to thrive in the harsh Highland environment and to provide large quantities of high-quality wool and meat meant that raising sheep suddenly became much more profitable than the traditional farming of the clansmen, and eager landlords decided that the old way of life had to go.

Tenants were cleared off the lands they had worked for generations to make way for sheep and large-scale agriculture. They were relocated to the coasts, where fishing and kelping were supposed to provide them with a better living, or forced to emigrate to Australia, New Zealand or Canada. Such clearances were carried out by landlords all over Scotland, but the sheer scale of the Sutherland clearances, with more than 5,000 people evicted from their homes, and the brutality of the Duke's agents, has ensured that they will remain singularly infamous in the annals of Scottish history.

Though much reviled, the Duke of Sutherland was not a bad man, but that most dangerous of men, a reformer. Sir Iain Moncreiffe of that Ilk put it well: 'Like so many reformers he was willing to dedicate his life and fortune to making other folk do something they found desperately disagreeable, for the sake of what he believed to be their future good.' The Duke was genuinely shocked by the conditions of his tenants and determined that they should be given the chance of a better life. And, indeed, many who settled in the New World soon found a quality of life far superior to any they could have aspired to in the barren highlands of their homeland.

On the summit of BEN BHRAGGIE there is a huge statue of the 1st Duke of Sutherland, erected in 1834, the year after he died, by 'a mourning and grateful tenantry to a judicious, kind and liberal landlord'. The inscription perhaps illustrates how detached from reality the great and the good can become.

Durness

Allt Smoo and Cape Wrath

DURNESS IS THE MOST NORTHWESTERLY VILLAGE ON MAINLAND BRITAIN, and also BRITAIN'S MOST REMOTE VILLAGE. A little to the east of the village, a steep track leads down to SMOO CAVE, which has THE LARGEST ENTRANCE OF ANY SEA CAVE IN BRITAIN. The main chamber, 200 ft (61 m) long and 110 ft (34 m) wide, is floodlit and echoes to the sound of Allt Smoo as it tumbles 80 ft (24 m) down a vertical shaft from the moorland above, into a deep pool in a second cave. There is a third cave further on, but these two inner chambers can only be reached by experienced potholers.

Fifteen miles (24 km) west of Durness is CAPE WRATH, THE MOST NORTHWESTERLY POINT ON THE BRITISH MAINLAND and ONE OF ONLY TWO 'CAPES' IN BRITAIN, the other being Cape Cornwall near Land's End. The name 'Wrath', although apposite for this place of wild weather, tempestuous seas and unforgiving rocks, actually means 'turning point' in Norse, for this is where the Viking ships would turn south on their journeys to the Western Isles or Ireland. The only way to reach Cape Wrath is to take a ferry from Durness across to the west side of the Kyle of Durness, and then walk or, in summer, take the minibus to the grey, granite lighthouse on top of the cliffs, 400 ft (122 m) above the sea. The road winds for 11 miles (18 km) across the lonely Parbh, made up of rocky peat bogs and heather, one of the last unspoilt areas of wilderness in Britain. Between Cape Wrath and Durness are the spectacular cliffs of CLO MOR, at 921 ft (281 m) THE HIGHEST CLIFFS ON THE MAINLAND OF BRITAIN.

Cape Wrath is NATO's foremost military training ground. It is so remote as to be the only place in Europe where military manoeuvres involving all three services together – army, navy and air force – can be carried out.

Carbisdale Castle

No Time

CARBISDALE CASTLE, which sits on a wooded hill overlooking the glorious Kyle of Sutherland, north of Bonar Bridge, was built from 1906 by Mary, Duchess of Sutherland. Lady Mary was the second wife of the 3rd Duke and lost most of the Sutherland estates to her stepson, after legal action over her husband's disputed will. With what she did inherit the Duchess built Carbisdale, in a prominent position where the new Duke could not fail to see it whenever he travelled to Dunrobin on the train. Not willing to 'give him the time of day', the Duchess had the clock tower designed with a clock on three faces only, with

Carbisdale Castle

nothing on the face that could be seen from the train. Like William Duff, in dudgeon over Duff House in Banff, the Duke would pull down the blinds of his carriage as he passed. Carbisdale Castle is now a youth hostel.

Well, I never knew this ABOUT SUTHERLAND

There is a memorial in DURNESS TO JOHN LENNON, who used to come here as a boy, on holiday with relatives.

In his report from the Battle of Balaclava in 1854, during the Crimean War, *Times* correspondent William Russell wrote that he could see nothing between the advancing Russian cavalry and the British except 'the thin red streak, tipped with a line of steel', of the 93rd. Thus did the 93RD SUTHERLAND HIGHLANDERS gain their immortal name 'THE THIN RED LINE', when they stood steadfastly in a line of two ranks and repelled, against all odds, the headlong charge of the Russian cavalry. It became a byword for British military valour.

The LOCH SHIN HYDRO ELECTRIC POWER SCHEME in central Sutherland is THE MOST NORTHERLY HEP SCHEME IN BRITAIN.

The open-cast coal-pit at BRORA, north of Dunrobin, opened in 1529 and was

THE FIRST COAL-MINE IN SCOTLAND. In 1839, the first settlers from Northern Scotland sailed for New Zealand from Brora, during the Sutherland Clearances.

Five miles (8 km) north of Brora, beside the road, is THE WOLF STONE, which commemorates the shooting in 1700 of the last wolf in Sutherland by the hunter Polson.

At 3,040 ft (927 m), BEN HOPE, south of Durness, is THE MOST NORTHERLY MUNRO, OR MOUNTAIN OVER 3,000 FT (914.4 M), IN BRITAIN.

HANDA ISLAND, off Scourie, is now an uninhabited nature reserve, but before 1846 it was populated by 12 families who elected their own parliament and appointed as queen the oldest widow in the community.

The EAS COUL AULIN waterfall which drops 660 ft (200 m) from Glas Bheinn to Loch Glencoul near Sutherland's west coast, is THE HIGHEST WATERFALL IN BRITAIN. The falls can be reached along a fairly steep footpath that starts from a small loch by the A894 about 3 miles (5 km) south of Kylesku, which takes you to the top of the falls with sensational views over Loch Glencoul and another waterfall across the glen. Or you can take a boat from Kylesku to the end of Loch Glencoul and see the falls from below.

Geologists from all over the world come to study KNOCKAN CLIFF, east of Lochinver, for its rare rock formation. Normally, older rocks are found underneath younger ones. At Knockan the old rocks of the cliff stand on top of a layer of younger rocks beneath, as a result of massive earth movements that thrust a huge tongue of very old rock up and over the newer rock. It is a fascinating sight.

LAIRG was the birthplace of SIR JAMES MATHESON (1796–1878), the trader and entrepreneur who co-founded the largest western conglomerate in Asia, Jardine Matheson. He began trading in India and then moved to China, where he teamed up with fellow Scot William Jardine (1784–1843), who was born in Lochmaben, Dumfriesshire. They prospered by trading in tea and smuggling opium from India into China from Hong Kong. The Chinese tried to put a stop to the trade and Matheson persuaded the English Prime Minister Lord Palmerston to intervene on Jardine Matheson's behalf. This was the start of the Opium Wars of the 1840s, which resulted in Hong Kong being ceded to Britain until 1997. Matheson returned home a very wealthy man. He bought the island of Lewis, where he built the mock Tudor Lews Castle and endeavoured to provide employment for the islanders, who were suffering from the ravages of the potato famine. He was knighted for his efforts.

WEST LOTHIAN

COUNTY TOWN: LINLITHGOW

West territory of *Loth*, grandfather of St Mungo

Hopetoun House, seat of the Marquess of Linlithgow and the largest country house in Scotland

Linlithgow

A Golden Palace

Even in ruin, LINLITHGOW PALACE, glowing golden on its hill above Linlithgow Loch, is impressive. There has been a royal manor here since the 12th century, but it was the Stuart who really seemed to love the place, starting with James I who began building what was to become the loveliest of all Scotland's royal palaces. His great-grandson James IV made sumptuous additions and, in 1512, James V was born in Linlithgow. The following year James V's mother Margaret stood on the roof of the Queen's Bower, a small octagonal turret in the northwest corner of the palace, watching in vain for her husband James IV to return from Flodden Field.

Almost 30 years later, in 1542, Mary, Queen of Scots was born in that same Queen's Bower. She was taken to Stirling Castle for safety when she was seven months old, and the Stuarts' love affair with Linlithgow was over. Mary stayed here briefly on her return from France, but her son James VI was indifferent and the last king to sleep in the crumbling palace was his son Charles I, in 1633. In 1746 the Duke of Cumberland's troops rested at Linlithgow on their way home from Culloden, and the Hanoverians' final insult was to burn down the Stuarts' once resplendent palace, by setting fire to the straw on which they had been sleeping.

The elaborate King's Fountain in the courtyard, which survived the fire, was built in 1538 for James V, and is THE OLDEST FOUNTAIN IN BRITAIN. On grand occasions this fountain was said to have flowed with wine, the last time being when Bonnie Prince Charlie stopped at Linlithgow on his way to Edinburgh in 1745.

Mary, Queen of Scots

Tragic Pawn

MARY, QUEEN OF SCOTS was born in Linlithgow Palace on 8 December 1542, and became Scotland's only Queen when she was six days old. She never saw her father, James V, who was dying, alone and depressed, at Falkland Palace, a broken man after defeat at the hands of Henry VIII at the Battle of Solway Firth. Mary's coronation as Queen of Scots took place at Stirling Castle in September 1543. She was nine months old.

Mary spent little more than a quarter of her life in Scotland, just 12 of her 44 years. She was a prisoner for half her life. Always at the mercy of events and people around her, she achieved very little of significance as a ruler. And yet she is the most famous and celebrated Scottish monarch of them all. Her tragic story touches the hearts of Scots around the world. During her brief time in the country, she must have travelled without respite, for every corner of Scotland, every village and town, every castle and every family has a cherished story of the time Queen Mary came to stay.

Her role as a political pawn began almost before she drew breath. Henry VIII of England saw Mary as a way to secure the Scottish throne for himself, by marrying her to his son Edward, a union that he attempted to enforce by sending his army into Scotland in what is known as the 'rough wooing'. Mary's mother, Mary of Guise, had other ideas.

In 1548 the six-year-old Mary sailed from Dumbarton castle for France with her companions, the 'four Marys' – Mary Beaton, Mary Seton (*see* East Lothian), Mary Fleming (*see* Lanarkshire) and Mary Livingstone – and in 1558 she married her childhood sweetheart, the Dauphin, heir to the French throne. Within a year her husband became François II and Mary was now Queen of two countries, aged just 16.

It was while she was in France that Mary traditionally changed her family name from Stewart to Stuart, as the French alphabet at that time contained no 'W'.

The Queen Returns

Double tragedy struck in 1560 when Mary's mother died and then, not long afterwards, her husband. She was now a 17-year-old dowager Queen, unwanted in France, and she returned to Scotland to begin her reign as the Queen of Scots. Beautiful, well read and polished, she soon won over her countrymen, all except John Knox, the implacable Protestant preacher who loathed Catholics and 'the monstrous regiment of women' in equal measure.

Mary was a passionate woman, and in 1565 she rashly married 'the lustiest and best proportionit lang man' she had ever met, her cousin Lord Darnley. She soon lived to regret it. Darnley, four years her junior, was debauched, a drunkard and a womaniser, and the marriage was not popular with the Scottish people. Darnley became irrationally jealous of Mary's relationship with her Italian secretary David Rizzio. On 9 March 1566, he and a group of rowdy young men broke into the Queen's apartments in Holyrood Palace, where she was hosting a supper party, and knifed Rizzio to death as he clung to Mary's skirts. His blood stains the floor at Holyrood still.

Mary was three months pregnant, and after such a trauma might have miscarried but, three months later on 19 June 1566, at Edinburgh Castle, she gave birth to a healthy son, the future James VI of Scotland and I of England.

Although she feigned to be reconciled to Darnley, the father of her child, Mary was now in love with another man, namely James Hepburn, 4th Earl of Bothwell. On 9 February 1567, Darnley was killed when the house where he was staying, Kirk o' Field, in Edinburgh, was reduced to rubble by an almighty explosion. Darnley's body was found lying outside in the garden. He had been strangled. Mary and Bothwell were immediately suspected of being behind the killing, and they escaped to Bothwell's castle at Dunbar. Here, Bothwell is alleged to have raped Mary, but whether she was a willing victim or not, they married at Holyrood on 15 May, just three months after Darnley's death. Mary was now on her third husband and the people of Scotland had had enough. They rose up and defeated Bothwell's men at the Battle of Carberry Hill in June. Bothwell fled to Denmark, where he died in gaol, and Mary was imprisoned at Lochleven Castle, where she was forced to abdicate in favour of her son James.

In one last desperate attempt to save her throne, Mary escaped from Lochleven (*see* Kinross-shire) and rallied her dwindling band of supporters, but they were defeated at the Battle of

Langside on 13 May 1568. Mary fled to England where she was held under house arrest by her cousin Elizabeth I until 1587. By then she had become a dangerous talisman for those wanting to unseat Elizabeth and was implicated in a number of plots. Even though probably innocent, Mary was led to the scaffold at Fotheringay Castle on 8 February 1587. It took two blows to sever her head from her body. Mary, Queen of Scots died in agony as she had lived in agony.

Queensferry

Overlooked

QUEENSFERRY is a venerable old burgh, overlooked by the awe-inspiring massiveness of the great Forth Railway Bridge, and hence by most travellers too. There scarcely seems room for a town between the steep hills and the broad river, and many of the houses perch on rocks right at the water's edge. The main street curls and bucks sinuously for half a mile or more, lined with tall, gabled houses that stretch and jostle with each other for a view of the water. Right underneath the bridge is the 17th-century Hawes Inn, where passengers would await 'the Queen's Ferry' to carry them across the Forth. The Queen referred to is Margaret, wife of Malcolm III 'Canmore', who, in 1071, guaranteed free passage for pilgrims travelling to Dunfermline and St Andrews. In room 13 of the Hawes Inn, above the entrance, Robert Louis Stevenson began writing *Kidnapped*. This is the inn where the loathsome Uncle Ebenezer and Captain Hoseason meet to plot the abduction of young Davie Balfour.

You can never really be alone in Queensferry. The whole town sits in the towering shadow of the railway bridge, and with 200 trains crossing every day, there is always someone looking down at you. The view of the bridge from Queensferry is like something out of Fritz Lang's *Metropolis*. The sky is made dark by vast, monstrous steel girders that grind and groan like a living thing every time a miniature train rattles across overhead, far, far above.

Forth Railway Bridge

The Best Bridge in the World

THE FORTH RAILWAY BRIDGE, THE WORLD'S FIRST MAJOR STEEL BRIDGE, THE LONGEST CANTILEVER BRIDGE IN BRITAIN, SECOND LONGEST IN THE WORLD and SCOTLAND'S BIGGEST LISTED BUILDING, is as much an internationally recognised symbol of Scotland as whisky or tartan or Edinburgh Castle. Designed by Sir John Fowler and Benjamin Baker and engineered by Renfrewshire's Sir William Arrol, it ranks as one of the wonders of the industrial world. The design is unique. When it was opened by the Prince of Wales, later Edward VII, on 4 March 1890, it was THE BIGGEST BRIDGE IN THE WORLD. The main span of 1,710 ft (521 m) was THREE TIMES LONGER THAN ANYTHING EVER BUILT BEFORE. The total length of the bridge is over a mile and a half, the height of the towers

is 330 ft (110.6 m) and the railway is 158 ft (48.2 m) above the high-water level. It took 4,000 men three and a half years to build it. Of these, 57 died, despite boats being stationed under each cantilever, which did save eight lives.

It is not pretty. William Morris called it 'the supremest specimen of all ugliness'. But our modern eye sees it as the embodiment of functional beauty. It is over 100 years old and yet casts a spell over even the most jaundiced of 21st-century travellers, who cannot fail to be awed by its raw bulk and force. It is enormous and preposterously over-engineered, but it was meant to be. Just over ten years earlier the graceful but delicate bridge over the River Tay had collapsed, taking a train and 75 lives with it, and the Forth Bridge was built to exude confidence and solidity. The cost was £3,200,000, or some £250,000,000 in today's money.

The Forth Railway Bridge has even given a phrase to the English language. A repetitive, unending task is often described as being 'like painting the Forth Bridge'. This arises from the fact that, for the first 100 years, the bridge's 135 acres of steel surface required continual painting. A new paint has now been developed designed to have a life span of at least 20 years.

Testament to the extraordinary impact of the Forth Railway Bridge is the way it completely overwhelms its younger neighbour, the slender, twin-towered suspension road bridge which was the longest outside America when it opened in 1964 and which, if it were anywhere else, would be a major attraction in its own right.

Bathgate

Birthplace of Oil

BATHGATE today seems like any other slightly run-down industrial town: a few shops, a couple of grand buildings donated by philanthropic Victorian barons, modern housing estates where there used to be factories. Bathgate, though, hides its light under a bushel. For here, in 1848, a spark was lit that would ignite around the world, spawning an industry that has made more millionaires, caused more wars, enriched and enslaved more nations and shaped the world more radically, both politically and economically, than any other single industry in history – the oil industry. And the man who lit that spark was JAMES 'PARAFFIN' YOUNG (1811–83).

In the early 19th century the Industrial Revolution was transforming the face of Britain. There was a race on to find a new kind of fuel that could power and lubricate all the new inventions, products and ideas that were appearing every day.

James Young, born in Glasgow, the son of a carpenter, was a chemist, and his quest was to find that new fuel. He first experimented successfully with a thick kind of bitumen that was seeping naturally from a coal-mine in Derbyshire, but the source quickly dried up.

Young then came across a similar type of cannel coal at the unfortunately named Boghead colliery near Bathgate, and discovered that a high yield could be extracted from it, producing crude oil, paraffin oil and wax, coke, gas and ammonium sulphate fertiliser – all of which were in great demand and could justify heavy investment. And so he set up THE WORLD'S FIRST OIL REFINERY, the Bathgate Chemical Works.

The First Oil Tycoon

Boghead's coal soon ran out too, but by then Young had found that he could extract oil more cheaply and efficiently from the abundant oil shale that West Lothian was sitting on. Young built a new plant at nearby Addiewell, and presumed to ask his old friend David Livingstone to lay the foundation stone. In 1865 he set up Young's Paraffin Light and Mineral Oil Company, selling oil and paraffin lamps around the world. For the next 15 years or so Scotland, and West Lothian in particular, was THE WORLD'S LARGEST OIL PRODUCER and James Paraffin Young THE WORLD'S FIRST OIL TYCOON.

He retired in 1870, a very rich man, built himself a fine villa at Wemyss Bay, and spent his money on educational endowments as well as financing the expeditions of his friend David Livingstone. He is buried in Inverkip. Young's Paraffin Light and Mineral Oil Company lives on as part of BP.

At the beginning of the 20th century, directly extracted crude oil from America and elsewhere began to undercut the West Lothian shale oil, and the industry fell into a gradual decline. The Bathgate Chemical Works closed in 1956. All that West Lothian had to show for its priceless contribution to the industrial world was a scattering of strange-looking pink 'bings', or mounds of spent shale, dotted across the countryside. Most have now been landscaped. Ironically, at about the same time as the last drop of shale oil was being extracted from West Lothian in 1962, the first oil and gas reserves were discovered beneath the North Sea. Scotland was not to be without oil for long.

You Are Feeling Drowsy
Bathgate was the birthplace of another pioneering James Young, SIR JAMES YOUNG SIMPSON (1811–70), THE FIRST MAN EVER TO BE KNIGHTED FOR SERVICES TO MEDICINE. His speciality was anaesthetics and he experimented with chloroform by inviting guests round for dinner and then dousing them to see at what stage they slid under the table. He pioneered the use of chloroform in childbirth – a radical idea that upset medical, moral and religious opinion until Queen Victoria used chloroform during the birth of Prince Leopold in 1853.

Well, I never knew this
ABOUT
WEST LOTHIAN

In 1944, the HOUSE OF THE BINNS, east of Linlithgow, became THE FIRST PROPERTY TO BE ACQUIRED BY THE NATIONAL TRUST FOR SCOTLAND UNDER THE COUNTRY HOUSES SCHEME. It is still the home of the outspoken former Labour MP for Linlithgow, TAM DALYELL (b.1932), who raised the crucial 'West Lothian question' during the debate over devolution. The 'West Lothian question' asks why, after devolution, Scottish MPs should be allowed to vote at Westminster on purely English issues, when English MPs cannot vote on West Lothian issues.

The village of ABERCORN, enfolded in the walls of Hopetoun House, was THE SEAT OF SCOTLAND'S FIRST BISHOPRIC, established in the 7th century.

BLACKNESS CASTLE, sited on a promontory jutting out into the Forth River, was designed to look like a ship. Archibald Douglas, who built the castle, suffered terribly from seasickness, an embarrassing weakness in his position as Lord High Admiral of the Scottish Fleet. So he promised his King, James V, that he would build a flagship for himself that the English couldn't sink and on which he would never be sick. He built Blackness Castle.

HENRY BELL, inventor of THE WORLD'S FIRST COMMERCIAL STEAMBOAT (*see* Dunbartonshire), was born at TORPHICHEN on 7 April 1767.

ROBERT LISTON (1794–1847), the first surgeon ever to perform an operation using a general anaesthetic, was born in ECCLESMACHAN, near Linlithgow.

ST MICHAEL'S CHURCH, adjacent to Linlithgow Palace, is SCOTLAND'S LARGEST PRE-REFORMATION CHURCH.

Kinneil House

DALMENY HOUSE, east of Queensferry, was THE FIRST TUDOR GOTHIC REVIVAL HOUSE IN SCOTLAND.

The Library at DALMENY is considered the birthplace of the Edinburgh Festival. The 6th Earl of Rosebery was Chairman of the newly formed Scottish Tourist Board and his wife an accomplished pianist. Together with friends they initiated a series of concerts and performances that would evolve into the great festival – the first concert being held in the Library at Dalmeny House.

ST CUTHBERT'S PARISH CHURCH in Dalmeny village dates from 1150, and is regarded as THE FINEST AND MOST COMPLETE ROMANESQUE CHURCH LEFT STANDING IN SCOTLAND.

The ceiling of the Parable Room at KINNEIL HOUSE, outside Bo'ness, is regarded as THE FINEST 16TH-CENTURY OAK CEILING IN SCOTLAND. In the grounds of the house, on the bank of the Gil Burn, where it runs through a precipitous gorge, is a small stone outhouse of great import. Here, in 1770, James Watt built his FIRST FULL-SCALE STEAM PUMPING ENGINE. Kinneil House was the home of Dr John Roebuck, an inventor and entrepreneur who was one of the leading lights of the Industrial Revolution in Scotland.

West Lothian can boast THE LARGEST SHOP IN EUROPE, the ASDA Walmart store in LIVINGSTON.

WIGTOWNSHIRE

COUNTY TOWN: WIGTOWN

Wiga's ton – Wig's village (Norse)

Twelfth-century Norman doorway of Whithorn Priory, on the site of the earliest religious establishment in Scotland

Wigtown

Town of Books

WIGTOWN, county town and, since 1997, Scotland's National Book Town, is a picturesque place set on a hill, with wide airy streets and a slightly dishevelled, scholarly feel to it. The big open square, where they used to pen the cattle at night, is now a bowling green and park, while dominating the east side of the square are the exotic pink County Buildings and Town Hall of 1863. Fresh sea breezes from the bay gust along the

High Street, and tug at the cobwebs on the bookshelves. The Book Shop on North Main Street, one of several bookshops in the town, is THE BIGGEST SECOND-HAND BOOKSHOP IN SCOTLAND.

On the salt marshes below is a stone monument marking the spot where, in 1685, two Covenanters, Margaret MacLachlan, a woman of 63, and Margaret Wilson, a girl of 18, were tied to stakes and left to drown, as the Solway tide swept in along the estuary of the River Bladnoch. The older woman was tied further out in the river so that the younger one might see her die, and repent. She refused, saying, 'I am one of Christ's children. Let me go.' And they did. The two Margaret martyrs are buried in the churchyard half-way up the hill beneath the words 'Requiescant in pace' – may they rest in peace.

On the southern slopes of Wigtown is the Bladnoch distillery, THE MOST SOUTHERLY DISTILLERY IN SCOTLAND.

The actor JAMES ROBERTSON JUSTICE (1905–75) was born in Wigtown. He was best known as the portly and irascible surgeon Sir Lancelot Spratt in the 'Doctor' comedy film series, and as Lord Scrumptious in the 1968 film of *Chitty Chitty Bang Bang*.

The Machars

Mysterious Churches

Wigtown is the guardian of the mysterious MACHARS, a wide peninsula thrusting into the Irish Sea. There are treasures and surprises to be found down every twisting lane. One such surprise can be found in the secluded ancient church of Cruggleton, encircled by a stone wall, and marooned on farmland beside the coast road to the Isle of Whithorn. Restored by the 3rd Marquess of Bute at the end of the 19th century, the interior boasts the finest early Norman arch in Galloway, but few people get to experience this lost treasure, for it sleeps behind a locked door, hidden by trees.

On the west coast of the Machars, near Monreith, are the ruins of KIRKMAIDEN CHURCH. Buried in the churchyard here is FRANÇOIS THUROT, a senior French naval officer whose body was washed up on Monreith Bay in 1760, after a sea battle against the English off the Isle of Man. Earlier in the year Commodore Thurot had captured Carrickfergus in County Antrim, Ireland, THE ONLY FRENCH VICTORY EVER ON BRITISH SOIL. Thurot, a protégé of Madame de Pompadour, apparently roamed far and wide, for he was well known in Sweden where he introduced the Order of Colvin, a Christian society connected to sailors and their traditions. Sweden is the only country where this order still exists, and in 1960 members of the order came over from Sweden and erected a plaque to Thurot in the churchyard. In 1967 a detachment of the French fleet came to honour him.

Many of the Maxwell family, local landowners, are buried beneath the chancel of the church at Kirkmaiden. On the hillside above there is a bronze otter, sculpted by Penny Wheatley, commemorating Gavin Maxwell, author of *Ring of Bright Water* (*see*

Glenelg, Inverness-shire), who was born nearby at the House of Elrig, a romantic, grey house set on lonely moorlands a little to the north, and very private. Maxwell wrote an autobiography called *The House of Elrig* about his childhood there, and returned to the area frequently, sometimes to be seen exercising his tame otter on the beach below Kirkmaiden.

The original Maxwell home was a tower house called The Dowies, which overlooked Monreith from on high. It was a proud boast of the family that from their property they could see five kingdoms – Scotland, England, Ireland, Man and the Kingdom of Heaven. The Dowies, or Old Place of Mochrum, now belongs to the Landmark Trust and can be rented.

Whithorn

Cradle of Scottish Christianity

WHITHORN WAS THE FIRST CHRISTIAN SETTLEMENT NORTH OF HADRIAN'S WALL and the site of SCOTLAND'S FIRST STONE CHURCH, built by ST NINIAN in the 5th century and dedicated to St Martin of Tours. St Ninian is THE EARLIEST KNOWN SCOTTISH SAINT, born in Galloway, most probably somewhere near Whithorn, and educated in Rome. His church, painted white so that it could be seen from a distance, was known as the CANDIDA CASA, or White House, from which Whithorn gets its name.

St Ninian was buried here, and over the next centuries Whithorn became a place of pilgrimage, with a succession of churches being constructed on the site, culminating in a mighty 12th-century cathedral and priory founded by Fergus, Lord of Galloway. The nave, with a fine carved doorway, and the crypt, are all that remain today. At the east end of the crypt, thought to be the site of St Ninian's grave, some remnants of a white plastered wall have been found. Unusually, the church buildings do not lie on a true east–west axis, an indication, perhaps, that St Ninian did not possess the means to align his Candida Casa accurately.

Towards the end of the 9th century a portion of the Lindisfarne Gospel was washed up on the shore near Whithorn, having been lost overboard from a boat attempting to take the body of St Cuthbert to Ireland, during the Norse raids. The Gospel was miraculously undamaged.

Royalty and Relics

Before the Reformation many of Scotland's monarchs paid a visit to Whithorn, James IV most frequently. In 1563 Mary,Queen of Scots made the last royal pilgrimage, for in 1581 an Act of Parliament banned such practices and slowly the town slipped into decline and forgetfulness.

Today, the wide, empty, sloping main street shows off a number of quite smart 18th-century houses, but the highlight is THE PEND, a medieval archway surmounted by the Royal Arms of Scotland dating from around 1500, one of the finest examples of the Stuart arms to be found in the whole country. The archway leads through to the cathedral ruins. Nearby there is a new parish church built in 1822 and a museum containing many of the relics excavated from the site over the years, including the Latinus Stone, dating from AD 450, THE OLDEST CHRISTIAN RELIC IN SCOTLAND.

The Pend

The significance of Whithorn in Scotland's story is immense and has been somewhat unfairly overshadowed by the more flashy Iona, which didn't come into existence until over half a century later. Although the town, at first glance, seems rather abandoned and forlorn – one half expects to see tumbleweed blowing down the street – there is a feeling that something deep and powerful happened here and a sense of awe that this unpretentious little grey town, on this bleak and windswept peninsula, is where it all began . . .

Three miles (5 km) to the south-east is the attractive little harbour village of the ISLE OF WHITHORN, now connected to the mainland by a causeway. This was where pilgrims from Ireland, from the Isle of Man, from England and from Europe, would land on their way to Whithorn.

Perched on a headland above the village are the ruins of St Ninian's chapel, dating from the 13th century and built on the site of an earlier chapel, where pilgrims would stop and give thanks for a safe voyage.

Close to the chapel is a stone seat that commemorates seven local fishermen who lost their lives when the fishing boat *Solway Harvester* sank, off the Isle of Man, in January 2000.

Three miles (5 km) away to the west, a beautiful walk beside a burn through deep green woods leads to a pebbly beach, at the far end of which is ST NINIAN'S CAVE, thought to be where the saint came for solitude and contemplation. There are seven crosses on the cave walls, pecked into the rock by pilgrims in the 8th century. It is quite fun to try and find them. The cave is remarkably undisturbed, no doubt because it is so difficult to reach, and the view and sense of seclusion have probably not changed since St Ninian's day. A service is held here once a year.

Final scenes of the cult 1973 film *The Wicker Man* were shot outside St Ninian's cave. The Wicker Man itself was erected on the cliff tops at Burrow Head to the south. Some wooden stumps from its legs can still be seen.

Well, I never knew this ABOUT WIGTOWNSHIRE

There have been more than 70 shipwrecks along the west coast of the Rhins in the last 150 years, the worst being on 31 January 1953, when the Stranraer to Larne ferry the *Princess Victoria* sank off Corsewall Point with the loss of 134 lives.

THE FIRST RECORDED SWIMMER OF THE NORTHERN CHANNEL was THOMAS BLOWER, who swam from Donaghadee to Portpatrick in 16 hours 7 minutes in 1947.

STRANRAER, the largest settlement in southwest Scotland, inherited the lucrative Irish ferry trade from Portpatrick in the mid 19th century, taking advantage of its sheltered position on Loch Ryan. Near the east pier is North West Castle, now a hotel but once the home of SIR JOHN ROSS (1777–1856), explorer of the North-West Passage across the top of Canada. He was born at Kirkholm, up in the north of the Rhins. In 1829 he discovered the northernmost point of mainland America and named it the Boothia Peninsula, after a patron of the expedition, Sir Felix Booth.

CAIRNRYAN, on the east coast of Loch Ryan, being significantly closer to Northern Ireland than Stranraer, is slowly taking over much of the ferry trade. In the Second World War, parts of the Mulberry harbours were constructed at Cairnryan, and in 1980 the aircraft carrier HMS *Ark Royal* was broken up here.

DRUMMORE, a collection of whitewashed cottages that run uphill from a sandy beach on the Rhins, is SCOTLAND'S MOST SOUTHERLY VILLAGE.

The MULL OF GALLOWAY, right on the tip of the Rhins, is THE MOST SOUTHERLY POINT IN SCOTLAND. And Scotland ends here in spectacular style with mighty cliffs 300 ft (90 m) high, views of Ireland, the Inner Hebrides, the Isle of Man and the Lake District, and a lighthouse designed by Robert Stevenson in 1830. The cliffs are home to sea birds of

all kinds and are now an RSPB reserve. The Mull of Galloway is further south than Durham.

One of Scotland's most unusual treats is the TIDAL FISHPOND at PORT LOGAN. In 1788 the Laird of Logan, ANDREW McDOUALL, began shaping a natural blow-hole into a larder to provide fresh fish for the kitchens of Logan House. The round pond, scooped out of the cliffs, is sheltered from the wind and the waves by a castellated stone wall. Over the years, the inhabitants of the pond have become quite tame, rising to the surface to be fed by hand. It can be quite an unnerving experience waiting for a large fish to explode out of the black depths and snatch the food from your hand. Favourite characters include TOD THE COD and HERBERT THE TURBOT.

Gazetteer

NTS: National Trust for Scotland
www.nts.org.uk Tel: 0131 243 9300

HS: Historic Scotland
www.historic-scotland.gov.uk Tel: 0131 668 8600

Aberdeenshire

Drum Castle NTS
3m west of Peterculter. 1m west of A93
Provost Ross's House NTS
Shiprow, Aberdeen
Balmoral Castle
8m west of Ballater off A93
Grounds open April to July
Other times guided tours by appointment
www.balmoralcastle.com
Craigievar Castle NTS
6m south of Alford off A980
Scottish Lighthouse Museum,
Kinnaird Head, Fraserburgh
Tel: 01346 511022
Old Slains Castle
1m north of Cruden Bay off A975

Angus

RSS Discovery
Discovery Point, Discovery Quay, Dundee.
Tel: 01382 201245
Signal Tower Museum, Arbroath.
Arbroath Harbour, on A92
Tel: 01241 875598
Kerr's Miniature Railway
West Links, Arbroath
James Barrie's Birthplace
9 Brechin Road, Kirriemuir
Tel: 01575 572646
Camera Obscura, NTS
Kirrie Hill, Kirriemuir
Glamis Castle
4m south of Kirriemuir off A928
www.glamis-castle.co.uk
Tel: 01307 840393
Edzell Castle and Gardens HS
8m north of Brechin. 1m west of B966
Mills Observatory
Glamis Road, Balgay Park, Dundee
Tel: 01382 435967
Finavon Dovecot
7m north of Forfar, off A90

Argyllshire

Inveraray Castle, Inveraray.
www.inveraray-castle.com
Tel: 01499 302203
Ardkinglas Estate and Woodland
Cairndow, Loch Fyne. Off A83
www.ardkinglas.com
Tel: 01499 600261
Dunadd Fort
3m north of Lochgilphead, west of A816

Ben Cruachan Visitor Centre
20m east of Oban off A85
www.visitcruachan
Tel: 01866 822618
Castle Tioram
On coast at the end of minor road north off A861
35m south of Mallaig.

AYRSHIRE

Burns Birthplace Cottage and Monument
Alloway, Ayr.
www.burnsheritagepark.com
Tel: 01292 443700
Ballochmyle Viaduct
Along footpath west off A76 where it crosses River Ayr
2m south of Mauchline
Laigh Milton Viaduct
Gatehead
3m west of Kilmarnock off A759
Culzean Castle NTS
12m south of Ayr off A719
Penkill Castle, Old Dailly
5m east of Girvan off B734
Visits by appointment only
Tel: 01465 871219
Loudoun Castle
Galston.
4m east of Kilmarnock on A71
www.loudouncastle.co.uk
Tel: 01563 822296
Crossraguel Abbey HS
2m south west of Maybole off A77

BANFFSHIRE

Duff House
Banff.
www.duffhouse.org.uk
Tel: 01262 818181
Craigellachie Bridge
½ m west of Craigellachie off A95
Macduff Marine Aquarium
11 High Shore, Macduff
www.macduff-aquarium.org.uk
Tel: 01261 833369

BERWICKSHIRE

Manderston
2m east of Duns on A6105
www.manderston.co.uk
01361 882010
Dryburgh Abbey HS
5m east of Melrose west of B6356 signposted on minor roads from St Boswells
Paxton House
5m west of Berwick-on-Tweed
1m south of B6461
www.paxtonhouse.co.uk
Tel: 01289 386291
Union Chain Bridge, Horncliffe
5m west of Berwick-on-Tweed
1m north of A698

BUTESHIRE

Mount Stuart, Isle of Bute
5m south of Rothesay, signposted off A844
www.mountstuart.com
Tel: 01700 503877
Rothesay Castle HS
Rothesay, Isle of Bute
Brodick Castle NTS
Brodick, Isle of Arran
Ascog Hall
3m south east of Rothesay, Isle of Bute, off A844
www.ascoghallfernery.co.uk
Tel: 01700 504555

Caithness

Castle of Mey
14m east of Thurso, off A836
www.castleofmey.org.uk
Tel: 01847 851473

Clackmannanshire

Alloa Tower NTS
Alloa Park, Alloa
Castle Campbell HS
1m north of Dollar
Menstrie Castle
Menstrie
4m east of Stirling off A91
Tel: 01259 213131

Dunfriesshire

Drumlanrig Castle
Thornhill
16m west of Moffat
Tel: 01848 331555
Robert Burns House
Burns Street, Dumfries
Tel: 01387 255297
Ellisland Farm (Burns Home)
4m north of Dumfries, east off A76
www.ellislandfarm.co.uk
Tel: 01387 740426
Caerlaverock Castle HS
7m south of Dumfries off B725
Ruthwell Cross
Ruthwell Church
¼ m north of B725 at Ruthwell 10m west of Annan
Duncan Savings Bank Museum
Ruthwell. 10m west of Annan
www.savingsbankmuseum.co.uk
Tel: 01387 870640

Museum of Lead Mining, Wanlockhead
15m north of Thornhill on B797
www.leadminingmuseum.co.uk
Tel: 01659 74387

Dunbartonshire

Dumbarton Castle HS
Denny Ship Model Experiment Tank
Castle Street, Dumbarton
Tel: 01389 763444
Argyll Motor Factory
(Loch Lomond Outlet Centre)
Main Street, Alexandria
Tel: 01389 710077
Hill House NTS
Upper Colquhoun Street, Helensburgh

East Lothian

Saltire Flag Heritage Centre
Athelstaneford
3m north of Haddington on B1343
Seton Collegiate Church HS
1m west of Longniddry, off A198
Preston Mill NTS
½ m north of East Linton off B1407
Dirleton Castle HS
Dirleton
2m west of North Berwick on B1345

Fife

Carnegie Birthplace Museum
Moodie Street, Dunfermline
www.carnegiebirthplace.com
Tel: 01383 724302
Culross Palace NTS, Culross
7m west of Dunfermline on A985
Falkland Palace NTS
Falkland, 4m north of Glenrothes on A912

Scotstarvit Tower HS
2m south of Cupar down track off A916

Deep World Centre
North Queensferry
www.deepseaworld.com
Tel: 01383 411880

HEBRIDES

Dunvegan Castle
Isle of Skye, Inverness-shire
www.dunvegancastle.com
Tel: 01470 521206

Flora Macdonald's Memorial
Kilmuir, Isle of Skye, Inverness-shire
5m north of Uig off A855

Iona Abbey HS
Iona, Argyllshire

Staffa NTS
Accessed by boat from Iona, Fionnphort, Mull or Oban

INVERNESS-SHIRE

Culloden Battlefield NTS
4m east of Inverness on B9006

Castle Urquhart HS
Northbank of Loch Ness, just south of Drumnadrochit on A82

Prince's Cairn
On north bank of Loch nan Uamh 10m south of Mallaig on A830

Seven Men of Moidart
North of Loch Moidart by A861, 3m south of Glenuig

Glenfinnan Monument (and Viaduct) NTS
On A830 15m west of Fort William

Cairngorm Mountain Funicular Railway
Mountain road of B970
10m south east of Aviemore

Aonach Mor Mountain Gondola
Nevis Range Ski Centre
West off A82 4m north of Fort William

West Highland Museum, Fort William
www.westhighlandmuseum.org.uk
Tel: 01397 702169

Commando Memorial
Beside A82 1m north of Spean Bridge, 7m north of Fort William

KINCARDINESHIRE

Crathes Castle NTS
16m north west of Stonehaven, 1m north of the A93

Dunnottar Castle
1m south of Stonehaven, off A92
www.dunechtestates.co.uk
Tel: 01569 762 173

Kinneff Church
8m south of Stonehaven, 1m east of A92

Fasque
5m north west of Laurencekirk off B974
www.fasque.com
Tel: 01561 340202

KINROSS-SHIRE

Kinross House
www.kinrosshouse.com

Loch Leven Castle HS
Accessed by ferry from west bank of Loch Leven at Kinross

KIRKCUDBRIGHTSHIRE

Broughton House NTS
12 High Street, Kirkcudbright

Dundrennan Abbey HS
6m south east of Kirkcudbright on A711

John Paul Jones Museum
12m south of Dumfries, 2m south of Kirkbean off A710
www.jpj.demon.co.uk
Tel: 01387 880613

Threave Castle HS
½ m walk from car park 1m west of Castle Douglas off A75

Cardoness Castle HS
1m south west of Gatehouse of Fleet off A75

Bruce's Stone, Glen Trool
4m east of A714 9m north of Newton Stewart

Orchardton Tower HS
On minor road off A711 4m south of Dalbeattie

Sweetheart Abbey HS
New Abbey
6m south of Dumfries on A710

David Coulthard Museum
Twynholm
4m north of Kirkcudbright on A75
www.davidcoulthardmuseum.co.uk

LANARKSHIRE

Pollok House NTS
Pollok Park
Glasgow
Tel: 0141 616 6410

Hamilton Mausoleum
Hamilton
Off Junction 6 of the M74
Tel: 01698 328232
Guided tours by appointment only

Leadhills and Wanlockhead railway
www.leadhillsrailway.co.uk

New Lanark Visitor Centre
New Lanark
www.newlanark.org
Tel: 01555 661345

Crookston Castle
South of Crookston village centre
5m south west of Glasgow off A761

MIDLOTHIAN

Edinburgh Castle HS
Tel: 0131 225 9846

Gladstone's Land NTS
477b Lawnmarket, Royal Mile, Edinburgh

Rosslyn Chapel
Roslin
10m south of Edinburgh city centre on B7006
www.rosslynchapel.org.uk
Tel: 0131 440 2159

MORAYSHIRE

Birnie church
4m south of Elgin on minor road east of B9010

NAIRNSHIRE

Cawdor Castle
6m south west of Nairn on B9090
www.cawdorcastle.com

Boath Doocot
2m east of Nairn off A96
Ardclach Bell Tower
10m south of Nairn on minor road south off A939

ORKNEY

Bishop's Palace and Earl's Palace HS
Kirkwall
Tel: 01856 871918

Skara Brae HS
8m north of Stromness on A967
Tel: 01856 841815

Maes Howe HS
9m west of Kirkwall on A965
Tel: 01856 761606
Ring of Brodgar HS
11m west of Kirkwall on B9055
Tel: 01856 841815
Italian Chapel
Lamb Holm, 7m south of Kirkwall off A961

PEEBLESSHIRE

Traquair House
Innerleithen
www.traquair.co.uk
Tel: 01896 830323
John Buchan Centre
Broughton
south end of village on A701
www.johnbuchansociety.co.uk
Tel: 01899 830205
Dawyk Arboretum
8m south west of Peebles off B712
www.rbge.org.uk

PERTHSHIRE

Scone Palace
2m north of Perth off A93
www.scone-palace.net
Tel: 01738 552300
Comrie Earthquake House
On minor road south of Comrie, 6m west of Crieff on A85
Blair Castle
Blair Atholl
8m north of Pitlochry on B8079
www.blair-castle.co.uk
Tel: 01796 481207
Doune Castle HS
3m west of Dunblane on A820
Tel: 01786 841742

ROSS AND CROMARTY

Hugh Miller's House NTS
Cromarty
Eilean Donan
8m east of Kyle of Lochalsh on A87
www.eileandonancastle.com
Tel: 01599 555202

ROXBURGHSHIRE

Jedburgh Abbey HS
Kelso Abbey HS
Floors Castle
1m north of Kelso
www.floorscastle.com
Tel: 01573 223333
Abbotsford
2m west of Melrose
www.scottsabbotsford.co.uk
Tel: 01896 752043
Melrose Abbey HS

SELKIRKSHIRE

Bowhill
3m west of Selkirk off B7039
Tel: 01750 22204

SHETLAND

Jarlshof HS
Sumburgh, Mainland 25m south of Lerwick
Tel: 01950 460112

STRLINGSHIRE

Wallace Monument
Abbey Craig
2m north east of Stirling off A907
www.nationalwallacemonument.com
Tel: 01786 472140

Stirling Castle HS
Tel: 01786 450000
Bannockburn Heritage Centre NTS
2m south of Stirling
Tel: 01786 812664
Falkirk Wheel
Lime Road, Falkirk off A803
www.thefalkirkwheel.co.uk
Tel: 01324 619888

Sutherland

Dunrobin Castle
1m north of Golspie on A9
Tel: 01408 633177

West Lothian

Hopetoun House
3m west of Queensferry on minor roads north off A904
www.hopetounhouse.com
Tel: 0131 331 2451
Linlithgow Palace HS
Tel: 01506 842896
Kinneil House Museum
Bo'ness
www.falkirk.gov.uk
Tel: 01506 778530
Blackness Castle HS
½ m east of Blackness off B903
Tel: 01506 834807
Dalmeny House
3m east of Queensferry off A90
www.dalmeny.co.uk
Tel: 0131 331 1888
House of the Binns NTS
3m north east of Linlithgow off A904
Tel: 0131 665 1546

Wigtownshire

Whithorn Priory HS
Whithorn
Tel: 01988 500508
Port Logan Fishpond
Port Logan
14m south of Stranraer on B7065
www.loganfishpond.co.uk

Index of People

Index of Places

Acknowledgements

My thanks to Hugh Montgomery Massingberd for his unflinching support and advice and to Ros Edwards for her guidance and help. Also to the team at Ebury, Carey Smith, Vicky Orchard and Caroline Newbury, for their vision, hard work and patience, and to Steve Dobell for his sensitive editing.

I would also like to thank Charles, Fiona and Rose Fletcher for their hospitality and insight.

And my love and thanks to Mai Osawa, whose extraordinary talent and grace are unfailing.